EXTERNAL DEGREES IN THE INFORMATION AGE
Legitimate Choices

Henry A. Spille
David W. Stewart
Eugene Sullivan

AMERICAN COUNCIL ON EDUCATION ★
ORYX PRESS ★
Series on Higher Education
1997

The rare Arabian oryx is believed to have inspired the myth of the unicorn. This desert antelope became virtually extinct in the early 1960s. At that time several groups of international conservationists arranged to have 9 animals sent to the Phoenix Zoo to be the nucleus of a captive breeding herd. Today the oryx population is over 1,000 and over 500 have been returned to the Middle East.

© 1997 by the American Council on Education and The Oryx Press
Published by The Oryx Press
4041 North Central at Indian School Road
Phoenix, Arizona 85012-3397

Published simultaneously in Canada
Printed and bound in the United States of America

∞ The paper used in this publication meets the minimum requirements of
the American National Standard for Information Sciences—Permanence
of Paper for Printed Library Materials, ANSI Z39.48-1984.

Library of Congress Cataloging-in-Publication Data
Spille, Henry A.
    External degrees in the information age : legitimate choices /
Henry A. Spille, David W. Stewart, Eugene Sullivan.
    p. cm. — (American Council on Education/Oryx Press series on
higher education)
    Includes index.
    ISBN 0-89774-997-9 (alk. paper)
    1. University extension—United States.   2. Distance education—
United States.   3. Degrees, Academic—United States.   4. Adult
education—United States.   5. Universities and colleges—United
States—Directories.   I. Stewart, David Wood, 1929–
II. Sullivan, Eugene J.   III. Title.   IV. Series.
LC6251.S75   1997
378.1'75—dc21   97-20531
                                                           CIP

CONTENTS

PREFACE

The purpose of this book is to provide a reliable and comprehensive guide for adults who are seeking degrees from accredited colleges and universities. It is also designed to help adult academic counselors and advisors; military educators; training and education personnel in business, industry, and labor unions; librarians; state government regulators of postsecondary education institutions; and external degree program directors and faculty members.

In developing this volume, we have built upon and updated our earlier work: *The Adult Learner's Guide to Alternative and External Degree Programs*, edited by Eugene Sullivan (Oryx Press, 1993); and *Diploma Mills: Degrees of Fraud*, by David Stewart and Henry Spille (Macmillan Publishing Co., 1988). The external degree programs that are the particular focus of this book are characterized by their responsiveness to the needs of contemporary adult learners. The institutions offering these programs typically make use of the rich variety of learning opportunities available in the Information Age, and they incorporate learning that takes place outside the traditional classroom into their degree programs. Unlike Sullivan's earlier *Guide*, this book does not include campus-based programs—a decision made, in part, because of the many inquiries we have received for information on campus-free degree programs. It is clear that today's learners, especially those with family and work responsibilities, are looking for programs that allow them to learn anytime and anywhere. The new electronic and digital technologies that have come into general use since the *Guide* was written in 1993 enable institutions to meet this new demand much more easily than before, and the need for campus-based alternative degree programs (such as "weekend colleges" and evening courses) has been greatly reduced.

Adult students, increasingly, look for programs that do not require travel to a campus and that offer flexible learning times—programs available through the Internet and other technologies. Institutions included in the book often use a cluster of technologies in offering a variety of degree programs, and they help adults consolidate credit earned in the past through approved job and military training and formal course work. External degree programs also provide off-campus learning opportunities, as well as a variety of student support services. Listed institutions meet most, if not all, of these features. In addition to being responsive to busy adult schedules, the new communication technologies provide a more individualized approach to the teaching and learning process, facilitate collaboration between students, and allow for closer connections with the learner's work environment.

It is no exaggeration to say that a revolution is occurring within higher education as colleges and universities develop programs specifically to serve adults—a group that is fast becoming the new mainstream of students. The increasing press for education by those who have family and employment responsibilities is no fad. Any individual who hopes to succeed (or even to survive) in today's highly competitive environment must develop and maintain a constant orientation to learning.

As never before, colleges and universities are urged to make themselves user-friendly for adult students—and many have responded with specially designed degree programs. The new telecommunications and computer technologies have made distance education a booming field, and it is now possible to earn degrees in some specialized fields without being required to leave work or home. Many other degrees can be completed with only minimal time spent in campus classrooms.

Unfortunately, however, the growth in the development of degree-granting programs designed for adults at accredited colleges and universities is being matched by the growth of programs at institutions that lack appropriate accreditation. Fast, easy degrees from these diploma mills—which frequently advertise in airline magazines and certain international newspapers, and maintain impressive Internet sites—pose an ominous threat to the reputations of legitimate adult degree programs at appropriately accredited universities. Many diploma mill degree programs are advertised as "nontraditional" and in the forefront of efforts to make higher education more useful and accessible to people with adult responsibilities. Deception and fraud often lurk in such an approach, which may not be understood by those unfamiliar with new developments in higher education. When abuses are publicly uncovered, innovative programs of all kinds may be tarnished in the public mind.

All too often, adults in search of higher education degrees have been misled by poor-quality directories containing incomplete or inaccurate information, leading them to make unwise decisions. In this guide, we have taken great care to ensure that prospective students are given the tools to make well-informed choices from among legitimate institutions.

In the initial pages of this book, readers are introduced to the new world of going to college. External degree programs are defined, and the basic instruments of nontraditional education are explained. The important but complex world of accreditation is sorted out in language that is easy to understand. Diploma mills—those corrupters of degree integrity—are defined, and their nefarious activities chronicled. Finally, the hallmarks of quality for adult degree programs are set forth, and guidelines for choosing the most suitable program are provided. The narrative is succinct but fact-filled, and it doesn't skimp on explanations of difficult subject matter. "Everything you need to know, but no more than you need to know" have been our watchwords.

Although many appropriately accredited institutions of higher education have responded to today's need for new approaches aimed at adult students, many others have not. That's why a guide to specific external degree programs constitutes the largest section of this volume. Institutions offering legitimately accredited external degree programs are listed by state. Included as appendixes are an alphabetical index of these institutions and an index to the fields of study they offer.

We thank the institutions that took the time to answer all of our survey questions. Thanks, too, go to state officials in charge of regulating institutions of postsecondary education who responded to our lengthy survey questionnaire and telephone follow-up.

We are also indebted to DoRita Alford for all of her work in managing the institutional information that came to us from our survey instrument, to Beatrice Wallace for her extraordinary competence in managing production of the narrative and completion of the state government survey instrument, to Richard Kraus for his valuable assistance with the survey of state government officials, and to James Murray for his many contributions, including valuable assistance in developing an appropriate title. Their commitment to the project and the hours they so graciously spent on it are deeply appreciated.

Henry A. Spille
David W. Stewart
Eugene Sullivan

PART ONE

CHAPTER 1

The New World
of Going to College

So you're thinking of returning to college to finish up what you started some years ago. Or maybe you're considering enrolling in college for the first time. You are not alone. Many thousands of American adults are having similar thoughts, and many have decided to proceed. The nation is better off because so many of its citizens are taking this courageous and exciting path.

In acquiring a college degree, you will enhance your knowledge and skills. If you have been parenting full time, a degree will help update your skills for a new or renewed career in the workplace. If you are currently employed, a college degree may help you qualify for a salary increase, job advancement, or job change. In these days of corporate downsizing, a degree may even help you keep your job. All of these are noble goals, but the best outcome of your collegiate experience may be a renewed sense of yourself. Purposeful learning as an adult can be fulfilling—and fun.

If you have not been at college for awhile, some pleasant surprises are in store. It is now possible to earn a degree while holding down a job or maintaining responsibilities in the home. More and more colleges and universities are making their programs and facilities increasingly user-friendly for adults. Conveniences such as the following have been incorporated into many adult degree programs:

- At some colleges, you can enroll and begin study at any time—you don't have to wait until the beginning of a semester or quarter.
- You may be able to receive credit for what you already know that is at a collegiate level and degree-relevant—there may be no need to take courses that duplicate prior learning. Knowledge acquired on the job or in the military can account for a significant share of such credit.

- You may not need to attend any classes during daytime hours on weekdays. Evening and weekend schedules for adults are becoming common.
- You may not have to attend any traditional classes to earn at least some of the credits toward your degree. A curriculum organized as "competencies," rather than as courses, can make this possible. You can acquire many of these competencies through independent study.
- You may be able to adapt the content of courses or programs of study to meet the specific needs of your work or personal life.
- You may be able to take some courses entirely by computer. Sophisticated software and interactive technology can put you in close touch not only with the instructor but also with fellow students as you pursue your work.

Can you afford the expense of going to college as an adult? There is often good news on this front, too. Many employers have programs of tuition assistance for their employees. Veterans may qualify for benefits, grants, or loans under either federal or state programs. Colleges and universities often provide scholarships or grants to individuals, and a small but increasing number of such opportunities are being earmarked for adult students.

All of this is good news, but some words of caution are in order. A host of "diploma mills" have sprung up to take advantage of unsuspecting adults (or to be used by the unscrupulous). Thousands of academic degrees these days are being awarded to people who have not acquired the knowledge and skills that should be expected of anyone who completes a program of study at the postsecondary level. Too many organizations operate—entirely legally—in states with very weak laws governing the organization and function of colleges and universities. Some of these diploma mills are even accredited—but by agencies that lack appropriate academic recognition and reputability.

The sheer number of decisions that need to be made by the wise consumer can appear daunting, and the opportunities for taking wrong turns are many. It's a good idea to do your homework about the external degree world well in advance of enrollment. We hope you can use this book as a starting point. Welcome to the world of higher education for the 21st century!

CHAPTER 2

External Degree Programs

What They Are and How They Work

An external degree program is any collegiate degree program designed primarily or exclusively for persons who have the characteristics and responsibilities of adults. At its simplest, it is a traditional degree program made more accessible by means of flexible scheduling of classes and creative approaches to the teaching and learning process.

External degree programs often are characterized by a limited period of campus residence or the absence of a residence requirement; instruction that is free of time and place requirements and makes extensive use of various communication technologies; assessments of prior learning with the potential for being granted college credit; student-designed (and faculty-approved) majors; and faculty who serve as learning facilitators, coaches, and mentors rather than as lecturers.

Many external degree programs are essentially degree-completion programs designed for those who have accumulated some college credits in the past. Many such programs are structured in an accelerated format that permits a degree to be completed in a shorter period of time than a comparable class-based degree. Prior learning assessment helps make this possible, as does flexible class scheduling that includes weekends, self-directed independent study, and study or learning related to the student's job.

Most external degree programs lead to a baccalaureate degree, although their use is fast expanding to the master's and doctoral degree levels. At these levels, the fields of business, education, allied health, and general studies currently are the areas of fastest expansion.

External degree programs for adults may be offered in various academic structures. The degree program may be the single mission of a freestanding institution, it may represent a major unit within a college or university, it may be an extension of other institutional services, or it may be a department or division within a larger college or university. Regardless of structure, however, the central concern of external degree program administrators is balancing quality and standards with access and program design to meet adult learners' needs. These concerns have been, and must continue to be, framed within the academic context of the higher education institutions offering the programs. While general institutional goals and standards must remain consistent for all academic programs, the policies, practices, and standards for external degree programs require particular attention.

BASIC INSTRUMENTS OF EXTERNAL DEGREE PROGRAMS

A number of terms have been introduced in the definition and description of external degree programs. Among them are the terms that define the basic instruments of adult degree programs:

- Assessment of prior learning
- Contract learning
- Competency-based curricula and degrees
- Learning outcomes
- Distance education

Assessment and Evaluation of Prior Learning

Adults entering degree programs may already have acquired learning from work, from life experiences, or from instruction either inside or outside of school or college classrooms. Such prior learning experiences can be divided into two categories:

- Formal classroom learning or sponsored learning, usually in the form of courses, programs, or modules offered by the military, corporations, labor unions, government agencies, professional and voluntary associations, and vendors.
- Learning acquired on an individual basis through work experience, reading, travel, or self-study.

By systematic assessment, colleges and universities can determine whether any of that prior learning was at a college level and is applicable toward a degree. Such learning must be documented, and then it must be assessed in the context of postsecondary education standards, using appropriate techniques.

According to studies conducted by the American Council on Education (ACE) and other organizations, in which representative samples of appropriately accredited American colleges and universities were surveyed, nearly all of them (97 percent) had policies permitting the award of some credit for learning acquired in noncollegiate settings. The most frequently used assessment technique for making these credit awards is testing; for instance, by use of standardized examinations such as the College Level Examination Program (CLEP).[1] Appropriate examinations also may be developed by academic departments or individual faculty members. Still another way in which prior learning is evaluated is by third-party assessments, such as those conducted by ACE. These third-party reviews are often required by colleges and universities for the evaluation of instruction sponsored by organizations other than accredited postsecondary education institutions.[2] In addition, qualified faculty members or others may be able to evaluate your occupational licenses or certification and conduct a hands-on evaluation of your knowledge, skills, and abilities to determine the college-level learning that you have acquired.

When it is done with integrity and in a professional manner, prior learning assessment is not a casual process. The student collects and presents information pertaining to prior learning in a systematic way, often in the form of a portfolio.[3] Learning for which the student is seeking credit is specifically identified and documented, and appropriate assessment techniques are applied by the faculty. Credit is not given on a wholesale basis; the faculty assigns it in relevant knowledge, skill, and ability areas, based on their subject matter expertise and the relationship of the prior learning to the student's program of study.

For determining whether a student should receive credit for prior formal instruction, a number of other tools are available. If you seek credit for your past formal education and training, you should be aware of the assessment tools that are most often employed so that you can question institutional officials about their use. You may need to be persistent to find out how prior formal training is evaluated at the institution in which you intend to enroll. The four most commonly used resources are[4]

- *College Credit Recommendations*, published by the University of the State of New York.
- *Guide to the Evaluation of Educational Experiences in the Armed Services*, published biennially in three volumes by the Oryx Press as part of the American Council on Education/Oryx Press Series on Higher Education.
- *The National Guide to Educational Credit for Training Programs*, published by the Oryx Press as part of the American Council on Education/Oryx Press Series on Higher Education.

- *Guide to Educational Credit by Examination,* edited by Joan Schwartz and published by the American Council on Education Center for Adult Learning and Educational Credentials.

All of these resources and methods—used by well-qualified faculty members, deans, registrars, and others, and administered under appropriate academic protocols—are being applied by most traditional American colleges and universities in awarding credit attained through formal but noncollegiate education and training. (In contrast, diploma mills are casual in their award of credit for noncollegiate formal training; see Chapter 4.)

Regular college credits may also have been earned previously by adults enrolling in degree programs. The college or university where credit was earned is referred to as the "sending institution." The institution reviewing this prior credit is referred to as the "receiving institution." If you have already earned college credit, you will need to determine the procedures and practices of the receiving institution that guide the acceptance and application of traditional transfer credit.

A student's credits for prior learning, when determined, are recorded on transcripts in accordance with the institution's record-keeping policies and procedures. Records are kept to demonstrate the consistency of the credit awards and to show the patterns of academic advising and other student services that were used and who used them. (All of these procedures for assessing prior learning are virtually absent, however, in the quickie machinery of the diploma mill; see Chapter 4.)

Contract Learning

Learning contracts are written agreements between an instructor and a student, under which both parties set forth their joint understanding of the terms and conditions of a learning project. Such agreements ordinarily include statements of what is to be learned (intended learning outcomes); how it will be learned; how, when, and by whom the learning will be assessed; what resources will be used; and the date of completion. Such contracts are being used increasingly in traditional classroom-based study, as well as in nontraditional programs designed for students with adult responsibilities.

Competency-Based Curricula and Degrees

Some traditional colleges and universities base prior learning assessments on competencies—units or modules of learning that are generally quite narrow in scope. (Courses, in contrast, usually address multiple skills, knowledges, and abilities.) The faculty assessors, for example, may break down a course into eight required skills, knowledges, and abilities. During the process of assessing prior learning, they may determine, for example, that the student has acquired competency in five of them, with the other three requiring further learning. The student may acquire these three competencies by enrolling in a course or part of a course, or by means of an independent or semi-independent activity agreed upon by the student and the faculty.

A few colleges and universities offer curricula and degrees that are based entirely on competencies, instead of on the number of courses taken and the credits accumulated. At these institutions, competencies—which must be demonstrated by students to qualify for graduation—usually are in both knowledge and skill areas, or they may be stated as generic abilities or as individual characteristics or attributes. Most often, they are assessed using multiple techniques, modes, and contexts, which almost always include demonstrations. Assessment is based on well-defined standards and criteria. Degree completion is based on satisfactory demonstration of the required skills, knowledge, or abilities.

Alverno College in Milwaukee, Wisconsin, has what is probably the best known competency-based (now referred to as "ability-based") college degree program in the United States. Alverno College defines competence as "a characteristic of the individual person, rather than a skill or an enumeration of tasks." In contrast to institutions that conduct their prior learning assessment in terms of narrow competencies, Alverno's competencies include general abilities in the following areas: communication, analysis, problem solving, valuing in decision making, social interaction, global perspectives, effective citizenship, and aesthetic responsiveness. But its graduates are required to demonstrate competence in more than these general abilities. A history major, for example, is required to achieve "a combination of specialized communication, analytical, and valuing abilities [to] make it possible for historians to 'do' history."[5]

Learning Outcomes

Learning outcomes are the skills, knowledge, abilities, and competencies that learners must acquire to complete a module, course, program, or other learning activity. For example, one of the learning outcomes of a course titled Introduction to Spreadsheet Applications may be: "Upon successful completion of this course, the student will be competent in integrating spreadsheet, graphing, database, and automated keystroke features. The student will demonstrate achievement of this outcome by performing the required integration."

Alverno College uses three levels of learning outcomes: institutional, major, and course. An example of an institutional learning outcome is: "Develop communication ability (effectively send and respond to communication for varied audiences and purposes)."[6] An example in a major (in this case, history) is: "Identifies and critiques the theories, concepts, and assumptions which historians have used to create coherent interpretations of the past." Finally, an example of a learning outcome from a course (in this case, Western World Views) is: "To use the conceptual frameworks of history to make independent interpretations of the development of Western assumptions, values, and cultural practices."[7]

Although learning outcomes are now widely used at all levels of education, they are especially relevant for adult learners who want to avoid duplication of prior learning, who want to know what they will be learning, and who want to know what will be expected of them in a given learning activity (module, course, tutorial, workshop, or independent project). Learning outcomes also help adult learners to match or compare their educational goals with what they will be learning and to ensure that progress is being made toward their degree or other educational objective.

Colleges and universities often have another set of learning outcomes—programmatic learning outcomes. These are comprehensive or program-wide in scope. Faculty and academic professionals determine outcomes for both a given learning activity and a program but often seek the involvement of adult learners in that determination. The learners themselves may identify additional individual outcomes for their learning experiences and programs.

As part of the achievement of programmatic learning outcomes, program faculty and academic administrators have a responsibility to assist adult learners in the acquisition of the depth and breadth of knowledge, skills, abilities, and competencies required for their specific degrees. They also are responsible for aiding the learners in the development of what now are often referred to as generic skills and abilities, such as communication, critical thinking, problem solving, learning to learn, and integration of knowledge. The development of these skills and abilities encourages learners to become more autonomous and self-directed lifelong learners. A good practice for students is to ask themselves periodically whether they are acquiring these necessary skills and abilities, especially for employment and further learning purposes, and, if not, to confer with faculty members and academic advisors about how to plan for and progress toward their acquisition.

Information about the assessment of learning outcomes may be useful to you. In most colleges and universities, assessment focuses on the content or subject matter of a module, course, or program. Probably the most frequently used modes of assessment at the undergraduate level are written tests—multiple choice and essay. Other modes of assessment also are frequently used for adult students, such as projects and/or reports done by a team of students, demonstrations, simulations, written statements of self-reflection on assumptions or issues, and the development or creation of a product. Regardless of the assessment mode used, however, criteria for successful performance always are established in advance. The faculty member should inform you of these criteria.

Distance Education

Correspondence study has been in existence for many decades, with communication between learners and the faculty and administrators at correspondence schools conducted largely through the postal service. Later, the telephone supplemented written communication. But in recent years, communication patterns have changed dramatically. Although the mail and telephone still are used, computers, videos, and other electronic devices have improved, enhanced, and increased correspondence study or distance learning between schools and learners.

A sign of the changing times is shifts within the former National Home Study Council (NHSC), which was established in 1926 as a voluntary association of correspondence schools. In 1994 it changed its name to the Distance Education and Training Council (DETC), mainly because of the changes in how its members were delivering instruction and communicating with their students.[8]

According to DETC, distance education—also called correspondence study or home study—is enrollment and study in an educational institution that provides lesson materials prepared in a sequential and logical order for study by learners on their own. After a lesson is completed, the learner returns it to the school by mail, fax, or computer transmission for assessment, correction, comments, grading, and subject matter guidance by the faculty member responsible for "teaching" the course. Corrected assignments are returned to the learner, again by mail, fax, or computer. A personalized learner-teacher relationship often develops through these exchanges.

In adult degree programs delivered at a distance, the role of teachers changes from that of classroom lecturers to facilitators of learning and mentors and coaches of learners. These teachers also become members of teams that develop curricula, design courses, and select technologies.

In searching for an adult degree program that meets your needs, you should not be surprised to find some programs are conducted using computers. This means of instructional delivery is becoming more and more common. Communication with the instructor and among learners is done on the computer. It is done asynchronously, at whatever times are convenient for each learner; in other words, not all learners are involved at the same time. Some early research results show that participants in such programs earn higher grades than their counterparts who are taking the same course in a formal classroom, and they tend to retain the learning outcomes longer. They also tend to be more active participants in "class" discussions. If you are comfortable using a computer or are willing to learn computer skills, you might find this form of instructional delivery to your liking.

All types of distance education are especially well-suited for persons who have adult responsibilities that leave them little time to attend regularly scheduled classes. Receiving instruction at a distance means that they do not have to give up their jobs, leave home, or lose income. Moreover, much of the instruction that is available at a distance is not degree related. Its purpose is to help adults learn new skills or upgrade skills to qualify for jobs or job promotions, or to provide avocational study.

In making a decision about pursuing instruction delivered at a distance, learners should use *Guiding Principles for Distance Learning in a Learning Society*.[9] The principles outlined in that publication, such as how the instruction is designed and the kinds of student support services that should be expected, will help them judge the quality and potential effectiveness of the instructional offering(s) that they are considering (see also Chapter 5).

NONTRADITIONAL DEGREE PROGRAMS

Sometimes external degree programs designed especially for adults are called "nontraditional." This label is used because the age, attendance pattern, employment status, and financial status of an adult enrollee tends to be different from that of the typical 18- to 22-year-old student. The value of the term is diminishing, however, because many 18- to 22-year olds now have some of the characteristics of older adult students—they may attend college part time and work full time or part time, may be married and/or have family responsibilities, and may be financially independent.

Degree programs can be nontraditional or unconventional in any of the following ways:

- The students may be employed adults, homemakers, adults motivated to study independently, individuals who cannot easily come to the campus, or those who cannot or do not wish to pursue a degree full time.
- The learning experience may take place off campus in a regional learning center or library, at home, or at the workplace.
- Institutional policies and procedures may provide extensive recognition of prior college-level learning, regardless of the way in which such learning was acquired.
- Instruction may be learner-centered, not teacher-centered.

- Instructional delivery may involve nonclassroom methods, programmed learning materials, and media such as computers, satellites, videocassettes, or television.
- The content of the courses may be either the same as that of courses taught on campus or different, but in either case, the learning outcomes are the same or comparable.
- The curriculum may be competency-based.
- The campus residency requirement may be reduced, waived, or eliminated.
- Students may participate extensively in designing their degree programs and learning experiences.
- The institutional arrangements for instruction or for student support services (such as academic advising and counseling) may incorporate contractual relationships with separate individuals or organizations (such as corporations, labor unions, or professional associations).

NOTES

1. The College Level Examination Program (CLEP) is owned by The College Board. For further information, write to The College Board, CLEP, Educational Testing Service, Princeton, NJ 08541; e-mail jpaine@ets.org; or visit The College Board's Web site at http://www.collegeboard.org.

2. ACE administers a process that includes assembling teams of faculty members from appropriately accredited colleges and universities who use their professional judgment in determining the comparability of learning acquired through offerings of these organizations and that acquired at appropriately accredited collegiate institutions. They also recommend semester hours of credit that should be awarded for that learning.

3. Portfolio assessment instruments and guides have been developed by the Council on Adult and Experiential Learning (CAEL). For more information on portfolio assessment, write to CAEL National Headquarters, 243 South Wabash Avenue, Suite 800, Chicago, Illinois 60604; or phone 312-922-5909.

4. For further information on the University of the State of New York's publication, write to the University of the State of New York, National Program on Noncollegiate Sponsored Instruction, Cultural Education Center, 5A25, Empire State Plaza, Albany, NY 12230; phone 518-434-0118; or e-mail natponsi@mail.nysed.gov.

For further information on the American Council on Education/Oryx Press Series on Higher Education, write to The Oryx Press, 4041 North Central, Suite 700, Phoenix, AZ 85012; phone 602-265-2651; fax 602-265-6250; e-mail info@oryxpress.com; or visit Oryx's Web site at www.oryxpress.com.

For further information on publications of the American Council on Education (ACE), write to the Publications Department, American Council on Education, One Dupont Circle, Suite 800, Washington, DC 20036; phone 202-939-9380; or visit the ACE Web site at www.acenet.edu.

5. Alverno College Faculty, *Liberal Learning at Alverno College*, 5th ed., 1992, 4; and Alverno College Faculty, *Ability-Based Learning Program: The History Major*, 1994, 1–8.

6. Alverno College Faculty, *Ability-Based Learning Program*, 1994, 2.

7. Alverno College Faculty, *Ability-Based Learning Program: The History Major*, 1994, 1–8.

8. For more information, write to DETC, 1601 18th Street NW, Washington, DC 20009; phone 202-234-5100; or visit the DETC Web site at www.detc.org.

9. *Guiding Principles for Distance Learning in a Learning Society* was published in 1996 by the American Council on Education. For further information, write to the Publications Department, American Council on Education, One Dupont Circle, Suite 800, Washington, DC 20036; or phone 202-939-9380.

CHAPTER 3

What You Should Know about Accreditation and State Regulation

I f you remember nothing else from this chapter, remember this: Consider enrollment *only* in colleges or universities that have accreditation from an agency recognized by the Council for Higher Education Accreditation (CHEA); its predecessor organization, CORPA; or the U.S. Department of Education.

Higher education institutions having CHEA-recognized and CORPA-recognized accreditation are listed in *Accredited Institutions of Postsecondary Education,* published annually by the American Council on Education,[1] and the U.S. Department of Education periodically publishes a listing of "Nationally Recognized Accrediting Agencies and Associations."[2] Don't be taken in by guides that purport to help you evaluate unaccredited institutions on your own. Too often such guides are written or published by persons having financial or other ties to unaccredited institutions that have very questionable standards.

If you want a high-quality education, don't enroll in an institution that has never been evaluated by an appropriate group of qualified educators. Degrees and credits awarded by institutions that do not have recognized accreditation are seldom, if ever, accepted by properly accredited colleges and universities. The U.S. military, as well as many employers, will not knowingly accept improperly accredited degrees in making determinations about hiring, salary increases, or promotion. Finally, holders of questionable degrees may find themselves unpleasantly surprised when someone blows the whistle on them. It's bad enough when the news moves through a person's workplace or social circle that his or her degree was awarded by a diploma mill. But the embarrassment has been compounded for some when it became part of an exposé in a newspaper or on radio or television.

THE ABCs OF ACCREDITATION

Accreditation is the voluntary system devised by the higher education community for evaluating the quality of an institution or academic program and for assisting the institution or program in maintaining and improving itself. Accreditation involves independent judgment by qualified outside persons that the institution or program achieves its own educational objectives and also meets the standards established by the body from which it seeks accreditation.

Anyone considering enrollment in an American college or university ought to understand the basic facts about the role of accreditation in protecting degree integrity—especially in the current era, during which the nation's accreditation enterprise is undergoing change. Here's what you need to know:

- First, accreditation is uniquely American.
- Second, accreditation comes in several varieties (regional, national, and specialized).
- Third, accrediting bodies that are generally accepted within the American higher education community are themselves "accredited" or recognized by appropriate review bodies.
- Fourth, much diploma mill fraud is aided and abetted by the dissemination of misleading information about accreditation.

Accreditation Is Uniquely American

Accreditation is a uniquely American process. In most countries of the world, the government—through a ministry of education—supervises and controls educational institutions. This is not true in the United States, where the federal government has never had such a role. Instead, U.S. educational institutions are "regulated" through a system of voluntary accreditation, which involves review of an institution's academic and other programs by nongovernmental bodies. It is this distinction that very often confuses persons from outside the United States, who sometimes assume that if an institution exists, the federal government must have authorized it and must be controlling its quality.

The Three Main Types of Accreditation

Accreditation comes in three major varieties: regional, national, and specialized. Of primary concern is regional accreditation, which is performed by eight organizations having this mission in various parts of the country.[3]

Regional

Regional accreditation focuses on an entire institution, not its individual programs. To say that College A or University B is accredited means that the accrediting agency has concluded that the institution as a whole meets its standards. Within the context of this overall review, a determination is made that it is likely the institution's individual programs are, to a reasonable degree, educationally sound.

National

National accreditation, in common with regional accreditation, focuses on an entire institution. However, national accrediting agencies, which are few in number, focus on institutions having very specialized missions.[4] For example, theological schools, Bible colleges, and institutions offering all instruction via correspondence or distance learning mechanisms may be accredited by national accrediting bodies rather than (or in addition to) those offering regional accreditation.

It is common for the staffs of diploma mills, which conduct most of their work at a distance, to tell prospective students that accreditation is not available to their institutions. That is untrue. The Accrediting Commission of the Distance Education and Training Council (DETC)[5] is a recognized national accrediting body that accredits correspondence and distance learning institutions. In addition, approximately 70 colleges and universities accredited by regional agencies offer thousands of courses in hundreds of subject matter areas under distance learning arrangements. Distance learning programs, if conducted under appropriate academic protocols, are entirely respectable and are becoming even more so—and they definitely can be accredited!

Specialized

Specialized accreditation, unlike regional and national accreditation, is program-specific. A specialized accrediting agency will review and accredit programs that prepare students for a profession or occupation (for example, in medicine, nursing, business, engineering, or teaching) within an institution holding regional or national accreditation. Some specialized accrediting bodies will, however, accredit professional programs at institutions not otherwise accredited. Generally these are independent institutions that offer only the particular specified discipline or course of study (such as art or music). Specialized accreditation may be of great importance if the program of study you plan to pursue is required for occupational licensure or certification. However, specialized accreditation is not available for some types of programs, and some highly respected professional programs may choose not to seek accreditation.

Recognized Accreditation

Accrediting bodies that are generally accepted within the American higher education community are themselves "accredited" or recognized by appropriate review bodies. Who "accredits" the accreditation bodies or assures that their standards and performance are satisfactory? This is a very important question. In the United States, this function currently is undergoing change. The Council for Higher Education Accreditation (CHEA) is a new organization formed to replace an earlier organization known as the Commission on Recognition of Postsecondary Accreditation (CORPA).[6] One of CHEA's purposes is to review accrediting bodies. Those that meet its standards are "recognized" as providing appropriate quality review functions.

Although the U.S. Department of Education may not authorize, approve, or in any way accredit colleges and universities, it does review accrediting agencies and publishes a list of nationally recognized accrediting agencies that it determines to be "reliable authorities" for judging the quality of education or training offered. Only students who are enrolled at institutions that have been accredited by agencies whose names appear on this list[7] are eligible for federal grants, loans, or other student financial aid.

Accreditation is, admittedly, an imperfect instrument—and by no means an absolute guarantee of quality. The American higher education community cannot be smug to the point of overlooking the shortcomings of accreditation. Still, an accredited institution has at least undergone review by a qualified outside academic team. It is a virtual certainty that no outright diploma mill could get past the review procedures currently in place at the nation's recognized institutional accreditation agencies.

Phony Accreditation

Much diploma mill fraud is aided and abetted by the dissemination of misleading information about accreditation. How do some diploma mills manage to get themselves accredited? It's easy. Anyone can form an accrediting agency simply by incorporating or otherwise registering in accordance with state laws. Questionable educational institutions often join together to obtain "accreditation" in this way. Sometimes the so-called accrediting entity is nothing more than a post office box or a phone line in someone's living room. Since accrediting organizations of this kind are not recognized by either CHEA or the U.S. Department of Education, their accrediting activities are not accepted within the mainstream higher education community.

STATE REGULATION OF COLLEGES AND UNIVERSITIES

Accreditation is not the sole means of protecting consumers against academic shoddiness or outright fraud. State governments also play a role—though not in accreditation, which is by definition a nongovern-mental function.

Because education is not mentioned in the U.S. Constitution's Tenth Amendment, it is one of the powers "not delegated to the United States and not prohibited to the states." Thus, education has become a state responsibility. State governments enact the laws under which colleges and universities may be organized and award degrees. Good state laws of this kind stipulate minimum standards—rather than the higher and more exacting standards that are properly inherent in accreditation. The most basic functions performed by states are those of incorporation and autho-rization to award degrees. Sometimes these functions are combined as one. The terms used by the various states in defining their roles are confusing—a fact very often exploited by diploma mills. Here's a quick guide through the maze.

Incorporation means that the organization has a right to exist. Each state has at least one incorporation or registration law under which individuals may organize for the purpose of engaging in commerce or receiving and disbursing funds. Depending on other state laws, incorporation or regis-tration may or may not mean that the organization is also authorized to call itself a college or university and to award degrees. The administrative responsibilities for incorporation are frequently assigned to a state's secre-tary of state or attorney general.

Authorization generally means that an organization not only has a right to exist (incorporation) but also has the right to award degrees at the most minimum level of organization and resources. Authorization is generally a responsibility of a state education agency. The following terms are also used in some states to describe incorporation, authorization, or some combination of the two functions: *acceptance, licensing, certification, recog-nition, appraisal, classification, registration, approval, chartering,* or even (adding the most to confusion) *accreditation.*

Approval, as a term, offers special opportunities for confusion. In Cali-fornia, this term refers to institutions that have been determined to meet minimum standards established by the state, and that have therefore been given authorization to operate and award degrees. In some instances, it is claimed that this process is equivalent to accreditation. However, the higher education community generally does not recognize approval by the California regulatory authorities as equivalent to accreditation by a CHEA-recognized or U.S. Department of Education–recognized accred-iting body.

Approval has an additional meaning that can cause confusion. Every state is required by the federal government to designate a "state approving agency" to certify that courses offered to veterans eligible to receive benefits under the G.I. Bills are provided by an institution accredited by an agency recognized by the U.S. Department of Education. This type of approval is a reference to courses rather than institutions.

The performance of state governments in encouraging quality control at the most basic level is decidedly uneven. Most states have strong laws that are adequately enforced, but some states have either weak laws or weak enforcement, and disproportionate numbers of unaccredited institutions sometimes flock to those states. Currently in this category are the states of Alabama, Hawaii, Idaho, Louisiana, Missouri, South Dakota, and Utah. The state of California was once a haven for diploma mills, but in recent years it has made progress in getting rid of many of them. California's statutes, while stronger than in the past, still reflect the powerful political presence of unaccredited (or improperly accredited) institutions in that state. Enforcement, however, is much improved. Still, political and legal pressures have in some instances prevented the state regulatory agency from closing down institutions that have questionable academic status, and strong pressures to weaken the statutes remain. Table 3.1 reports the results of a survey of state regulatory agencies having responsibility for oversight of higher education institutions.

What is important to remember in this tangle is that *no service provided by any state replaces, or is equivalent to, accreditation.*

NOTES

1. CHEA assumed the accreditor-recognition functions of its predecessor organization, the Commission on Recognition of Postsecondary Accreditation (CORPA), on January 1, 1997. The edition of *Accredited Institutions of Postsecondary Education* being published for 1996–1997 includes institutions recognized by both CORPA and CHEA. Beginning with the 1997–1998 edition, only CHEA recognition will apply. Copies of this directory are available from The Oryx Press; for more information write to The Oryx Press, 4041 N. Central Avenue, Suite 700, Phoenix, AZ 85012; phone 602-265-2651; fax 602-265-6250; or e-mail info@oryxpress.com.

2. The U.S. Department of Education's listing is published in the *Higher Education Directory*, published annually by Higher Education Publications, Inc., 6400 Arlington Blvd., Suite 648, Falls Church, VA 22042; phone 703-532-2300.

3. The regional institutional accrediting bodies that have met or exceeded CORPA standards are listed below. CHEA, CORPA's successor, also recognizes these agencies. For more information on these groups, see Appendix B in *Accredited Institutions of Postsecondary Education* (details in note 1).
- Middle States Association of Colleges and Schools, Commission on Higher Education
- New England Association of Schools and Colleges, Commission on Institutions of Higher Education
- New England Association of Schools and Colleges, Commission on Technical and Career Institutions
- North Central Association of Colleges and Schools, Commission on Institutions of Higher Education
- The Northwest Association of Schools and Colleges, Commission on Colleges
- Southern Association of Colleges and Schools, Commission on Colleges

- Western Association of Schools and Colleges, Accrediting Commission for Community and Junior Colleges
- Western Association of Schools and Colleges, Accrediting Commission for Senior Colleges and Universities

4. The national institutional accrediting bodies that have met or exceeded CORPA standards are listed below. CHEA, CORPA's successor, also recognizes these agencies. For more information on these groups, see Appendix B in *Accredited Institutions of Postsecondary Education* (details in note 1).

- American Association of Bible Colleges, Commission on Accrediting
- Accrediting Bureau of Health Education Schools
- Accrediting Commission for Career Schools/Colleges of Technology
- Accrediting Council for Independent Colleges and Schools
- Association of Advanced Rabbinical and Talmudic Schools, Accreditation Commission
- The Association of Theological Schools in the United States and Canada, Commission on Accrediting
- Council on Occupational Education (formerly SACS-COEI)
- Distance Education and Training Council (formerly National Home Study Council, NHSC)

5. See Chapter 2, note 8.

6. CORPA turned over its accreditor-recognition functions to CHEA on January 1, 1997. See note 1.

7. See note 2.

TABLE 3.1

Summary of State Statutes Governing Regulation of Degree-Granting Colleges and Universities

STATUTORY PROVISION	AL*	AK	AZ	AR	CA**	CO	CT	DE	DC
Minimum Criteria	Yes	Yes	Yes	Yes	Yes	No, but must be accredited	Yes	Yes	Yes
Site Visit by Regulatory Agency	Yes for out-of-state; no for in-state	Yes	Yes	Yes	Yes	No, visit required by accrediting body	Yes	Yes	Yes, initial
Religious Exemption	Yes, provided they offer only religious degrees; no for out-of-state	No	Yes	Yes, provided they offer only religious degrees	Yes, provided they offer only religious degrees	No, authorization is needed	No	No	No
Review of Finances	Yes	Yes	Yes	Yes	Yes	Yes	Yes	No, accreditation financial review used	Yes
Surety Bond Required	Yes, $10,000	Yes	Yes, $15,000 non-accredited	No	No, must pay into Tuition Recovery Fund	No	No	No	Yes
Recruiters of Students	Yes	Yes, if on commission	No	No	Yes, permit required	No	No	Yes	Yes
Advertising Regulated	Yes	Yes	Yes	Yes	Yes	No	Yes	Yes	Yes
Periodic Reauthorization Required	Yes	Yes	Yes	Yes	Yes	No	Yes	Yes	Yes
Out-of-State Activities Monitored	Yes	No	No	Yes	Yes	Yes	Yes	n/a	Yes
Out-of-State Institutions Regulated	Yes	Yes	Yes	Yes	Yes	Yes	Yes	Yes	Yes
Penalties for Violation	Yes	Yes	Yes	Yes	Yes	Yes	Yes	No	Yes
Consumer Protection Laws Apply	Yes	Yes	Yes	Yes	Yes	Yes	Yes	Yes	Yes
List of Authorized Institutions Maintained	Yes	Yes	Yes	Yes	Yes	Yes	Yes	Yes	Yes

* State statutes are relatively weak.
** California once had weak statutes that encouraged the organization and growth of numerous unaccredited institutions. Current statutes are a great improvement and assertive enforcement also deserves commendation. Progress continues to be made, but some questionable unaccredited institutions remain in operation.

TABLE 3.1, continued

SUMMARY OF STATE STATUTES GOVERNING REGULATION OF DEGREE-GRANTING COLLEGES AND UNIVERSITIES

STATUTORY PROVISION	FL	GA	HI**	ID	IL	IN	IA*	KS	KY
Minimum Criteria	Yes	Yes	No	Yes	Yes	Yes	No, registration only	Yes	Yes
Site Visit by Regulatory Agency	Yes	Yes	No	No	Yes, if board finds cause	Yes	No	Yes	Yes
Religious Exemption	Yes	Yes	n/a	No	No	Yes	No	Yes, from licensing but subject to degree granting requirements	No
Review of Finances	Yes	Yes	No	No	Yes	Yes	No	Yes	Yes
Surety Bond Required	No	Yes	No	Yes, based on number of students	No	Yes	No	Yes	Yes
Recruiters of Students	Yes	Yes	No	No	Yes	Yes	Yes	Yes	Yes
Advertising Regulated	Yes	Yes	Yes	Yes	Yes	Yes	No	Yes	Yes
Periodic Reauthorization Required	Yes	Yes	No	Yes	No	Yes	No	Yes	Yes
Out-of-State Activities Monitored	No	Yes, if complaint received	No	No	Yes	Yes	No	Yes	No
Out-of-State Institutions Regulated	Yes	Yes	No	No	Yes	Yes	No	Yes	Yes
Penalties for Violation	Yes	Yes	Yes	Yes	Yes	Yes	Yes	Yes	Yes
Consumer Protection Laws Apply	Yes	Yes	Yes	Yes	Yes	Yes	Yes	Yes	Yes
List of Authorized Institutions Maintained	Yes	Yes	Registration required for unaccredited institutions, but not enforced	Yes	Yes	Yes	No	Yes	Yes

* State statutes are relatively weak.
** Hawaii (and South Dakota) have exceptionally weak statutes.

TABLE 3.1, continued

SUMMARY OF STATE STATUTES GOVERNING REGULATION OF DEGREE-GRANTING COLLEGES AND UNIVERSITIES

STATUTORY PROVISION	LA*	ME	MD	MA	MI	MN	MS	MO*	MT
Minimum Criteria	Yes	Yes	Yes	Yes	Yes	Yes	Yes	Yes	No
Site Visit by Regulatory Agency	Yes	Yes	Yes	Usually	Yes	Not required by statute but customary	Sometimes	No, because no visits are made before a license is obtained by the school. Once license is issued, visits are made, but not on a regular basis.	No
Religious Exemption	Yes	No	Yes	No	No	Yes	No	Yes	No
Review of Finances	Yes	Yes	Yes	Yes	Yes	Yes	Yes	Yes	No
Surety Bond Required	Yes, $10,000	No	Yes	No	Yes for associate degree solicitation	Yes for for-profits; no for nonprofits	No	Yes	No
Recruiters of Students	No	No	No	No	Yes	Yes	No	No	No
Advertising Regulated	Yes	No	Yes	Yes	No	Yes	No	Yes	No
Periodic Reauthorization Required	Yes	No	No	No	No	Yes	Yes	Yes	No
Out-of-State Activities Monitored	No	Yes	No	No	Yes	No	No	No	No
Out-of-State Institutions Regulated	Yes	Yes	Yes	Yes	Yes	Yes	Yes	Yes	No
Penalties for Violation	Determined by attorney general	Yes	Yes	No	Yes	Yes, minimal	Yes	Yes	No
Consumer Protection Laws Apply	Yes	Yes	Yes	Yes	Yes	Yes	Yes	Yes	Yes
List of Authorized Institutions Maintained	Yes	Yes	Yes	Yes	Yes	Yes	Yes	Yes	No

* State statutes are relatively weak.

TABLE 3.1, continued

SUMMARY OF STATE STATUTES GOVERNING REGULATION OF DEGREE-GRANTING COLLEGES AND UNIVERSITIES

STATUTORY PROVISION	NE	NV	NH	NJ	NM	NY	NC	ND	OH
Minimum Criteria	Yes	Yes	Yes	Yes	Yes	Yes	Yes	Yes	Yes
Site Visit by Regulatory Agency	No for out-of-state; yes for non-public in-state	Yes	Yes	Yes	Yes	Yes	Yes	No	Yes
Religious Exemption	No	No	No	No	Yes	No	Yes	No	No
Review of Finances	No for out-of-state with programs in NE; yes for new non-public in-state	Yes	Yes	Yes	Yes	Yes	Yes	Yes	Yes
Surety Bond Required	No	Yes, $10,000	No	Selected cases	Yes, in-state $5,000; out-of-state $10,000	No	Yes	Yes	No
Recruiters of Students	No	Yes	No	Yes	Yes	Yes	Yes	Yes	No
Advertising Regulated	No	Yes	Yes	Yes	Yes	Yes	Yes	Yes	No
Periodic Reauthorization Required	No	Yes	Yes	Yes	Yes	Yes	Yes	Yes	Yes
Out-of-State Activities Monitored	No	No	No	No	No	No	Yes	No	No
Out-of-State Institutions Regulated	Yes	No	Yes	Yes	Yes	Yes	Yes	Yes	Yes
Penalties for Violation	No	Yes	Yes	Yes	Yes	No	Determined by attorney general	Yes	Yes
Consumer Protection Laws Apply	Yes	Yes	Yes	Yes	Yes	No	Yes, under attorney general	Yes, under attorney general	Yes
List of Authorized Institutions Maintained	Yes	Yes	Yes	Yes	Yes	Yes	Yes	Yes	Yes

TABLE 3.1, continued

SUMMARY OF STATE STATUTES GOVERNING REGULATION OF DEGREE-GRANTING COLLEGES AND UNIVERSITIES

STATUTORY PROVISION	OK	OR	PA	PR	RI	SC	SD*	TN	TX
Minimum Criteria	Yes	Yes	Yes	Yes	Yes	Yes	No	Yes	Yes
Site Visit by Regulatory Agency	Yes	Yes	Yes	Yes	Yes	Yes	No	Yes	Yes
Religious Exemption	No	Yes, from some standards if religious degree title approved	No	Yes	Yes	Yes	No	No	No
Review of Finances	Yes	Yes	Yes	Yes	Yes	Yes	No	Yes	Yes
Surety Bond Required	No	Yes	Yes, minimum unencumbered endowment of $500,000	Yes	Yes, may be required	Yes $10,000 minimum	No	Yes, $10,000 in state; $20,000 out-of-state	No for degree-granting authority; yes for proprietary school operation
Recruiters of Students	No	Yes	No	No	Yes	Yes	No	Yes	Yes
Advertising Regulated	No	Yes	No	Yes	Yes	Yes	No	Yes	Yes
Periodic Reauthorization Required	Yes	Yes	Yes	Yes	No	Yes	No	Yes	Yes
Out-of-State Activities Monitored	No	Yes	No	No	No	No	No	Yes	Yes
Out-of-State Institutions Regulated	Yes	Yes	Yes	Yes	Yes	Yes	No	Yes	Yes
Penalties for Violation	No	Yes	Yes	Yes	Some, but not all	Yes	No	Yes	Yes
Consumer Protection Laws Apply	Yes	Yes	No	Yes	Yes	No	Yes	Yes	Yes
List of Authorized Institutions Maintained	Yes	Yes	Yes	Yes	Yes	Yes	No	Yes	Yes

* South Dakota (and Hawaii) have exceptionally weak statutes.

TABLE 3.1, continued

SUMMARY OF STATE STATUTES GOVERNING REGULATION OF DEGREE-GRANTING COLLEGES AND UNIVERSITIES

STATUTORY PROVISION	UT*	VT	VA	WA*	WV	WI	WY
Minimum Criteria	Yes	No	Yes	Yes	Yes	Yes	Yes
Site Visit by Regulatory Agency	No	No	Yes, as needed	Yes	Yes	Yes	Yes
Religious Exemption	Yes	Yes	Yes, provided only religious degrees are offered	Yes	No	Yes	Yes
Review of Finances	Yes	Yes	Yes	Yes	Yes	Yes	Yes
Surety Bond Required	No	No	No	Yes	Yes	Yes	Yes
Recruiters of Students	Yes	No	No	Yes	Yes	Yes	Yes
Advertising Regulated	Yes	Yes	Yes	Yes	Yes	Yes	Yes
Periodic Reauthorization Required	Yes	Yes	Yes	Yes	Yes	Yes	Yes
Out-of-State Activities Monitored	No	No	Yes	No	No	No	Yes
Out-of-State Institutions Regulated	No	Yes	Yes	Yes	Yes	No	Yes
Penalties for Violation	Yes	Yes	Yes	Yes	No	Yes	Yes
Consumer Protection Laws Apply	Yes	Yes	Yes	Yes	Yes	Yes	Yes
List of Authorized Institutions Maintained	Yes	No	Yes	Yes	Yes	Yes	Yes

* State statutes are relatively weak.

CHAPTER 4

Diploma Mills

What They Look Like
and How to Avoid Them

If you follow the advice given elsewhere in this volume—that you consider enrollment *only* in institutions that have accreditation by an agency recognized by CHEA, CORPA, or the U.S. Department of Education—you can skip this chapter about diploma mills. You may want to be aware, however, of the nature of these highly questionable institutions, which are extensively involved in the world of higher education.

What is a diploma mill? Basically, this term refers to a person or an organization that sells degrees or awards degrees without an appropriate academic base and without requiring sufficient academic achievement at the postsecondary level. It is not necessarily illegal under state and federal laws to operate a diploma mill, so consumers need to be wary.

What constitutes an "appropriate academic base"? There is no precise formula; colleges and universities can exist in a variety of sizes and forms and still qualify as real colleges and universities. But at the core of all such institutions must be a total resource base that is substantial enough to enable the institution to fulfill its mission. The faculty should have academic or professional credentials appropriate for teaching the subject matter and/or for assessing students' acquisition of learning. The curriculum should reflect sound planning by persons who are thoroughly familiar with the field of study. There should be an adequate library or learning resource center, or arrangements should be in place for students to use other appropriate library facilities. Instructional support services, such as academic advising and computer services, also need to be available. Academic records should be maintained and stored under appropriate protocols. The institution's financial base should be sufficient to enable it to pay its employees and acquire resources necessary to provide effective instruction.

What does it mean to require "sufficient academic achievement at the postsecondary level"? This means that before awarding a degree to a student, an institution should do more than collect money and grade a few papers. Course requirements should specify achievement at the postsecondary education level, and assessment procedures should be in place to determine whether students have, indeed, acquired skills or knowledge beyond those required for high school graduation and at a level consistent with the degrees being sought. If the institution offers external degrees or does not itself offer instruction, adequate procedures should be in place to ensure that students have attained college-level learning under the sponsorship of other institutions and organizations or through the use of appropriate assessment methods.

DIPLOMA MILL CHARACTERISTICS

Diploma mills exist in several forms. At its simplest, the diploma mill has few academic pretensions. It simply awards a diploma or degree to a person upon payment of a fee and does not require any demonstration of the achievement of college-level learning. More common these days is the diploma mill that will grant a degree to those who meet requirements that emulate those ordinarily specified at legitimate colleges and universities—but that are far less demanding. These marginal organizations often thrive by advertising their programs as tailored to meet the unique needs of adult learners. Their promotional literature cites the inadequacy (often real enough) of many mainstream institutions in developing programs that are truly designed for adults.

Although some diploma mills are blatantly exploitative commercial enterprises run by people who have no regard for academic values, others are headed by individuals who are honest and well-intentioned but who do not have the background, resources, or competence necessary to organize and administer an institution awarding postsecondary-level degrees. Unaccredited institutions offering religious degrees frequently fall in this category. The basic program may be respectable enough in its outlines, but instruction is likely to be thin at best and academically unsound.

How do you know a diploma mill when you see one? Outlined below are some characteristics that are often associated with diploma mills.

Name and Address

- The organization has a name similar to a well-known college or university.
- The address suggests a prestigious location.

- Mail is received only at a post office box, often the address of a mail-forwarding service.
- The organization frequently changes its address, sometimes moving from state to state.
- The organization's name includes adjectives that convey undue prestige. For example, *United States* or *U.S.* may be used in the name of a college or university to suggest official government sanction, particularly to persons outside the United States. The word *international* is also frequently used as a means of suggesting prestige or as justification for far-flung program activity.

Catalog and Promotional Literature

- A showy front cover on a catalog or promotional piece intentionally gives a false impression. For example, a striking photo of a handsome building in the organization's home city may be left unidentified so that a reader will mistakenly conclude that it is part of the campus.
- Narrative in the catalog and promotional materials is filled with errors in spelling, grammar, and syntax. (A PhD in "Scared Theology" is promised in one catalog; another advertises its "batchelor's" degrees.)
- The catalog is filled with extravagant or pretentious language; for example, one in our collection makes generous and often inappropriate use of such words as *didactics* and *symposia*.
- The catalog is long on canned phrases in Latin and short on clear English. Latin may be used extensively on the letterhead, as well.
- Catalog text states that each student's dissertation is placed on file in the Library of Congress. (In reality, the Library of Congress uses commercial subscription services to acquire information about dissertations and lengthy research papers. Its acquisition of dissertations, of course, implies no certification of quality.)
- A photograph of a diploma appears in the catalog or promotional literature. (We have never seen a diploma pictured in the catalog of a legitimately accredited college or university.)
- A sample copy of a diploma is used in promotional mailings to prospective students.
- The catalog lists as "faculty" individuals who neither teach nor provide any other services to the institution. (In some instances, these individuals may not even know they are listed as faculty by the organization.)
- There is a preoccupation with degree identification for individuals listed in the catalog or promotional literature. For example: *John Doe, Chancellor, PhD, EdD, BSEd, MAR, DD, LHD, LLD.*

- The catalog lists honorary degree holders, and even photographs showing the awarding of honorary degrees to prominent local (perhaps even internationally known) figures.
- Affiliation with an accredited American institution is falsely claimed or implied. (This is especially common in advertisements appearing in foreign publications.)
- The catalog contains advertisements for school paraphernalia (such as rings and T-shirts).
- Subject matter has an inappropriate religious dimension. ("Religious" engineering courses, for example, are offered by one institution that claims exemption from state regulation on religious grounds.)

Policies, Procedures, and Requirements

- Little or no selectivity is practiced in admissions. Frequently, no admissions requirements are listed, and there is no evidence that the organization has the services available to support operation under a sound open-admissions policy. If an open-admissions policy exists, there is no evidence that appropriate criteria for graduation have been established.
- Catalog descriptions of programs vary grossly from the reality of the programs actually offered.
- A wide range of degrees is offered, with a dazzling array of impressive titles. Frequently, a special degree title not listed in the catalog can be obtained without evidence that the institution has the resources to support this type of individualized major.
- Degree requirements, if any, are few and are often unspecified.
- Assessment of learning outcomes or achievement is minimal or nonexistent.
- Professional advanced degrees may be acquired without clearly established examination for requirements or assessment designed to assure mastery of knowledge and skills in the field.
- Degrees can be obtained in far less time than ordinarily would be required for completion of a similar program at a legitimately accredited institution. Degrees are awarded within a few weeks or months from the time of enrollment, without evidence that the institution has a legitimate program for assessing prior learning, supporting self-directed study, and providing the other essentials of a sound external degree program.
- Degrees not listed in the catalog can be created "to order."
- Degrees can be backdated.
- For a fee, official state or federal government "verification of transcript" is offered. (State and federal governments in the United States do not verify transcripts.)

- Dissertations, rather than being structured analyses based on original research, may take the form of a shallow analysis or a description of various aspects of a person's job or current life situation. Dissertations are accepted with misspelled words and grammatical errors.

- Dissertations or other scholarly works are not defended before acknowledged scholars in the field.

- Quantity, rather than quality, is emphasized in evaluating dissertations. For example, one institution boasts about the number of pages in a dissertation written by one of its students. Another requires a dissertation of 25,000 words.

- Papers and dissertations may be submitted in a language other than English.

- A previously written book or article can qualify as a dissertation or thesis.

- Student work is not done under appropriate academic or professional supervision.

- In telephone conversations or correspondence with prospective students, answers are provided for only the most routine questions.

- One diploma reproduction service uses simulated diplomas for a legitimate college or university with a written disclaimer so placed that it can be completely covered by a frame.

Faculty, Administration, and Staff

- Governing boards do not exist or are composed of persons unqualified to serve in such positions. Some persons listed as board members may not know of their "appointment" to the board.

- Long lists of degrees typically follow the names of all officials.

- No full-time personnel with appropriate academic qualifications serve as professional educators or administrators in academic programs.

- Many or all faculty lack appropriate advanced degrees from generally recognized and legitimately accredited higher education institutions. A number of faculty members may hold advanced degrees from the diploma mill itself or from similar organizations.

- Some individuals listed as faculty members neither teach courses nor provide any other services for the institution.

- Part-time staff, most of whom are full-time employees of other organizations, are used extensively to provide instruction or academic services. No evidence exists that such persons have strong ties to the organization or that they function under appropriate orientation, supervision, and evaluation procedures. Also, such staff members may not meet the same or comparable requirements for professional, experiential, and scholarly preparation as their full-time counterparts teaching in the same discipline.

External Degree Program Abuses

- Great emphasis is placed upon granting credit for work experience or life experience—but without appropriate mechanisms for assessing that experience in terms of college-level learning.
- Little emphasis is given to relating prior experience and learning to specified degree requirements.
- Assessment of prior learning is offered free to prospective students on a casual mail-order basis, with an implicit promise that much more credit than is anticipated may be awarded upon actual enrollment.
- Credit for experience is offered based on time spent on a job without any effort to determine skills or knowledge acquired, qualifications to perform, or theoretical understanding of content.
- Credit is granted for prior learning based on "clock hours" or "seat time" spent in a class.
- Credit for work or life experience depends upon the level of degree wanted, with more credit granted if the student is seeking a higher-level degree. (The objective is to keep students enrolled and paying tuition over a longer period of time.)
- Terms such as *nontraditional, alternative,* and *innovative* are used generously to gloss over a multitude of academic shortcomings.
- It may be claimed or implied that respected assessment instruments are used—such as those offered by the Council for Adult and Experiential Learning (CAEL), the College-Level Examination Program (CLEP) of the College Board, or the American Council on Education (ACE)—when this is not in fact the case.
- Many of the organization's degrees are awarded to students in remote locations (for example, Pakistan, India, Nigeria, or Bolivia) where it is unlikely that appropriate local support services exist.
- Assertions that the institution is at the forefront of efforts to make higher education more accessible are coupled with unsupported assertions that traditional institutions make no efforts in this direction.

Authorization, Approval, and Accreditation

- The organization is not accredited by an agency recognized by CHEA, CORPA, or the U.S. Department of Education. Promotional materials may, however, report that the organization is accredited—although that accreditation is by agencies that do not have such recognition.

- The organization claims accreditation by an agency having a name very similar to that of another agency generally recognized as legitimate.
- The false statement that accreditation is not available to institutions that offer nontraditional instruction or distance learning appears in catalogs or promotional literature.
- The organization is located in a state having weak statutes (or inadequate enforcement of statutes) governing the authorization of colleges and universities (see Table 3.1).
- The words *licensed, state-authorized,* or *state-approved* are used ambiguously or deceptively to suggest that the organization has undergone a process of academic review comparable to accreditation.
- The organization is authorized under the laws of one state but has its principal base of operation in another state or even in a foreign country.
- The institution is located in a nation having very few higher education institutions, with most students being residents of other countries.

Fiscal

- Tuition and fees are typically on a per-degree basis rather than a per-semester, per-quarter, or per-course basis. For example, a bachelor's degree might cost $1,200; a master's degree, $2,000; and a doctoral degree, $2,600. Frequently, this information is stated on application forms and most or all of the payment is expected in advance.
- Prospective students may be sent letters urging them to "enroll now" before an increase in fees or tuition takes effect. These letters may be sent routinely to anyone whose reply to an earlier letter is not received within a given period of time.
- Prospective students who do not respond to a recruiting letter are sent another letter notifying them that they have qualified for a fellowship, scholarship, or grant that will mean a lowered tuition upon enrollment.
- A scholarship may be offered simply because someone is a resident of a third-world country.
- Expenses beyond tuition (such as the cost of books, exam fees, and survey completion fees) are stated in fine print.
- Arrangements can be made for the institution to deduct monthly tuition payments from an individual's bank account.

Facilities

- The organization operates from a single room in a private home or office building and has no formal arrangements for use of educational facilities and services that it does not own.

- The organization does not maintain a library of sufficient breadth and depth to support its programs, nor is there provision for access to non-owned libraries. No guidance for using libraries or other resources is provided to students.

CHAPTER 5

Choosing
an External Degree Program
Hallmarks of Quality

The fundamental shift from the Industrial Age to the Information Age has affected higher education along with every other institution and organization in society. The driving force is technology, especially the blending of the various telecommunications technologies with the computer. This is a turbulent and even dangerous time for all institutions. Hugh L. McColl, the chief executive of NationsBank, puts it this way: "[Technology] is like a tidal wave. If you fail in the game, you're going to be dead."

PRINCIPLES TO CONSIDER
IN CHOOSING A DEGREE PROGRAM

While there have been varying degrees of responsiveness to this change by colleges and universities, there is no doubt that technology is having a major impact on all of higher education. With this in mind, the American Council on Education and the Alliance: An Association of Alternative Programs for Adults published *Guiding Principles for Distance Learning in a Learning Society*.[1] This booklet was written for providers of distance-learning programs and accreditation agencies, but it is also useful to prospective students in all types of adult degree programs. *Guiding Principles* covers five key areas: learning design, learner support, organizational commitment, learning outcomes, and technology. We hope you can make use of these principles as you choose an institution for an external degree program.

Learning Design

Learning activities should be designed so that

- The planned learning experiences are appropriate to the subject material.

- The learning to be gained meets the goals of the student.
- The student has some control over the pace and time of the instruction.
- There are flexible opportunities for interaction with the instructor, as well as with other students.

Learner Support

Learner support should provide

- Convenient access to such services as counseling, financial aid information, and library resources.
- Consideration of the student's preferred way of learning, as well as his or her learning setting (such as the workplace).
- Information about course prerequisites, student performance evaluation criteria, and any equipment or technical requirements for the course before the student begins.
- Orientation to the degree program and, if needed, specific training in electronic research and communication skills.

Organizational Commitment

Organizational commitment is evidenced by

- A clear mission statement outlining program goals and values.
- Financial and administrative resources to support the program.
- A research and program evaluation component to ensure effectiveness and currency.
- Investment of institutional resources in faculty and staff professional development.
- Promotion and reward policies that recognize faculty and staff involvement in the program.

Learning Outcomes

Learning outcomes should be the focus of the program by having

- Learning activities organized around outcomes that are clearly demonstrable.
- Assistance to students framed by expected learning outcomes.
- Students participating, whenever possible, in the determination of learning outcomes and how they are to be achieved.
- Assessment of student progress related directly to learning outcomes, course content, and the instructional methods.

- Regular review of learning outcomes to assure their clarity, utility, and appropriateness.

Technology

There is a technology plan and an institutional structure that addresses

- Learning goals and activities.
- Necessary technical requirements.
- Security systems to protect the information shared in learning activities.
- Ease of interactivity among students, faculty, and staff.
- Accessible and understandable technology that is appropriate to the learning to be achieved.
- Training needs of students, faculty, and staff in the uses of the technologies employed in the learning activities.

QUESTIONS TO ASK BEFORE ENROLLING IN A DEGREE-GRANTING PROGRAM

As you consider enrolling in a particular external degree program, you might begin by asking how the program deals with the five key areas addressed in *Guiding Principles*. Whether or not the program is familiar with the ACE/Alliance booklet, you will want to find out whether it offers the education that is right for you. For each of the five principles, questions are suggested below that you may want to ask yourself or raise with officials in the program that you are considering. You may also have other questions of your own. The main thing is to obtain as much information as you need before making the important decision about your future education.

Learning Design

Do you understand how and what you are to learn in the planned learning activity? Does it seem appropriate and doable? Will you be able to engage in the learning activity at a time and place that is good for you? Will you be able to relate some of your course work to your job? Will you be able to communicate on a regular basis with the instructor and, if you wish, with other students?

Learner Support

Do you feel you will need some help in taking on the role of a student? If so, how will the institution assist you by way of orientation and training? Are you clear about any prerequisites and/or learning skills you must have before you begin the program? Will you be able to talk about ways that you like to learn with your instructors?

Organizational Commitment

Does the program have a mission statement? If so, does it state in clear terms why the program exists? Does the statement seem appropriate in relation to your educational goals? Is there information available that describes all the resources in place to make it an effective program? Does the program have ways of evaluating how well it meets student goals?

Learning Outcomes

Are there learning outcomes spelled out for the course(s) you plan to take? If so, will you have an opportunity to discuss them in light of your own learning goals? Do you understand how learning outcomes will relate to the assessment of your performance as a student in the program?

Technology

Does the program have a technology plan? Are the program's technologies relevant to your educational goals? How does the program plan to keep up with the latest technological changes? Does the plan provide for easy access to faculty, other students, and program staff? Is training available, if needed, in the use of electronic technologies?

QUESTIONS TO ASK
THROUGHOUT YOUR ACADEMIC WORK

After enrolling in a degree program, there are two questions that you and your program need to ask throughout your enrollment:

- How is the program doing as your partner in learning?
- How are you doing as a partner in your learning enterprise?

Guiding Principles provides the context for joint reflection on these two questions that are vital to the successful realization of your academic goals and plans. This is especially important in programs that emphasize independent, self-directed study, and various distance learning technologies.

NOTE

1. For further information, write to the Publications Department, American Council on Education, One Dupont Circle, Suite 800, Washington, DC 20036; or phone 202-939-9380.

PART TWO

CHAPTER 6

Institutional Listings

This section lists 140 legitimately accredited external degree programs. Readers should bear in mind that all information in this directory has been supplied by the institutions themselves. External degree programs listed in *The Adult Learner's Guide to Alternative and External Degree Programs,* edited by Eugene Sullivan (Oryx Press, 1993), were asked to complete and return a questionnaire that asked for program information. Questionnaires were also sent to other external degree programs that became known through sources such as references in magazine articles and education journals. The 140 programs that returned completed questionnaires are included in this section. Most of the program data were collected in 1996, and the information is based on programs offered in the 1995–96 academic year. The editors have assumed that the information supplied was factual and accurate.

Listings are not meant to be comparative in nature, nor is a listing in this directory meant to be an endorsement of any institution by the Oryx Press or by the American Council on Education.

HOW TO USE THIS DIRECTORY

This directory section offers key information needed to understand the scope and purposes of each listed external degree program. Institutions are listed alphabetically by state. Following the directory are two related indexes, one of Fields of Study, the other an Alphabetical List of Institutions.

Each directory entry contains the following information:

- Degree(s) offered
- Program mission statement

- Accreditation
- Admission requirements
- Credit hour requirements
- Minimum campus time
- Tuition and fees
- Credit awards for prior learning and for standardized examinations
- A narrative program description

The data offered in each entry should help prospective students determine the most appropriate institutions to meet their needs. It also will assist those who counsel adults in both school and work settings; librarians providing information to patrons who inquire about degree programs for adults; college and university administrators who plan degree programs; decision-makers in accrediting bodies and state degree program approval agencies; and others interested in the field of external education. Each entry begins with the name of the institution, followed by the degree(s) offered and the program mission statement. Also provided are phone and fax numbers and, when available, Internet addresses. While the book uses the generic term "external" in the title, it should be noted that institutions use a variety of terms, including "outreach program" and "online program."

Below is a more detailed description of the information provided in the sections on Accreditation, Credit Requirements, Minimum Campus Time, Tuition and Fees, Credit Awards for Examinations, Credit Awards for Prior Learning, and Description.

Accreditation

All of the institutions included in this book are accredited by an agency recognized by the Council for Higher Education Accreditation (CHEA), the Commission on Recognition of Postsecondary Accreditation (CORPA), or the U.S. Department of Education.

CHEA is a nonprofit membership organization of colleges and institutions. It is supported by member institutions and regional, national, and specialized and professional accrediting bodies. Established in 1996, CHEA serves as a national advocate for voluntary self-regulation through accreditation. One of CHEA's missions is to promote academic quality through the formal recognition of higher education accrediting bodies (previously conducted by CORPA). CHEA is committed to coordinating research and debate to improve accreditation, collecting and disseminating data and information about accreditation fostering communication between and among accrediting associations and the higher education community, and promoting innovation in accreditation policies and practices.

Although institutional accreditation indicates that the basic foundation for quality education programs is present, it is only a partial indicator. For just as quality cannot be "inspected" in a manufacturing process, neither can it be "accredited" in an education program. Rather, quality must be built into the detailed processes of teaching, learning, and program administration; indeed, it resides in the details. (For more information, see Chapter 3.)

Minimum Campus Time

This is time that must be spent on campus to meet degree requirements. Some institutions do not require any campus time.

Tuition and Fees

Tuition is generally the cost per credit hour, although the total semester, quarter, or annual cost may sometimes be given. A normal three-hour course would cost three times the per-credit charge. For example, if the per-credit cost is $200, a regular course would total $600. Many public institutions have a higher tuition cost for out-of-state students. In addition to tuition, there are often a number of fee charges covering such items as registration, graduation, and course materials. Because the information was collected well before the date of publication, many costs will have increased somewhat.

Credit Awards for Examinations

Many of the programs in the directory award credit for passing standardized examinations. A number of such examinations currently are available for institutional credit-by-examination programs. Probably the most widely recognized series of such tests is The College Board's College-Level Examination Program (CLEP). Other examinations are available through the Defense Activity for Non-Traditional Education Support (DANTES), American College Testing (ACT) program, and other organizations. Most are designed to gauge comprehension of subject matter corresponding to a single college course; some are more general in scope. Institutions may also offer their own institutionally developed examinations as a basis for awarding credit.

Credit Awards for Prior Learning

Frequently, adult learners achieve college-level learning in settings outside of the traditional classroom. Many institutions with external degree programs award academic credit for prior learning when that learning is assessed by qualified faculty members, judged comparable to learning outcomes expected in the program, and found relevant to the learner's program of study.

Prior or extra-institutional learning occurs in military service, through courses sponsored by an employer, or by independent study. Various types of extra-institutional learning have been evaluated for academic credit purposes by the American Council on Education (ACE). Descriptions of this learning, along with ACE credit recommendations, may be found in *Guide to the Evaluation of Educational Experiences in the Armed Services; National Guide to Educational Credit for Training Programs;* and *Guide to Educational Credit by Examination.* (See Chapter 2.)

Another way institutions validate prior learning is through portfolio assessment techniques. Assessment instruments and guides developed by the Council on Adult and Experiential Learning are often used for this purpose. (See Chapter 2, note 3.)

Traditional institution-based transfer credit may also be accepted by an external degree program.

Description

This section includes, whenever possible, information about program elements essential to learning such as: student support services access to distance-education opportunities, as well as access to academic resources at a distance; opportunities for interaction with faculty and between students; opportunities for self-designed courses and for relating learning experiences to one's job or local community; and the ways the institution evaluates the effectiveness of its program.

ABBREVIATIONS AND ACRONYMS

AA	Associate of Arts	AGS	Associate of General Studies
AALS	Associate of Arts in Liberal Studies	AP	Advanced Placement
AAS	Associate in Applied Science	AS	Associate of Science
		BA	Bachelor of Arts
ABET	Accreditation Board for Engineering and Technology	BALS	Bachelor of Arts in Liberal Studies
		BBA	Bachelor of Business Administration
ACE	American Council on Education	BCS	Bachelor of Continuing Studies
ACRL	Association of College and Research Libraries	BFA	Bachelor of Fine Arts
ACT	American College Testing	BGS	Bachelor of General Studies
AND	Associate Degree in Nursing	BIS	Bachelor of Independent Studies

BLS	Bachelor of Liberal Studies		MALS	Master of Arts in Liberal Studies
BM	Bachelor of Music		MAT	Master of Arts in Teaching
BPA	Bachelor of Public Administration		MAT	Miller Analogies Test
BS	Bachelor of Science		MBA	Master of Business Administration
BSCS	Bachelor of Science in Computer Science		ME	Master of Engineering
BSET	Bachelor of Science in Engineering Technology		MEd	Master of Education
			MFA	Master of Fine Arts
BSIT	Bachelor of Science in Industrial Technology		MHR	Management of Human Relations
BSN	Bachelor of Science in Nursing		MLA	Master of Liberal Arts
			MM	Master of Management
BSPS	Bachelor of Science in Professional Studies		MN	Master of Nursing
			MPA	Master of Public Administration
BSW	Bachelor of Social Work		MPH	Master of Public Health
CAI	Computer-Assisted Instruction		MPS	Master of Pastoral Studies
CIS	Computer Information Systems		MRE	Master of Religious Education
			MS	Master of Science
CLEP	College Level Examination Program		MSEd	Master of Science in Education
COPA	Council on Postsecondary Accreditation		MSHA	Master of Science in Health Administration
DANTES	Defense Activity for Non-Traditional Education Support		MSW	Master of Social Work
			NLN	National League for Nursing
EdD	Doctor of Education		NTE	National Teacher Examination
EMBA	Executive Master of Business Administration		PACE	Program for Adult College Education
GED	Test of General Educational Development		PhD	Doctor of Philosophy
			PONSI	Program of Noncollegiate Sponsored Instruction
GMAT	Graduate Management Admission Test		ScD	Doctor of Science
GRE	Graduate Record Examination		TOEFL	Test of English as a Foreign Language
MA	Master of Arts		WCC	World Community College
MAE	Master of Arts in Education			

ALABAMA

Auburn University

Graduate and Outreach Program
303 Ramsey Hall
Auburn University, AL 36802
Phone: 334-844-5300
Fax: 334-844-2519
E-mail: jcbrandt@eng.auburn.edu

Degrees Offered
Master's degrees in Aerospace, Chemical, Civil, Computer Science, Electrical, Industrial, Mechanical, and Materials Engineering; Master of Business Administration (MBA)

Program Mission
To respond to requests by industry to provide graduate engineering courses for their employees.

Accreditation
Southern Association of Colleges and Schools

Admission Requirements
Bachelor of Science or Bachelor of Arts from accredited university or college. GRE score for Engineering or GMAT for Business.

Credit Hour Requirements
45–48 quarter hours Engineering and 58–87 quarter hours MBA

Minimum Campus Time
Engineering, two-hour oral exam before graduating; MBA, one oral seminar presentation

Tuition and Fees
$202 per credit hour; $130 registration each quarter; $25 application fee; $20 graduation fee; and $50 late registration fee

Credit Awards for Examinations
None

Credit Awards for Prior Learning
Transfer credits from accredited, degree-granting institutional exams

Description
Students must be within 3- to 4-day mail range. Can be military overseas if they have an APO address.

Advising, book purchasing, registration available 7:45 am–4:45 pm Monday–Friday.

There are videotaped lectures of on-campus courses.

Academic resources are accessed through the Internet.

Interaction between faculty and students is through telephone and e-mail.

Program effectiveness is determined by surveys of distance learners conducted each year. Quality is assured by maintaining the same standards for distance students as for those on campus.

Southern Christian University

Extended Learning Program
1200 Taylor Road
Montgomery, AL 36117
Phone: 800-351-4040
Fax: 334-271-0002
E-mail: scu@wsnet.com

Degrees Offered
Bachelor of Science in Biblical Studies; Bachelor of Arts in Biblical Studies; Master of Arts in Biblical Studies; Master of Science in Ministry; Master of Science in Counseling; Master of Divinity

Program Mission
To meet the educational needs of ministers and other qualified persons interested in religious instruction who are unable to at-

tend classes on campus because of distance, employment obligations, or family responsibilities; to strengthen the churches and related institutions in various locations by upgrading the effectiveness of their leadership; and to promote evangelism and enrich the lives of individuals and families by making available instruction in the Bible and related areas.

Accreditation
Southern Association of Colleges and Schools

Admission Requirements
Undergraduate: high school diploma or GED; Graduate: Bachelor's degree and GRE or MAT scores. Two letters of recommendation.

Credit Hour Requirements
Bachelor of Science, 192 quarter hours; Bachelor of Arts, 192 quarter hours; Master of Arts, 54 quarter hours; Master of Science in Ministry, 54 quarter hours; Master of Science in Counseling, 50 quarter hours; and Master of Divinity, 120 quarter hours

Minimum Campus Time
None

Tuition and Fees
Tuition $135 per quarter hour, ELP fee $55 per quarter hour, and registration fee $150 per quarter

Credit Awards for Examinations
None

Credit Awards for Prior Learning
Transfer credits from accredited, degree-granting institution

Description
The Extended Learning Program is a distance learning delivery system that brings the instructor and the classroom to the student. It combines traditional instruction with modern-day technology to ex-

tend educational opportunity beyond the limits of Southern Christian University's campus. This delivery system offers students who live outside commuting distance or who have inflexible work schedules the opportunity to take courses at their places of employment or in the convenience of their homes.

Students are provided the same access to Southern Christian University library resources as are those who come to campus. Both e-mail and the campus WATS line may be used to contact the library for needed books or journal articles. Library staff sends materials out to students upon request. Library staff will also provide assistance with computer searches on requested topics. Extended Learning students enroll in courses currently being offered by the university, view videotapes of class instruction rushed to them after each class session by priority mail, interact with instructors by written notes and toll-free telephone calls, and complete the same assignments on the same schedule as on-campus students. Library resources needed are made available through arrangements with theological libraries in the student's local area or are mailed to them from Southern Christian University's library.

Most students are ministers, and the courses relate to the ministry. Some degree programs require internships.

Program effectiveness is determined through such measures as the regular review, which is a part of an on-going institutional effectiveness program.

The University of Alabama
Educational Telecommunications

Box 870388
Tuscaloosa, AL 35487-0388
Phone: 205-348-9278

Fax: 205-348-0249
E-mail: ctingle@ccs.ua.edu

Degrees Offered
Master of Science in Engineering, Aerospace Engineering, Electrical Engineering, Mechanical Engineering, Civil Engineering, and Environmental Engineering

Program Mission
To offer various educational formats for working professionals to continue their education without leaving their jobs or disrupting their lives.

Accreditation
Southern Association of Colleges and Schools; Accreditation Board for Engineering and Technology (ABET)

Admission Requirements
Graduate or Bachelor's degree and entrance exam; 3.0 GPA for last 60 hours. No entrance exam if degree is from an accredited institution. If not, score of 1500 on GRE required. Conditional admission for up to 12 semester hours, after which regular admission must be sought to continue degree work.

Credit Hour Requirements
Electrical Engineering, 32 including thesis and seminar; Aerospace Engineering, 24 hours plus thesis or 33 hours without thesis; Mechanical Engineering, 24 hours plus thesis or 33 hours without thesis; Environmental and Civil Engineering, 24 hours plus thesis or 33 hours without thesis

Minimum Campus Time
None

Tuition and Fees
$150 per semester hour and $25 registration per semester

Credit Awards for Examinations
CLEP general exams; CLEP subject exams; DANTES subject tests; College Board AP exams; and Defense Language Institute proficiency tests

Credit Awards for Prior Learning
Transfer credits from accredited, degree-granting institution

Description
Learning formats include Quality University Extended Site Telecourses (QUEST), which delivers classes via videotape to a student's place of employment; intercampus interactive telecommunications system (IITS), which is a network of conference rooms connected by compressed-video technology allowing live interaction; and National Technological University (NTU), which is a private, nonprofit institution that services the needs of busy, highly mobile engineers and scientists via satellite technology. The university is committed to extending its resources through distance learning.

Students support services are available Monday–Friday 8:00 am–4:45 pm.

Students access academic resources through interlibrary loan, e-mail, Internet services, and computer software, as needed.

Interaction with faculty is by telephone during office hours and e-mail.

Interaction between students is by e-mail or live video conferencing.

Each division has a directed individual study course number allowing "special problems" studies.

To determine program effectiveness, evaluations are completed on every course by faculty, on-campus students, distance students, and site coordinators.

The University of Alabama
New College External Degree Program

P.O. Box 870182
Tuscaloosa, AL 35487
Phone: 205-348-6000
Fax: 205-348-7022
E-mail: info@extdegree.nc.ua.edu

Degrees Offered
Bachelor of Arts in Humanities, Human Services, Social Sciences, Communication, Natural Sciences, Administrative Sciences, and Applied Sciences

Program Mission
To assist adult students who have not completed an undergraduate degree and whose educational needs cannot be met by residential programs.

Accreditation
Southern Association of Colleges and Schools

Admission Requirements
Students must be residents of the United States, be 22 years of age or older, have a high school diploma or GED score of 45 or more, have educational goals attainable through the program, and have competency in writing, the ability to read discerningly, and the ability to assume the primary responsibility for learning. There is generally a waiting list to attend an on-campus orientation seminar of about 18 months to two years.

Credit Hour Requirements
128 semester hours are required for graduation, with at least 32 semester hours of University of Alabama (UA) credit gained after official admission to the program

Minimum Campus Time
Three-day, on-campus orientation seminar

Tuition and Fees
$450 orientation; $93 per semester hour; $95 annual participation fee; $200 prior learning; $150 modified prior learning

Credit Awards for Examinations
ACT-PEP: Regents College Examinations Program; CLEP general exams; CLEP subject exams; DANTES subject tests; ACE-evaluated certification exams

Credit Awards for Prior Learning
Transfer credits from accredited, degree-granting institution; ACE military recommendations; ACE/PONSI recommendations; portfolio type assessment

Description
Student support services are available via phone, voice mail, regular mail, and e-mail, Monday–Friday, 8:00 am–5:00 pm. Students must file a yearly degree plan. All course work is coordinated through an advisor. When requested, prospective students on waiting list receive a transcript review before entering program.

Except for the initial three-day orientation seminar required for all students, the program is designed to be completed with no on-campus courses; through distance learning methods such as faculty-designed out-of-class learning contracts, student-designed out-of-class learning contracts, independent studies (correspondence courses), videotaped courses, summer institutes, and weekend seminars.

Students have access to interlibrary loans and to UA network.

Faculty work one-on-one with students and track progress in out-of-class learning contracts. Staff advisors also track students through their yearly degree plans and by reviewing all learning contracts.

Listserv/chat rooms are available for communication between all students.

Learning can be related to various contexts of the student's life through out-of-class learning contracts. Examples include: the Alabama Renaissance Fair, project management of system development, white collar crime, stress and employees working swing shift and night shift jobs, and stream reclamation. All were self-designed out-of-class learning contracts. Out-of-class learning contracts may apply, if appropriate, to any of the areas of the curriculum.

Students develop depth study in interdisciplinary areas rather than having a single-discipline major. Students, therefore, design their own curriculum plan with help of an advisor to assure core curriculum areas are included and overall plan is academically sound.

To determine program effectiveness the Dean of New College meets weekly with the program director to assess activities and the Dean receives monthly reports on financial administration and academic areas of the program. Annually, program staff assesses all areas and plans academic program for following year.

The University of Alabama in Huntsville

Engineering Management/Distance
    Learning Programs
EB 120
Huntsville, AL 35899
Phone: 205-895-6976
Fax: 205-895-6608
E-mail: westbrook@ebs330.eb.uah.edu

Degrees Offered
Master of Science in Engineering, Engineering Management option; Doctor of Philosophy, Engineering Management option

Program Mission
To provide, and continuously improve, the following services to engineering management graduate students and industry partners: state-of-the-art education in engineering management theories and practices, flexible customer service for working professionals, and effective communication of information through innovative technology and distribution processes.

Accreditation
Southern Association of Colleges and Schools; Accreditation Board for Engineering and Technology (ABET)

Admission Requirements
Graduate of ABET-accredited engineering program; five years experience or currently employed in a U.S. firm; 3.0 GPA for undergraduate work; 1500/2400 score on GRE, or 50/100 score on MAT. Current résumé is helpful in assessing experience in engineering field.

Credit Hour Requirements
Master's 36 credit hours; PhD 84 credit hours

Minimum Campus Time
PhD, 18 semester hours; Master's, possibly two three-hour courses

Tuition and Fees
Tuition by location from campus, $520–$695 per three-credit-hour course

Credit Awards for Examinations
Each case is evaluated on an individual basis

Credit Awards for Prior Learning
Transfer credits from accredited, degree-granting institution

Description
Office open from 8:30 am–5:00 pm Monday–Friday. Instructors available through phone, mail, e-mail, via videotape, and in

person. Faculty will make visits to industry locations during semester.

Distance education opportunities include videotaped courses, short courses for "refresher" before taking required courses.

Students at their industry location meet as a class when possible to view the videotapes. When traveling, they view tapes independently. A proctor administers the exams and sends homework into the department. Industry partner provides the necessary VCR equipment and location.

Instructors routinely direct questions to distance students and make them feel a part of the live class. Instructors address concerns of distance students as well as on-campus students on tape.

Interaction between students is provided through team projects. Students from across the country may be paired up as a "team." Class rolls are distributed; students may contact each other when necessary. Students participate in team projects and case studies related to their own work experiences.

One master's course requires attendance on campus for one weekend. During this time, students meet for dinner and, the next day, participate in "Labor Negotiations" for "Labor Relations for Engineers," a course taught each summer semester. Another course, "Modern Manufacturing/Production Systems" meets one weekend to visit industry locations and participate in labs.

Program effectiveness is determined through evaluations distributed to all students, both distance learning and on campus. Final grades typically have been higher for distance learning students.

United States Sports Academy

One Academy Drive
Daphne, AL 36526
Phone: 334-626-3303
Fax: 334-626-3874
E-mail: Admin@USSA-Sport.USSA.edu

Degrees Offered
Master of Sport Science in Sport Coaching, Sport Management, Sport Fitness Management, and Sport Medicine

Program Mission
To provide both traditional and innovative professional growth opportunities in higher education that are sports-specific for students with diverse needs through a variety of courses dedicated to the betterment of sport throughout the world.

Accreditation
Southern Association of Colleges and Schools

Admission Requirements
Bachelor's degree; GRE or MAT; official college transcripts; three letters of recommendation; personal statement; and résumé

Credit Hour Requirements
Master's degree, 60 quarter hours

Minimum Campus Time
Master's program may be taken off campus except for sports medicine classes, which must be taken on campus. Also, all comprehensive exams must be taken on campus.

Tuition and Fees
Master's degree—residential courses, $125 per quarter hour; distance learning, $150 per quarter hour.

Credit Awards for Examinations
None, except for departmental challenge exams

Credit Awards for Prior Learning
Transfer credits from accredited, degree-granting institution

Description
Advising and student support services are available 8:00 am–5:00 pm Monday–Friday.

Academic resources are available through local libraries, the Academy library, and Internet resources. All distance learning students are required to have computer equipment that will interact with the Academy and its online services.

Students are required to interact with faculty on a regular basis through electronic mail, telephone, and/or fax. Students are required to discuss papers and projects with faculty members before beginning them and also during the writing process.

Learning experiences may be related to the contexts of a student's life. For example, a student may wish to do a project for marketing the city's baseball team and then work with the team's owners to implement the project.

Individualized study courses are available to students, and professors work with students to make sure work is of graduate quality.

Program effectiveness is determined by grades, student surveys showing satisfaction with the program, and jobs earned by graduates.

ARIZONA

Prescott College

Adult Degree Program
220 Grove Avenue
Prescott, AZ 86301
Phone: 520-776-7116
Fax: 520-776-5151

Degrees Offered
Bachelor of Arts in Management, Education, and in a wide variety of liberal arts areas

Program Mission
To provide a structure and atmosphere in which students gain competence, self-direction, and insight while fulfilling personal goals. Learning is viewed as an ongoing process. The program recognizes that adult learners are different from their younger counterparts. Adults have been learning throughout their lives—via their personal relations, and through their reading and contemplation of the world. Through these experiences, they have gained unique insight and understanding. Often, adults are highly motivated to learn and have specific and personal goals they wish to achieve. The Adult Degree Program recognizes this, and helps students design learning experiences to meet individual goals.

Accreditation
North Central Association of Colleges and Schools

Admission Requirements
Completed application, educational goals essay, two letters of recommendation, high school or GED diploma, and interview

Credit Hour Requirements
No specific number of quarter hours, as program is competency-based. Range is approximately 180–210 quarter hours.

Minimum Campus Time
Two weekends, one in orientation and one in liberal arts seminar

Tuition and Fees
$6280 per year for 36–46 quarter units

Credit Awards for Examinations
CLEP general exams; CLEP subject exams; DANTES subject tests; College Board AP

exams; Defense Language Institute proficiency tests; and ACE-evaluated certification exams

Credit Awards for Prior Learning
Transfer credits from accredited, degree-granting institution; portfolio type assessment; and department/institutional exams

Description
Each student has an advisor who is in close communication with the student throughout his or her program. Advisors are available according to individual student schedules.

The entire adult degree program is based on independent mentored study.

The library works with students, through use of the Internet, interlibrary loans, and personalized assistance.

Students are assigned an individual advisor who is a member of the adult degree program faculty. Students work with college-approved mentors in their local community. The program design allows for close interaction between students and their advisor and mentors.

Students are given networking lists to help them contact each other. Individual advisors may introduce students in the same geographic area to give students the opportunity to work with each other.

Learning experiences may be related to the contexts of a student's life. In the human services area, for example, a student who works at a human services agency might do a program evaluation as part of course in research methods and statistics. Another student in environmental studies might create a recycling program for his or her community as part of an environmental planning course.

All students design an individualized degree program. Students design their overall curriculum as well as individual courses.

Program effectiveness is determined through such measures as retention rates, surveys of graduates, satisfaction surveys, and placement studies, as well as ongoing program review by faculty and staff.

Rio Salado
Community College

Distance Learning
640 N. First Avenue
Phoenix, AZ 85003
Phone: 602-223-4201
Fax: 602-223-4329
E-mail: distance@rio.maricopa.edu

Degrees Offered
Associate of Arts; Associate of Applied Science; Associate of General Studies

Program Mission
To offers the associate's degree to any student unable to participate in traditional campus real-time classes.

Accreditation
North Central Association of Colleges and Schools

Admission Requirements
Admission into English, reading, or math classes by an assessment test score only

Credit Hour Requirements
64 credits

Minimum Campus Time
None

Tuition and Fees
$34 per credit hour and $5 registration fee for Maricopa County residents. Out-of-state residents with six hours or less add $25 for fees. Students from other counties in Arizona must get permission from their community college.

Credit Awards for Examinations
ACT-PEP: Regents College Examinations Program, CLEP general exams, CLEP subject exams, DANTES subject tests, College Board AP exams, ACE-evaluated certification exams

Credit Awards for Prior Learning
Transfer credits from accredited, degree-granting institution; ACE military recommendations; ACE/PONSI recommendations; department/institutional exams

Description
Student support services include tutoring in person, hotline phone tutoring, block tutoring, and special services seven days a week; personal and career counseling five days a week, 8:00 am–5:00 pm; testing, scholarship counseling, and financial aid counseling all by appointment.

Distance education opportunities include print-based, audiocassette, videocassette, online, Internet, teleconference, Imagenet, videoconference network, and mixed media.

Students may utilize any of the Maricopa Community Colleges for library materials as well as access library materials via computer from any of the college's computer labs or on their personal computer using a modem. Software may be accessed in the college's four computer labs.

Voice messaging is utilized by instructors to post a weekly memo as well as for students to leave messages 24 hours a day.

Interaction between students is voice messaging for each class section 24 hours a day. "Grapevine" voice messaging for each language student 24 hours a day. Teleconferencing for synchronous class meetings and review sessions.

A major project in the MGT 253 course, for students who own and operate a business, is developing a business plan for their company. Other courses include assignments that can be work related.

The FLEX program, which was piloted in the summer of 1995 and readily accepted by students, allows students to enroll at various times and accelerate the course if desired.

Program effectiveness is determined through such measures as student retention rate, growth of program, student evaluation of each course taken, peer evaluation of instructor by faculty chair, and accreditation of Rio Salado by the North Central Association of Colleges and Schools.

University of Arizona Extended University

Master of Arts in Library Science
F. S. Griego, Floor 3
Main Gate Center
Tucson, AZ 85721
Phone: 520-621-1031
Fax: 520-621-3269
E-mail: fsg@u.arizona.edu

Degrees Offered
Master of Arts in Library Science

Program Mission
To contribute to the advancement of library science and information management through research and teaching.

Accreditation
North Central Association of Colleges and Schools; American Library Association

Admission Requirements
Bachelor's degree, transcripts, two letters of recommendation, and GRE

Credit Hour Requirements
MA, 36 semester units; PhD, 48 semester units and dissertation

Minimum Campus Time
12 semester units

Tuition and Fees
$770 per three-unit course

Credit Awards for Examinations
None

Credit Awards for Prior Learning
Transfer credits from accredited, degree-granting institution

Description
The program is weighted in technology and emphasizes theoretical constructs of library and information science.

Advising and support services are available anytime via Internet and by phone during business hours, 8:00 am–5:00 pm Monday–Friday. Distance opportunities include: e-mail, videotape lectures, internships, and independent study. Students access academic resources via the Internet, e-mail, and library. Students are required to subscribe to general School of Library Science listserv, the individual course listserv each semester, and they will have professor's Internet address. Course listserv provides participation grade.

Internships are available. Independent study units may be earned provided student has access to local library or information resource center.

Program effectiveness is determined through such measures as tracking student graduation. There is a 90-plus percent graduation rate and 90-plus percent of graduates are hired upon completion of degree.

University of Phoenix

Center for Distance Education
4065 E. Elwood Street
Phoenix, AZ 85040

Phone: 602-921-8014
Fax: 602-894-2152
E-mail: cdeinfo@apollo1.uophx.edu

Degrees Offered
Associate of Arts through credit recognition (military personnel only); Bachelor of Science in Business/Administration; Bachelor of Science in Business/Management; Bachelor of Science in Business/Information Systems; Bachelor of Science in Business/Accounting; Master of Business Administration; Master of Business Administration–Technology Management; Master of Arts in Organizational Management; Master of Arts in Education; Master of Nursing; certificate programs

Program Mission
To provide high-quality education to working adult students. The University of Phoenix is a private, for-profit higher education institution. It identifies educational needs and provides— through innovative methods including distance education technologies—educational access to working adults, regardless of their geographical location. The university provides general education and professional programs that prepare students to articulate and advance their personal and professional goals.

Accreditation
North Central Association of Colleges and Schools

Admission Requirements
Undergraduate—High school graduation or GED certificate; a minimum of 24 transferable semester credits from regionally accredited institutions; current employment or access to an appropriate organizational environment that will allow completion of program course work; at least 23 years of age; completion of the university's Comprehensive Cognitive Pre-Assessment; and an acceptable score on the Test of English as a Foreign Language (TOEFL) for non-native speakers of English.

Graduate—An undergraduate degree from a regionally accredited, or candidate for accreditation, college or university; a minimum GPA of 2.5 on the degree-posted transcript; post–high school work experience related to the graduate degree program for which the student is applying; current employment or access to an appropriate organizational environment that will allow completion of program course work; completion of the University's Comprehensive Cognitive Pre-Assessment; and an acceptable score on the Test of English as a Foreign Language (TOEFL) for non-native speakers of English.

Credit Hour Requirements
Associate of Arts through credit recognition, 60 semester hours; BS in Business/Administration, Business/Management, and Business/Information Systems, 120 semester hours; BS in Business/Accounting, 126 semester hours; MB in Administration and Administration/Technology Management, 51 semester hours; MA in Organizational Management, 49 semester hours; MA in Education, 37 semester hours; Master of Nursing, 39 semester hours; and certificate programs—18 semester hours

Minimum Campus Time
None

Tuition and Fees
AA, $530 per credit hour; Undergraduate tuition, $265 per credit hour; Graduate tuition, $295 per credit hour; and application fee, $50

Credit Awards for Examinations
ACT-PEP: Regents College Examinations Program; CLEP general exams; CLEP subject exams; DANTES subject tests; College Board AP exams; ACE-evaluated certification exams

Credit Awards for Prior Learning
Transfer credits from accredited, degree-granting institution; ACE military recommendations; ACE/PONSI recommendations; portfolio type assessment

Description
The Center for Distance Education employs a team of enrollment advisors and academic counselors who provide support to students beginning with the first step in the admission process, through their degree programs, to graduation. Students can communicate with staff through phone, fax, e-mail, and mail. The center offers extended business hours, Monday–Friday 8:00 am–6:00 pm. Students may also e-mail requests to: request@bsdi.uophx.edu or conduct their own searches by utilizing the Electronic Info/News Center on the university's home page (http://www.uophx.edu).

The Learning Resource Center functions as an electronic library by performing bibliographic searches and document retrieval for students, staff, and alumni. The center has electronic access to millions of citations in hundreds of online and CD-ROM databases. The center is also home to extensive microfiche and CD-ROM collections carefully aligned to the university's programs.

The center also provides professional statistical processing assistance during the completion of student's major research projects.

The University of Phoenix Adult Learning Outcomes Assessment (ALOA) project is one of the most comprehensive personal and educational assessments of working adults at any accredited college or university in the nation. The principal purpose of the project is to provide students with useful information about their educational achievements and needs.

The Alumni Network provides services and benefits both to current students and to university graduates. The alumni group offers seminars, workshops, and courses; maintains a scholarship program; and participates in several career opportunity referral services. The national office is open from 8:00 am–5:00 pm Monday–Friday.

The center offers directed-study courses. Students communicate with staff and faculty by telephone, e-mail, fax, or mail.

The curriculum developed for each course utilizes appropriate texts, supplemental readings, and a course module. The course module is used in conjunction with the faculty member's course syllabus and indicates the required outcomes for the course. Students working toward these course outcomes can also utilize the Learning Resource Center to access outside sources for their research activities.

Students are required to make weekly contact with their faculty members in order to meet the university's attendance requirements. This contact can include submission of course assignments, faxes, telephone calls, e-mail communications, and letters. Weekly attendance is reported by faculty members and logged by the university.

Students are required to attend a tele-conferenced orientation at the beginning of their program. This orientation acquaints students with other Center for Distance Education students and covers university academic and operational policies. Additional student interaction is limited due to the nature of the program.

Course curriculum is designed to integrate academic theory and current professional practices, and its application to the workplace. The courses are designed to enhance the working adult student's involvement, and student work-related projects constitute a primary method of learning.

In addition to the ALOA project, the university's system for assessing and managing the quality of educational process and providing feedback for the improvement of those processes is known as the Academic Quality Management System (AQMS). The AQMS comprises the following components: student end-of-course survey, faculty end-of-course survey, student comment analysis system, faculty grading practices, academic quality management system decision support software, internal customer service survey, registration/graduation survey, and comments to the chair. This provides a broad base of decision-support information pertaining to the management of academic quality and effectiveness.

CALIFORNIA

California College for Health Sciences

222 West 24th Street
National City, CA 91950
Phone: 619-477-4800
Fax: 619-477-2257
Internet: http://www.cchs.edu

Degrees Offered
Associate of Science in Respiratory Technology; Respiratory Therapy; Early Childhood Education; Medical Transcription; Electroencephalograph; Allied Health; Business Administration; and Finance. Bachelor of Science in: Health Services; Marketing; and Accounting. Master of Science in Community Health Administration; and Wellness Promotion.

Program Mission
CCHS is dedicated to adult learning. Specializing in health services degree programs, CCHS will be expanding to offer business, finance, marketing, and accounting degree programs.

Accreditation
Distance Education and Training Council; Joint Review Committee Respiratory Therapy Education

Admission Requirements

High school diploma; specific requirements for each degree program. Six months' experience for Respiratory Technologist. Certification in Respiratory for Respiratory Therapist program.

Credit Hour Requirements

Associate of Science, 60 semester hours; Bachelor of Science, 120 semester hours; Master of Science, 36 semester hours

Minimum Campus Time

None

Tuition and Fees

$100 per credit plus $35 registration fee for college courses. $1990 respiratory programs and $2200 EEG program.

Credit Awards for Examinations

ACT-PEP: Regents College Examinations Program; CLEP subject exams; College Board AP exams; CLEP general exams; and DANTES subject tests

Credit Awards for Prior Learning

Transfer credits from accredited, degree-granting institution; ACE/PONSI recommendations; ACE military recommendations; and portfolio type assessment

Description

Student advisement can be accessed 7:30 am–5:00 pm PST, Monday–Friday. Students can obtain course support in any program by instructors credentialled in the specific subject area.

CCHS provides independent study courses and limited student services by e-mail.

There is open enrollment for all courses, enrolling students to enroll at any time during the year.

The course materials sent to students contain all necessary information; however, students will need to access library facilities to search required information. Students may access advisors for clarification.

CCHS offers a buddy system, which is used to pair-up students upon request.

Student feedback and quarterly student completion rates are used to determine program effectiveness.

California Institute of Integral Studies

Integral Studies Doctorate
9 Peter Yorke Way
San Francisco, CA 94109
Phone: 415-674-5500
Fax: 415-674-5555
Internet: http://www.ciis.edu

Degrees Offered

Doctorate in Integral Studies with an area of concentration in Learning and Change in Human Systems

Program Mission

To develop scholar-practitioners who can conduct research on the process of transformative change in human systems.

Accreditation

Western Association of Schools and Colleges

Admission Requirements

Completion of master's degree; exceptions will be made for candidates of unusual promise who have demonstrated advanced learning in areas relevant to goal of the program. Skills and competencies in chosen field; willingness to work both independently and collaboratively and to participate in experiential learning community.

Credit Hour Requirements

90 quarter hours

Minimum Campus Time

Three days per month; two residential seminars (6 days) per year

Tuition and Fees
$310 per unit; 9 units per quarter; 3 quarters per year. $75 registration fee per quarter. $300 residency fee for yearly intensives.

Credit Awards for Examinations
None

Credit Awards for Prior Learning
None

Description
Student services 9:00 am–5:00 pm Monday–Friday by phone, fax, or via e-mail anytime.

Distance education opportunities include online course work, independent studies, and online electives.

All seminars and advising are conducted online or by phone. The library can be accessed online.

Interaction between faculty and student includes computer conferencing, e-mail, and online folders (which hold continuing discussions about mutual interest areas).

Learning experiences may be designed to relate to various contexts of the student's life. Some examples are: analysis of the mental models guiding their employing institution, cooperative inquiry within community or organization, and synergetic inquiry within community or organization.

Some degree requirements may be met through group-designed courses. Individuals can take 16 units (of 90) independently (i.e., through independent study).

Program effectiveness is determined through such measures as monthly feedback on progress; annual "empowerment evaluation" of each group; faculty assessment of each student annually; faculty assessment of collective demonstrations; and measures of expanded consciousness, awareness of personal worldview, capacity to reflect alone and within collective, and capacity to plan and carry out rigorous research.

During the program, students progressively assume more leadership in the process; faculty transition from teachers to consultants and coaches.

California State University, Dominquez Hills
Division of Nursing

1000 E. Victoria Street
Carson, CA 90747
Phone: 310-243-3596
Fax: 310-516-3542
E-mail: kjohnstan@dhux20.csudh.edu

Degrees Offered
Bachelor of Science in Nursing; Master of Science in Nursing

Program Mission
To offer distance learning programs in nursing, in California and nationally.

Accreditation
Western Association of Schools and Colleges; National League for Nursing

Admission Requirements
Licensure as a registered nurse in the United States; at least 56 transferable units; GPA 2.0 or greater. May begin class work before applying and before acceptance.

Credit Hour Requirements
BSN, 53 semester units of nursing support and integrated nursing courses. MSN, 36 semester units for all but family nursing practitioner, which is 52 semester units.

Minimum Campus Time
None

Tuition and Fees
National—$210 per unit with added online/course costs; state of California—$532, 0–

6 units and $865, 7 or more units; nonresident—$246 per unit

Credit Awards for Examinations
ACT-PEP: Regents College Examinations Program; CLEP general exams; CLEP subject exams; DANTES subject tests; College Board AP exams; New York Regents College Exams

Credit Awards for Prior Learning
Transfer credits from accredited, degree-granting institution

Description
In California, students physically attend class in 170 different sites throughout the state. The same program is offered by satellite and videotape across the nation.

Student support services available 7:00 am–6:00 pm Monday–Friday and 10:00 am–2:00 pm Saturday. 8:30 am–5:00 pm Monday–Friday, 800-344-5484.

Distance education opportunities in the national program include satellite delivery, videotape, voice mail, bulletin board service, e-mail, and online library services.

In the California program, where classes in real time and real space are offered, limited e-mail and online library services are available.

Online literature and computer/fax delivery services are available for both programs. Students must have computer and modem with computer software. (Students must have beginning computer skills.) Initial class introduces how to complete literature search, etc. 1-800-HELP line available to national students.

Assignments to meet course requirement are integrated into syllabi for student-to-student discussion and student-to-instructor interactions by Internet and voice mail.

To provide for student interaction, the national program has a bulletin board service.

Preceptored courses have integrated theory-clinical experiences in the student's locale. Student selects and nominates preceptor whose qualifications meet course guidelines. Instructor must pre-approve preceptor and agency.

Learning contracts are used to individualize instruction and provide students with a high degree of control over their learning and as a tool to plan for performance course learning experiences. Students may pursue a higher-level objective, one that subsumes one or more of the required course objectives, if they already have had experience with the lower-level objective. Students also may add their own objectives that are complementary to the course objectives, but not required. The learning contract gives the student a great deal of control over the time, place, and pace of the field experience, subject to negotiation with, and approval by, both the instructor and the preceptor.

Program effectiveness is determined through such measures as surveys of student perception of instructor effectiveness, and surveys of graduates.

California State University, Dominquez Hills
HUX Master of Arts Program

SAC II/Room 2126
1000 E. Victoria Street
Carson, CA 90747
Phone: 310-243-3741
Fax: 310-516-3971
E-mail: huxonline@dhvx20.csudh.edu

Degrees Offered
Master of Arts in Humanities

Program Mission
To offer an external degree program for anyone presently holding a bachelor's de-

gree, who prefers an individualized approach to advanced education rather than traditional classroom courses on college campuses.

Accreditation
Western Association of Schools and Colleges

Admission Requirements
Bachelor of Arts or Bachelor of Science from accredited university; GPA of 3.0 (at least 2.5 for conditional admission); TOEFL required in some cases. Intellectual autobiography showing strength of writing ability and ability to conceptualize also required

Credit Hour Requirements
30 semester hours

Minimum Campus Time
None

Tuition and Fees
Courses $120 per unit; $55 application fee; $35 graduation fee; $60 books per semester

Credit Awards for Examinations
None

Credit Awards for Prior Learning
Transfer credits from accredited, degree-granting institution, up to 9 units. Units may not be more than five years old at time of graduation from HUX program.

Description
Students receive advising from coordinators and from their course instructors. Telephone numbers are provided on all syllabi. These hours vary each semester, as coordinator and faculty also teach on campus.

Distance education opportunities include independent study courses; audiotapes for music courses; some courses are online; eventually, all courses will be online. E-mail is used by majority of faculty.

Some independent studies may be done as art internships (museum work, etc.). Some assignments in some art courses may be fulfilled by writing about architecture or works in museums in student's location.

Up to three courses of independent study are allowed.

Program effectiveness is determined by evaluations by Dean of Extended Education, HUX Committee, HUX faculty, and accreditation. All new courses must receive approval of school and university curriculum committees, Dean of Extended Education and College of Arts and Sciences, and Associate Vice President of Academic Planning.

The Fielding Institute

2112 Santa Barbara Street
Santa Barbara, CA 93105
Phone: 800-340-1099
Fax: 805-687-9793
Internet: http://www.fielding.edu

Degrees Offered
Doctor of Philosophy (PhD) in Clinical Psychology, Human and Organization Development; Doctor of Education in Educational Leadership and Change; Master of Arts in Organizational Design and Effectiveness

Program Mission
To offer networked distance learning opportunities for midcareer professionals at the graduate level.

Accreditation
Western Association of Schools and Colleges

Admission Requirements
Accredited bachelor's degree, previous academic and professional experience in the field to which one is applying. For the psychology program only: students must reside in the continental United States (excluding Hawaii) or Canada.

Credit Hour Requirements
None

Minimum Campus Time
Students must attend a one-week orientation session in Santa Barbara, CA. Other academic and research sessions are offered throughout the year in various locations. Various academic, clinical, and research requirements. Request individual program brochures for details.

Tuition and Fees
Annual tuition is $10,200

Credit Awards for Examinations
None

Credit Awards for Prior Learning
None

Description
The Human and Organization Development program is an interdisciplinary program in the applied social and behavioral sciences. The Clinical Psychology Program provides a traditional doctoral-level curriculum that meets the psychology licensing standards in most states. Educational Leadership and Change is a cohort-based program for individuals who wish to provide leadership for creating change within educational systems in conjunction with an EdD program. Organizational Design and Effectiveness is a master's-level program for professionals who want to provide effective leadership for the future in their workplace and community.

Faculty/student cluster groups and administrative and support staff are available for advising.

All academic work is done on an individualized, self-directed basis; electronic seminars offered.

Extensive training and assistance provided for online learning resources, electronic databases, library access, research skills, etc.

Students have extensive interaction with a local faculty advisor, and a communications system is in place for learning opportunities with a national network of faculty.

Students interact by means of an electronic learning community, as well as numerous opportunities for face-to-face interaction.

Individual interests and needs can be negotiated within the boundaries of the curriculum design.

Frequent feedback mechanisms are built into the learning model. Regular, periodic self-studies and surveys are conducted.

The Fielding Institute model was developed to accommodate the learning styles and needs of midcareer, midlife students. Important elements are: contract-based learning, competence-based assessment, student initiative, building on existing learning and experience, collaborative learning, flexible scheduling, integration of theory and practice, and a commitment of multicultural and global awareness.

Loma Linda University School of Public Health

Office of Extended Programs
Nichol Hill, Room 1706
Loma Linda, CA 92350
Phone: 909-824-4595
Fax: 909-824-4087
E-mail: ttamayose@sph.llu.edu

Degrees Offered
Master of Public Health, areas of emphasis include Health Administration, Health Promotion and Education, and International Health

Program Mission
To meet the needs of qualified individuals seeking to develop graduate-level competencies in public health but who, for a

variety of reasons, do not chose to become full-time, on-campus students.

Accreditation
Western Association of Schools and Colleges

Admission Requirements
Baccalaureate degree from an accredited institution, with a GPA of 3.0 or above. An applicant whose GPA is less than 3.0 may be considered if current GRE scores have been submitted. Each program has specific prerequisite courses. Applicants are encouraged to contact each department for details. As face-to-face interviews with each applicant are not always possible, arrangements must be made with the particular department to which the individual is applying.

Credit Hour Requirements
MPH in Health Administration, minimum 49 quarter units; MPH in Health Promotion and Education, minimum 51 quarter units; and MPH in International Health, minimum 55 quarter units

Minimum Campus Time
Course sessions are conducted at each off-campus site on a regularly scheduled basis. With the exception of format, courses offered off campus are regular School of Public Health courses. They carry the same credit units as on-campus courses. Each course consists of a 10-week module with independent study assignments. Halfway through the module, an intensive student/instructor session of three to five days is scheduled at the off-campus instruction center. Similarly structured courses are offered on campus during the summer quarter. Students have the option to register for these on-campus courses.

Tuition and Fees
Tuition is currently $325 per unit; $25 application fee

Credit Awards for Examinations
None

Credit Awards for Prior Learning
Transfer credits from accredited, degree-granting institution

Description
Health Administration: The MPH program with an emphasis in health administration provides an understanding of healthcare management issues and skills within the broad perspective provided by an introduction to the public health sciences. It is designed for healthcare professionals who expect to advance into administrative responsibilities and those without healthcare professional degrees who plan a career in healthcare management. The student will be prepared for careers in either public- or private-sector healthcare management.

Health Promotion and Education: This program is designed around the specific needs of the individual who wants an emphasis in health promotion and who has the appropriate experience or training.

International Health: The MPH program with an emphasis in international health prepares professionals to apply their skills in solving the special problems of developing countries and disadvantaged groups in the U.S. population. The program is ordinarily from five to six quarters in length for full-time students. Off-campus students may complete the program by taking the public health core requirements at an off-campus site and the international health requirements at Loma Linda University during summer sessions. Courses are offered during the summer in the block format of three- to five-day sessions with pre- and postsession assignments. Scheduling is done to enable a student to meet all international health requirements in four consecutive summer sessions.

The MPH program with an emphasis in health promotion and education is limited to licensed health professionals.

Upon admission into a degree program, each student is assigned an academic advisor—a faculty member in the student's major department. When questions arise relating to curriculum or policy requirements, students may refer to the SPH Bulletin, program curriculum outline, academic advisor, and if necessary, the Director of the Office of Admissions and Academic Records. At the beginning of each fall quarter, orientation and advisement sessions are scheduled for all new students. Extended campus program students are welcome but not required to attend. Other facilities are available to assist students in excelling toward their academic goals. They include: Student Assistant Program "Avenue," 909-799-6050; University Counseling Center, 919-824-4507; Teaching Learning Center, 919-478-8625.

Most courses in the extended campus format are offered at a location distant to Loma Linda. Students are encouraged to take as many of these courses as possible at the site to which they are assigned. There have been instances where students fly to other locations (including Loma Linda) to complete course work. There are a limited number of independent study units available for an MPH degree.

Students obtain library resources through their place of employment (e.g., hospitals, clinics, public health departments), local libraries (university, college, and community), and the Del Webb Library at Loma Linda University either by written request or by toll-free telephone number. The campus library has installed CD-ROM databases that are now available to students. All students are required to be computer literate and have access to computers at home or through their workplace.

Every course taught in the extended campus format requires a faculty member to meet with students in a classroom situation for a specified number of contact hours. An academic advisor is also assigned to each site location. Periodically, this advisor will go to the site for advisement opportunities. Advisors and course instructors are also available by telephone, e-mail, written correspondence, and fax.

Many of the courses taught in the extended campus format include group projects and assignments. Much emphasis is placed on student interaction within group as well as individual situations. Students also develop their own study groups.

Many courses allow students to complete projects from work environments, including grants, papers, statistical analyses, group activities, and independent study projects.

The school conducts periodic surveys of its graduates including those in the extended campus program to determine program effectiveness.

National University

Extended Studies Institute
4141 Camino del Rio South
San Diego, CA 92108
Phone: 619-563-7370
Fax: 619-563-2515
E-mail: esi@nunic.nu.edu

Degrees Offered
Bachelor of Business Administration; Bachelor of Science in Nursing; Global Master of Business Administration

Program Mission
To make higher education degree programs available to adult students who cannot, for various reasons, attend the university's regular on-site programs.

Accreditation
Western Association of Schools and Colleges

Admission Requirements
High school diploma or GED equivalent

Credit Hour Requirements
BBA, 180 quarter hours; BS Nursing, 180 quarter hours; and Global MBA, 60 quarter hours

Minimum Campus Time
A summer intensive is required for Global MBA

Tuition and Fees
Tuition for video teleconferencing programs is $715 per course

Credit Awards for Examinations
ACT-PEP: Regents College Examinations Program; CLEP general exams; CLEP subject exams; DANTES subject tests; ACE-evaluated certification exams

Credit Awards for Prior Learning
Transfer credits from accredited, degree-granting institution; ACE military recommendations; ACE/PONSI recommendations; departmental/institutional exams

Description
Courses and degree programs offered through the Extended Studies Institute are delivered through a variety of distance education technologies to students' homes, community colleges, and businesses.

Student admission advisors are available from 9:00 am–8:00 am Monday–Friday and 9:00 am–4:00 pm Saturday. These advisors are able to assist with scheduling, financial aid questions, and other student concerns. The Extended Studies Institute is also staffed with individuals who track student progress and ensure that assignments and exams are handled properly and efficiently.

Video teleconferencing courses incorporate e-mail and desktop video units for interaction between students and between faculty and students outside of class time. The Global MBA is an independent study format and incorporates CD-ROM, World Wide Web, e-mail, and video teleconferencing in the delivery of the course.

Academic services are accessed through the Internet and video teleconferencing over a proprietary phone network or through outside service providers. Many courses are taught in conjunction with other institutions. Therefore, students have access to computer resources at their local institution.

Video teleconferencing interaction is incorporated into the two-way audio and video technology. Interaction for the Global MBA is part of the course design. Students from institutions around the world are expected to work jointly on portions of the case studies.

The design of each course encourages students to draw on their work and life experiences.

Program effectiveness is determined by comparing similar on-site programs to the distant programs. Attitudinal surveys are also administered to students at the end of each course.

Pacific Oaks College

Human Development
5 Westmoreland Place
Pasadena, CA 91103
Phone: 818-397-1351
Fax: 818-577-6144

Degrees Offered
Master of Arts in Human Development

Program Mission
To promote social justice and respect for diversity. With roots in early childhood education, the focus is on the preparation

and continuing education of professionals who work with children and families.

Accreditation
Western Association of Schools and Colleges

Admission Requirements
Bachelor's degree of 60 or more semester units meeting all transfer requirements, for MA/ABLE (Assessment by Life Experience). Admission is limited to students at least 35 years of age with five or more years of leadership experience in human services.

Credit Hour Requirements
30 semester units (up to 42 units for MA/ABLE students)

Minimum Campus Time
Two to four weeks (one week at a time or two weeks at a time). Classes are available in Pasadena, Seattle, and the San Francisco area.

Tuition and Fees
$455 per credit and $30 student service fee per semester

Credit Awards for Examinations
CLEP general exams; CLEP subject exams

Credit Awards for Prior Learning
Transfer credits from accredited, degree-granting institution; portfolio type assessment

Description
Most students enroll part-time, integrating study with work and family lives. Computer technology increases the connection with students at a distance.

Areas of competence in the program: life cycle theory, social/political contexts of development, communication, research, implementation in work with children and/or adults.

Admissions advising, financial aid, program advising by distance learning faculty. Offices are open 8:30 am–4:30 pm Monday–Friday. Voice mail, mail, fax, and e-mail can also be used.

Distance education opportunities include computer mediated classes (online asynchronous e-mail meetings) and independent study by mail (limited).

Students may access the library catalog by computer; books may be borrowed by mail; software for online instruction is provided as needed.

Faculty advise distance students and teach online classes that are highly interactive.

Action and research projects in classes and the master's project are based on topics of the student's choice from the student's job or community environment. Credit is given for observation and fieldwork.

Independent studies are self-designed, based on fieldwork/journaling and/or reading.

Program effectiveness is determined by continual monitoring by faculty and student participants in a dialogue process, review by institutional committee on distance learning, and program completion by students.

Saybrook Institute

Graduate School and Research Center
450 Pacific Avenue
San Francisco, CA 94133
Phone: 800-825-4480
Fax: 415-433-9271
E-mail: blittleton@igc.apc.org

Degrees Offered
Master of Arts in Psychology; Master of Arts in Human Science; Doctor of Philosophy in Psychology; Doctor of Philosophy in Human Science. Interest areas: Clinical Inquiry, Consciousness Studies, Health

Studies, Organizational Inquiry, Systems Inquiry, Social Philosophy and Political Psychology, and Peace and Conflict Resolution Studies

Program Mission

To provide a unique and creative environment for graduate study, research, and communication in humanistic psychology and human science, focused on understanding and enhancing the human experience. Applying the highest standards of scholarship, the Saybrook Institute is dedicated to fostering the full expression of the human spirit and humanistic values in society.

To accomplish this mission, the institute offers an innovative, individualized, and rigorous distance learning opportunity. It also encourages ongoing research to develop more valid and effective methodologies for building a meaningful body of knowledge about human experience.

Accreditation

Western Association of Schools and Colleges

Admission Requirements

Graduation from an accredited college or university. PhD in psychology must hold the Master's in Psychology or Counseling. Interview may be required. Attendance at residential orientation conference. Also, academic writing sample, personal statement, three letters of recommendation, official transcripts, and curriculum vitae.

Credit Hour Requirements

Master's, 31 units; PhD, 72 units

Minimum Campus Time

Students are required to attend a five-day residential orientation conference and two residential conferences each year (weeklong)

Tuition and Fees

Academic year tuition (September–August) is $10,500. Costs for course materials are not included. Conference fees are approximately $600 including room and board. Travel costs vary.

Credit Awards for Examinations

None

Credit Awards for Prior Learning

Transfer credits from accredited, degree-granting institution; department/institutional exams

Description

Regular office hours are 8:30 am–4:30 pm Monday–Friday. Director of Academic Counseling offers direct support to students. Faculty advisors assigned. Support provided through Internet also. Staff and faculty available at residential conferences. Dean of Students accessible.

Regional seminars are offered. Learning guides and course readers provide a framework for courses. All faculty and staff are accessible by e-mail as well as through electronic conferences established for specific student interests. Fax available.

There is full electronic access to faculty and staff. Web site currently in development, as well as expansion of teaching/learning modes. Students can contact faculty through long-distance phone calls, as well as through fax and ground mail.

Student representatives are involved in administration, faculty, and board committees. Students interact with each other through electronic conferences as well as at meetings. A student newsletter is published bimonthly.

There is flexibility for relating learning experiences to various contexts of the student's life with the approval of faculty.

Independent studies may also be developed with a maximum of nine credits with faculty approval.

Program effectiveness is determined through course and program completion rates, evaluations of courses, and conferences. Faculty Research and Development Committee also assesses program effectiveness.

COLORADO

College for Financial Planning

Master of Science Degree
4695 S. Monaco Street
Denver, CO 80237-3403
Phone: 303-220-1200
Fax: 303-220-5146

Degrees Offered
Master of Science, with an academic emphasis in the area of personal financial planning

Program Mission
To provide graduate-level study in four crucial personal financial planning areas: wealth management, estate planning, retirement planning, and tax planning.

Accreditation
North Central Association of Colleges and Schools; Distance Education and Training Council

Admission Requirements
Bachelor's degree from a regionally accredited college or university; promise of the ability to succeed in graduate studies related to personal financial planning; undergraduate financial services background.

Credit Hour Requirements
36 semester credit hours

Minimum Campus Time
None

Tuition and Fees
$75 program application processing fee and $525 for each three-credit course

Credit Awards for Examinations
None

Credit Awards for Prior Learning
Transfer credits from accredited, degree-granting institution; ACE/PONSI recommendations

Description
Student support services include an assigned academic advisor. Course instructors, registrar's office all accessible by mail or phone 8:30 am–5:00 pm Monday–Friday.

All course study materials are offered in print. Students are provided informal feedback through the answering of open-ended review questions as well as formal feedback through the mandatory completion of interim (open-book) examinations.

Currently, there is no separate access to the College's library by students, although it is anticipated that online delivery may be available soon.

Interim examinations are required for each course in addition to proctored exams at over 200 sites in the United States.

Program effectiveness is determined through such measures as course evaluation forms, large scale surveys of students and alumni, achievement on course examinations, survey of employers of graduates, independent certification examinations, and student attrition studies.

Colorado Electronic Community College

9125 E. 10th Drive
Aurora, CO 80010
Phone: 303-340-2401
Fax: 303-340-5876
E-mail: sb_marybeth@mash.colorado.edu

Degrees Offered

Associate of Arts; Associate of Science

Program Mission

To deliver the associate of arts and associate of science degrees through telecommunications technology.

Accreditation

North Central Association of Colleges and Schools

Admission Requirements

16 years or older is desirable

Credit Hour Requirements

60 semester hours

Minimum Campus Time

None

Tuition and Fees

$120 per credit hour, $25 course registration, $25 voice mail fee, and $25 telelicense fee

Credit Awards for Examinations

ACT-PEP: Regents College Examinations Program; CLEP general exams; CLEP subject exams; DANTES subject tests; College Board AP exams; Defense Language Institute proficiency tests; ACE-evaluated certification exams

Credit Awards for Prior Learning

Transfer credits from accredited, degree-granting institution; ACE military recommendations; ACE/PONSI recommendations; portfolio type assessment; and department/institutional exams

Description

In collaboration with Jones Intercable and other partners, the Colorado Community College and Occupational Education System College offers a full range of general education-transferable curriculum through television, telephone, the Internet, CD-ROM, and videoconferencing to Colorado and national audiences, thereby facilitating access to higher education to every citizen.

All student services, including financial aid, career exploration, and special population support, are provided by phone. Information is also provided on a Web site. Every student is assigned a voice mail box number to communicate with professors and classmates. Faculty/students also communicate through e-mail. Phone service is 7:00 am–7:00 pm. Other communication is asynchronous (therefore 24 hours/day).

Distance education opportunities include telecourse broadcasts, print materials, and videotape rental. Some courses are available through the Internet. All course work is provided asynchronously.

Students have access to all Colorado Community College libraries. Networked Colorado Area Regional Library system also available online.

Students are provided with their own personal voice mail box. They have the option of allowing other students within their class to access their voice mail boxes, and to share e-mail addresses. Faculty create distribution lists on e-mail as well.

Co-op experiences are available where students on the job can receive college credit.

As an elective, students may research a general education topic and work with a faculty member for reading and assignments required.

All general curriculum in the Colorado Electronic Community College is standardized and completely transferable between community colleges. Also, the general education core is accepted completely by all public four-year colleges and universities in Colorado. If general education is completed, a graduate is accepted as a junior in good standing and need not take any more general education requirements.

Program effectiveness is determined through such measures as student evaluations of faculty, phone surveys conducted by advising office, mailed exit surveys, retention rates, completion rates, and satisfactory performance rates.

Colorado State University

Colorado SURGE
Division of Continuing Education
Fort Collins, CO 80523
Phone: 970-491-5288
Fax: 970-491-7885
E-mail: inquiries@vines.colostate.edu

Degrees Offered
Master of Science in Computer Science; Master of Business Administration; Master of Science in Management; Master of Science in Engineering (Civil, Chemical, Electrical, Environmental, and Mechanical); Master of Education in Human Resource Development

Program Mission
To offer master's degrees via videotape in business, engineering, computer sciences, statistics, and human resource development.

Accreditation
North Central Association of Colleges and Schools; Accrediting Board for Engineering and Technology (ABET)

Admission Requirements
Varies by program—usually, bachelor's degree, GMAT or GRE

Credit Hour Requirements
32–36 semester hours

Tuition and Fees
$300–$350 per credit

Credit Awards for Examinations
CLEP general exams; CLEP subject exams; College Board AP exams

Credit Awards for Prior Learning
Department/institutional exams

Description
Student advising is available from departments 8:00 am–5:00 pm Monday–Friday. Distance education opportunities are provided through videotaped lectures. Students may access the librarian available via telephone, fax, e-mail, and the university computer via modem. Students and instructors communicate via fax, letters, telephone, and e-mail. Some student group projects are required.

International School of Information Management

Distance Learning University
501 S. Cherry, Suite 350
Denver, CO 80222
Phone: 303-333-4224
Fax: 303-336-1144
E-mail: istm@admin.com

Degrees Offered
Master of Business Administration; Master of Science in Information Management

Program Mission
To offer nonresidential graduate degrees through guided self-study or online interactive technology.

Accreditation
Distance Education and Training Council

Admission Requirements
Bachelor's degree, résumé, transcripts, $35 application fee, and three letters of recommendation

Credit Hour Requirements
50 credit units

Minimum Campus Time
None

Tuition and Fees

Online interactive program, $250 per unit and total tuition, $12,500. Guided self-study program, $190 per unit and total tuition, $9500.

Credit Awards for Examinations

ACE-evaluated certification exams

Credit Awards for Prior Learning

Transfer credits from accredited, degree-granting institution; portfolio type assessment; credit by exam

Description

Admissions office open Monday–Friday 8:00 am–5:00 pm (can leave messages 24 hours a day). Faculty is accessible to the students by phone, e-mail, and fax.

Distance learning opportunities include a private online server and guided self-study correspondence courses using mail, fax, and e-mail.

Software, study guides, and course materials are sent from International School of Information Management to the student.

Students are encouraged to utilize their work/career experience in their assignments and capstone project.

Program effectiveness is determined through such measures as sending course evaluation surveys to both students and faculty. Also, a faculty advisor oversees all of the courses.

National Technological University

700 Centre Avenue
Fort Collins, CO 80526
Phone: 970-495-6400
Fax: 970-484-0668

Degrees Offered

Master of Science in Chemical Engineering, Computer Engineering, Computer Science, Electrical Engineering, Engineering Management, Hazardous Waste Management, Health Physics, Management of Technology, Manufacturing Systems Engineering, Materials Science and Engineering, Software Engineering, Transportation Systems Engineering, and special majors

Program Mission

To serve the advanced educational needs of graduate engineers, technical professionals, and managers using advanced educational and telecommunications technology and to award degrees and certificates at the master's level to qualified candidates.

Accreditation

North Central Association of Colleges and Schools; Accreditation Board for Engineering and Technology (ABET)

Admission Requirements

Admission criteria differ slightly by degree program but the basic requirements are a BS degree in engineering from an ABET-accredited engineering program and a cumulative undergraduate GPA of at least 2.9 on a 4.0 scale. Work experience and in-house classes are considered.

Credit Hour Requirements

Chemical Engineering, Engineering Management, Hazardous Waste Management, Manufacturing Systems Engineering, Materials Science and Engineering, Software Science, Electrical Engineering, and Transportation Systems Engineering—33 semester credit hours. Computer Engineering and Computer Science—30 semester credit hours. Health Physics—32 semester credit hours. Special majors—36 semester credit hours. Management of Technology—45 semester credit hours.

Minimum Campus Time

Management of Technology degree program requires six one-week residencies; Hazardous Waste Management requires one summer session laboratory

Tuition and Fees

Tuition is $530 per credit for credit registration; $430 per credit for audit registration

Credit Awards for Examinations

None

Credit Awards for Prior Learning

Transfer credits from accredited, degree-granting institution

Description

Each student admitted to a degree program is assigned an advisor. Because students and advisors are separated geographically, they keep in contact via e-mail, telephone, and fax and have no time constraints.

Courses are delivered via satellite to downline sites in business, industry, and the military. Courses are available only to students located at sites with employer sponsorship.

Academic resource services are provided by the teaching institutions and the students' employers. Students access these services electronically, by fax, or by mail.

Interaction between faculty and students takes place by electronic mail, World Wide Web, telephone, and fax.

The Management of Technology degree requires a work-related field project. The Engineering Management, Hazardous Waste Management, Health Physics, and Transportation Systems Engineering degrees all require a work-related capstone project.

Program effectiveness is measured by means of questionnaires that are sent to students after each course. These are collected and evaluated by an independent consulting firm annually.

Pikes Peak Community College

External Degree Completion Program
5674 S. Academy Boulevard
Campus Box 33
Colorado Springs, CO 80906-5498
Phone: 719-540-7225
Fax: 719-540-7614
E-mail: jordan@ppcc.cccoes.edu
Internet: http://www.ppcc.cccoes.edu

Degrees Offered

Associate of General Studies; Associate of Applied Science, Fire Science Technology; Associate of Applied Science, Aviation Maintenance Technology

Program Mission

To recognize that people working in business, industry, government, and the military can achieve college-level learning through nontraditional and experiential learning methods.

Accreditation

North Central Association of Colleges and Schools

Admission Requirements

As an "open door" institution, Pikes Peak Community College has no admission requirements. Students do take a placement test to determine the course level in which they may enroll.

Credit Hour Requirements

Associate of General Studies, 60 semester hours; AAS, Fire Science Technology, 69 semester hours; AAS, Aviation Maintenance Technology, 75 semester hours

Minimum Campus Time

None

Tuition and Fees

In-state tuition $52.25 per credit hour; out-of-state tuition $233.75 per credit hour; student and registration fees $29–$49 based on hours taken; graduation fee $15; off-campus independent study tuition $60 per credit hour

Credit Awards for Examinations

ACT-PEP: Regents College Examinations Program; CLEP general exams; CLEP subject exams; DANTES subject tests; College Board AP exams

Credit Awards for Prior Learning

Transfer credits from accredited, degree-granting institution; ACE military recommendations; ACE/PONSI recommendations; and portfolio type assessment

Description

Through the Credit for Prior Learning Program, the student's past experiences are evaluated and credit awarded, a Plan for Degree is issued, and the student finishes the required course work through one of the available distant learning methods.

Student support services are available from 8:00 am–5:00 pm Monday–Friday. Students may reach the Credit for Prior Learning Office of the Division of Extended Studies by calling 719-540-7225 or 800-777-9446. Information is available through the PPCC WWW site.

Distance education opportunities include independent study, interactive television, the Internet, telecourses, and FM radio. An online writing lab (OWL) is also available to students through the Internet.

Courses given through distant learning options are designed to have faculty-student interaction as part of the class. This interaction can be via e-mail over the Internet, via the telephone for interactive television courses, and via voice mail for independent study courses.

Internet courses are designed for e-mail interaction between students. Interactive television courses also provide for student contacts. Independent study courses must have instructor-student contact via voice mail on a regular basis.

Students may take guided individual study. These courses may be based on the student's job or other experience. This type of course is limited to six hours of credit and must be applicable to the student's degree program.

Program effectiveness is measured through such means as student surveys after graduation, community and employer surveys, license examinations passed, needs assessment surveys, and job placements.

Regis University

School for Professional Studies
3333 Regis Boulevard
Denver, CO 80221-1099
Phone: undergraduate 800-967-3237;
    graduate 800-727-6399
Fax: 303-964-5539; 303-964-5538
Internet: http://www.regis.edu

Degrees Offered

Bachelor of Arts in many majors through guided independent study; Teachers' Education through guided independent study; Bachelor of Science in Business Administration through televised learning/video and voice mail; Master of Arts in Liberal Studies through guided independent study; Master of Arts in Liberal Studies Professional Counselor Licensure; Master of Arts in Liberal Studies Teacher Certification

Program Mission

To serve two general groups: those who wish to complete a program leading to a degree, and those who seek specialized training or knowledge to increase their competence in their current occupation or profession or to prepare themselves for a new occupation or profession. The School for Professional Studies develops and administers degree programs and credit courses for both traditional and nontraditional learners. These offerings take place on and off campus and respond to a variety of learner needs.

Accreditation
North Central Association of Colleges and Schools

Admission Requirements
Undergraduate—application, three years work experience, college-level writing skills, high school diploma or equivalent, transcripts, admissions fees. Graduate—application, transcripts of bachelor's degree from a regionally accredited college/university, admissions essay, letters of recommendation, and admissions fees.

Credit Hour Requirements
Undergraduate, 128 semester hours; graduate Master of Arts in Liberal Studies, 36 semester hours; and MA in Community Leadership, 35 semester hours

Minimum Campus Time
None

Tuition and Fees
Undergraduate guided independent studies, $247 per semester hour; televised learning, $192 per semester hour (in state) and $175 per semester hour (out of state). Graduate MLS, $255 per semester hour.

Credit Awards for Examinations
ACT-PEP: Regents College Examinations Program; CLEP general exams; CLEP subject exams; DANTES subject tests; Defense Language Institute proficiency tests; ACE-evaluated certification exams

Credit Awards for Prior Learning
Transfer credits from accredited, degree-granting institution; ACE military recommendations; ACE/PONSI recommendations; portfolio type assessment; department/institutional exams; and technical credit

Description
Student support services available include academic advising, faculty contact, and financial aid. Business office hours are Monday–Friday 8:30 am–5:00 pm; library and bookstore open Monday–Saturday 8:30 am–5:00 pm; registration 24 hours via fax, telephone Monday–Friday 8:30 am–5:00 pm; and voice mail in televised learning.

Distance education opportunities include e-mail, voice mail, guided independent study, videotapes (in undergraduate televised learning degree).

Dayton Memorial Library at Regis University and the Colorado Area Regional Library are available through telephone and fax. Undergraduate televised learning degree uses voice mail between faculty and students, and students with one another.

Guided independent study uses local course consultants and advising contact by telephone with faculty of record, and fax. Televised learning degree uses voice mail and fax.

In the undergraduate televised learning degree through televised/video courses, a voice mail system connects students with faculty and one another.

Learning experiences may be designed to relate to various contexts of the student's life. A student may, for example, design a human resource manual for his or her organization or workplace. Self-designed courses, where applicable, must have approval of faculty and must be accomplished with a course consultant.

A university-wide outcomes study program assesses program outcomes. Biannual assessment exists for televised learning/video learning program at the undergraduate level. Other measures to determine program effectiveness include faculty assessment, orientation, and development before teaching, student evaluation process, university-wide outcomes studies, focus groups, accreditation visits, and specialized outcomes studies comparing learning methods.

University of Colorado

Center for Advanced Training in Engineering and Computer Science (CATECS)
Campus Box 435
Boulder, CO 80309
Phone: 303-492-6331
Fax: 303-492-5987
E-mail: micucciv@spot.colorado.edu

Degrees Offered
Master of Science (MS) in Aerospace Sciences; Master of Education (ME) in Aerospace Sciences; ME in Computer Science; MS and ME in Electrical and Computer Engineering; MS and ME in Mechanical Engineering; ME and MS in Telecommunications; ME in Engineering Management

Program Mission
To provide quality, graduate-level education to working professionals via distance learning modalities so they can achieve their educational goals.

Accreditation
North Central Association of Colleges and Schools; Accreditation Board for Engineering and Technology (ABET)

Admission Requirements
Bachelor's degree in engineering from an accredited university; GPA of 3.0 or higher; need to request admission from department concerned (each department's eligibility requirements may vary slightly)

Credit Hour Requirements
Typically 30 semester hours

Minimum Campus Time
Varies among departments. Usually minimal if at all.

Tuition and Fees
CATECS tuition is $996 for a three-credit graduate course

Credit Awards for Examinations
None

Credit Awards for Prior Learning
Transfer credits from accredited, degree-granting institution

Description
Courses can be taken for credit or non-credit; for professional development or for application to a graduate degree program.

Advising available from individual departments 8:00 am–5:00 pm Monday–Friday.

Distance education opportunities include videotaped lectures; live, microwave TV broadcast within 75 miles of Boulder, CO. Some courses feature the use of listservs on e-mail where students can interact with other students.

Students registered with CATECS may access the University of Colorado computer network for course-required transactions.

Faculty provide office hours and are usually accessible via fax or e-mail.

In lieu of a thesis, most degree programs have student write a capstone project, which can be related to the student's job.

University of Southern Colorado

External Degree Completion Program
2200 Bonforte Boulevard

Pueblo, CO 81001
Phone: 719-549-2316
Fax: 719-549-2438
E-mail: rstubenr@uscolo.edu

Degrees Offered
Bachelor of Science in Social Science

Program Mission
To provide a flexible degree completion and opportunity to adult students.

Accreditation
North Central Association of Colleges and Schools

Admission Requirements
High school completion or equivalent or college transfer

Credit Hour Requirements
128 semester hours

Minimum Campus Time
None

Tuition and Fees
$125 enrollment fee; $85 yearly maintenance fee; $70 per credit tuition; and $50–$75 videotape fees for selected courses

Credit Awards for Examinations
ACT-PEP: Regents College Examinations Program; CLEP general exams; CLEP subject exams; College Board AP exams

Credit Awards for Prior Learning
Transfer credits from accredited, degree-granting institution; ACE military recommendations; department/institutional exams

Description
Complete advising services available at sites during normal work hours. Advising available from campus by telephone, e-mail, and fax 8:30 am–5:00 pm Monday–Friday, 8:30 am–6:30 pm Thursday.

Distance education opportunities include videocourses, videotaped lectures, independent study (correspondence) courses, PBS telecourses, and courses on the Internet.

Students learning at a distance access academic resources through interlibrary loan and the Internet.

All faculty provide appropriate telephone numbers, e-mail, office hours, as a part of course syllabi. A toll-free number to administration office is provided to students.

If students wish to communicate with others, a release is required and then e-mail and mailing addresses are forwarded to participating students.

Some degree requirements may be met through self-designed independent study courses. Field experience credits also available.

Program effectiveness is determined through such measures as follow-up surveys of graduates.

CONNECTICUT

Charter Oak State College

66 Cedar Street
Newington, CT 06111
Phone: 860-666-4595
Fax: 860-666-4852
E-mail: charter_oak@comment.edu
Internet: http://www.ctstateu.edu/
~charteroak

Degrees Offered
Bachelor of Arts; Bachelor of Science; Associate in Arts; Associate in Science. The bachelor's degree is a general studies degree with many concentration options. One of the most popular is the individualized studies concentration that allows students to combine professional studies with the

liberal arts and sciences into cohesive courses of study that meet career and/or personal needs

Program Mission

To provide a way for adults to earn a college degree outside the traditional classroom.

Accreditation

New England Association of Schools and Colleges

Admission Requirements

To enroll, a student must have completed nine college-level credits.

Credit Hour Requirements

AS and AA require a minimum of 60 credits; BS and BA require a minimum of 120 credits

Minimum Campus Time

None

Tuition and Fees

Application fee $30; in-state enrollment $360, out-of-state enrollment $540; annual advisement and record maintenance in-state $250, out-of-state $380; concentration proposal review $225; graduation $115

Credit Awards for Examinations

ACT-PEP: Regents College Examinations Program; CLEP general exams; CLEP subject exams; DANTES subject tests; College Board AP exams; Defense Language Institute proficiency tests; ACE-evaluated certification exams; GRE subject exams.

Credit Awards for Prior Learning

Transfer credits from accredited, degree-granting institution; ACE military recommendations; ACE/PONSI recommendations; portfolio type assessment; department/institutional exams; contract learning; and credit for certain professional certifications and licenses

Description

Each enrolled student is assigned to an advisor who is a specialist in his or her field of study. A student may visit an advisor in person, or call, fax, or e-mail. Advisor is available Monday–Friday 8:30 am–4:30 pm. The advisor works with the student to plan the remainder of the degree program, including the concentration proposal, which must be submitted to a faculty committee in the discipline. Charter Oak uses the services of a mail-order bookstore.

Students have e-mail opportunities with advisors. COSC offers Independent Guided Study (IGS) courses that are available using textbooks, videotapes, and a COSC mentor. Five or six courses are offered each semester; students can complete the course faster than the semester with permission of the mentor. The mentor can be reached by phone or e-mail.

Established in 1973, Charter Oak State College (COSC) is the State of Connecticut's external college degree program. Because COSC is an external degree program, it does not have a library. Academic resources are available at local libraries and at a mail-order book store through which COSC works. COSC advisors direct students to learning skills services at other institutions. COSC may use the library resources of any state college or university.

Students are assigned a mentor for each IGS course who is available to that student at a designated time each week. Faculty also approve each student's concentration plan. Advisors act as the intermediary between faculty and students.

Students taking IGS courses may have each other's telephone number and/or e-mail address; alumni are available to speak with students; a COSC bulletin board for students on the Internet is planned. A student council represents student interests and hosts regional meetings among students.

Students may earn credit through contract learning. Under the guidance of faculty mentors, students prepare contracts that delineate what they will study, the resources they will use, and the methods by which their knowledge will be assessed. This process allows students who cannot access courses offered by colleges and universities, either because of scheduling conflicts or availability, to develop a contract to learn the equivalent knowledge.

Program effectiveness is determined through such measures as persistence rates, graduation rates, professional advancement of graduates, baccalaureate program acceptances (for associate grads), graduate school acceptances (for bachelor's degree grads), licensure and certification exams passed, and percent favorable rating of program by students.

COSC students and alumni report that personal service of academic advisors and the flexibility of the credit-earning options are its hallmarks.

DELAWARE

University of Delaware

FOCUS/Distance Learning
217 John M. Clayton Hall
Newark, DE 19716
Phone: 800-833-6287
Fax: 302-831-3292
E-mail: mary.pritchard@mvs.udel.edu

Degrees Offered
Bachelor of Science in Human Resources with a major in Hotel, Restaurant, and Institutional Management (HRIM); Bachelor of Science in Nursing for Registered Nurses (BSN)

Program Mission
To provide access to university courses to nontraditional students whose geographic location, work schedules, or personal responsibilities prevent them from attending traditional campus classes.

Accreditation
Middle States Association of Colleges and Schools; National League for Nursing

Admission Requirements
High school diploma, GED, or successful completion of college courses; BSN-RN license

Credit Hour Requirements
BS, HRIM 120 credit hours; BSN, 125 credit hours

Minimum Campus Time
BSN, three weekends on campus; BS with major in HRIM, two 10-day on-campus institutes

Tuition and Fees
Work site rates: undergraduate, $188 per credit hour; graduate, $522 per credit hour. Non-work-site resident: undergraduate, $161 per credit hour; graduate, $214 per credit hour. Non-resident: undergraduate, $447 per credit hour; graduate, $596 per credit hour.

Credit Awards for Examinations
College Board AP exams

Credit Awards for Prior Learning
Transfer credits from accredited, degree-granting institution and department/institutional exams

Description
The majority of courses are available on videotape. Students have the same requirements as on-campus students and are expected to follow the semester schedule for course completion.

Access counselors guide returning adult students through counseling and testing services (301-831-2741). Hours are Monday–Wednesday 8:00 am–6:30 pm, Thursday 8:00 am–8:00 pm, and Friday 8:00 am–5:00 pm. FOCUS/Distance Learning office provides information and registration assistance. Students can call 302-831-3146 locally or 800-UD-FOCUS 8:00 am–4:30 pm, 800-833-6287 Monday–Friday.

Distance education opportunities include videotaped lectures; live, interactive lectures (limited to specific receive sites); and external studies courses print-based format.

Students access academic resources through interlibrary loan; videotapes on learning skills are available.

Toll-free number maintained for student access to faculty from 8:00 am–4:30 pm Monday–Friday. Students can call 1-800-UD-FOCUS (833-6287) and will be transferred to their faculty member.

The FOCUS/Distance Learning system is designed to bridge the distance between student and university. A proactive staff tries to make sure that students' problems are successfully resolved.

Program effectiveness is determined through student retention statistics, student course evaluations, and survey in development.

FLORIDA

Brevard Community College

World Community College
1519 Clearlake Road
Cocoa, FL 32922
Phone: 407-632-1111
Fax: 407-634-3724
E-mail: info@a1.brevard.cc.fl.us

Degrees Offered
Associate of Arts in General Studies; Associate of Science in one of the following 10 fields: Criminal Justice, Drafting and Design, Electronic Engineering Technology, Fire Science Technology, Hazardous Materials Technology, International Business Management, Legal Studies, Marketing Management, Radio and Television Broadcast Programming, or Solar Energy Technology

Program Mission
Through partnerships with the Community College for International Development and Electronic University Network, Brevard Community College offers distance learning courses online via America Online (AOL) through a new consortium called the World Community College (WCC).

Accreditation
Southern Association of Colleges and Schools

Admission Requirements
Educational records (high school or GED diploma). Students must have access to America Online. Degree-seeking students may have to take placement tests to be placed in appropriate course levels for English, mathematics, and reading.

Credit Hour Requirements
60 credit hours

Minimum Campus Time
None

Tuition and Fees
One-time application fee of $20; Florida resident $185 for courses with video, $135 for courses without video component; out-of-state resident $455 for courses with video, $405 for courses without video component

Credit Awards for Examinations
CLEP general exams; CLEP subject exams; DANTES subject tests; College Board AP

exams; ACE-evaluated certification exams; portfolio type assessment

Credit Awards for Prior Learning

Transfer credits from accredited, degree-granting institution, ACE military recommendations, ACE/PONSI recommendations, portfolio type assessment, department/institutional exams, regionally accredited correspondence courses

Description

WCC offers instruction to students anytime and anywhere around the world where AOL is accessible. Distance Learning students have the opportunity to experience conventional aspects of campus life, activities, support services, and courses leading to entire degree programs in a virtual environment that is readily available, easy to use, and complemented by a vast array of electronic resources.

Online students have access to advising and student support services via America Online at any time. The operating hours for services are 8:00 am–5:00 pm Monday–Friday, however students may leave e-mail or voice mail messages at any time.

Distance education opportunities include telecourses; two-way audio/video courses, televised interactive education, and online courses.

Academic resources are available to students online.

Course lessons require interaction between faculty and students in online courses. E-mail and chat capabilities through America Online facilitate student interaction.

Measures are being designed to accurately determine program effectiveness.

Embry-Riddle Aeronautical University

Independent Studies
600 S. Clyde Morris Boulevard
Daytona Beach, FL 32119-3900
Phone: 800-359-3728
Fax: 904-226-7627
E-mail: dammerl@cts.db.erau.edu

Degrees Offered

Associate of Science in Professional Aeronautics and Aviation Business Administration; Bachelor of Science in Professional Aeronautics and Aviation Business Administration; Master of Aeronautical Science (MAS) with specialization in either Management or Operations

Program Mission

To provide high-quality aviation undergraduate and graduate degree programs through the use of specially developed Embry-Riddle independent study courses to working adult civilian and military aviation professionals who are unable to attend traditionally scheduled classes to meet their higher educational needs.

Accreditation

Southern Association of Colleges and Schools; Accreditation Board for Engineering and Technology (ABET)

Admission Requirements

Undergraduate: high school or GED diploma. Graduate: bachelor's degree from accredited college or university.

Credit Hour Requirements

Associate of Science in Aviation Business Administration, 63 semester hours; Associate of Science in Professional Aeronautics, 63 semester hours; Bachelor of Science in Aviation Business Aeronautics, 126 semester hours; Bachelor of Science in Professional Aeronautics, 126 semester hours;

Master of Aeronautical Science, 36 semester hours

Minimum Campus Time
None

Tuition and Fees
Undergraduate—$140 per credit hour, plus the cost of course materials and shipping fees. Graduate—$285 per semester hour, plus the cost of textbooks and shipping fees.

Credit Awards for Examinations
ACT-PEP: Regents College Examinations Program; CLEP general exams; CLEP subject exams; DANTES subject tests; College Board AP exams; Defense Language Institute proficiency tests; ACE-evaluated certification exams, for graduate programs

Credit Awards for Prior Learning
Transfer credits from accredited, degree-granting institution; ACE military recommendations; ACE/PONSI recommendations; portfolio type assessment; department/institutional exams

Description
Each student is assigned an academic advisor who will assist them in the pursuit of their degree. The advisors will provide students with contact information on faculty and staff who may assist the student during the course. Also, graduate students can transmit e-mail messages that are received and responded to by the advisors within one working day.

Undergraduate: Each course includes the textbook, a specially developed study guide, and a set of audio- or videocassette tapes. Graduate: Using state-of-the-art instructional methods and techniques students interact electronically with faculty, staff, and fellow students. The university has established a private forum on CompuServe to facilitate communications between faculty/students and student/student. Because Embry-Riddle's independent study program requires electronic interaction, all students must have access to the following equipment: IBM-compatible (preferably 386 or later model) or Macintosh personal computer system with monitor; hard drive system sufficient to load spreadsheet and word processing software; 3.5 floppy drive; letter-quality printer capable of printing graphics; a modem that will support 1200 or higher baud rate; and VCR and television for videotapes.

Students in the undergraduate program may contact the university library through e-mail or by telephone. Students in the graduate program are provided access to library support through the CompuServe Forum.

Undergraduate: Feedback on examination or papers is provided. Graduate: Student and faculty interaction is facilitated through the CompuServe Forum. Students, faculty, and staff are required to respond to all messages within one week of original transmission. Faculty are encouraged to review all messages at least three times per week.

Graduate: Student to student interaction is encouraged. Using the CompuServe Forum students find the exchange of messages simplistic.

An undergraduate student may be permitted to select a topic related to work for the courses requiring a research paper. Graduate students are encouraged to write papers on topics familiar to them. Papers that cover personal work or learning experiences are shared with other students by the professor.

This program is offered to potential students on an international basis. At the present time the program has students in over 25 countries on six different continents.

Program effectiveness is determined through such measures as completion rates.

Graduate: The program is a mirror image of the on-campus programs offered by Embry-Riddle. A recent comparison analysis found that there was no significant difference between on-campus and independent study outcomes.

Institute of Physical Therapy

Master of Science in Physical Therapy
170 Malaga Street
Saint Augustine, FL 32084
Phone: 904-826-0084
Fax: 904-826-0085

Degrees Offered
Master of Science in Physical Therapy

Program Mission
To provide an educational opportunity that allows the physical therapist to develop specialized clinical competencies that enhance patient care beyond basic professional preparation and experiences. In this manner, the institute's advanced master of science program develops both the professional and the profession. The institute places a high priority upon the need to maintain an active attitude of inquiry, and to become a critical thinker and a reflective practitioner.

Accreditation
Distance Education and Training Council

Admission Requirements
Bachelor of Science in Physical Therapy; passed certification acceptable to institute; maintained at least a B average in certification courses; official transcripts from all institutions of higher education; minimum GRE scores of 900 taken within five years; and interviews

Credit Hour Requirements
45 quarter hours

Minimum Campus Time
Seven to nine weeks, i.e., two separate three-week residencies, and a third residency of from one to three weeks, depending on the student's remaining academic needs. Additionally, six days manual therapy certification.

Tuition and Fees
$195 per course; approximate total tuition and fees $14,625

Credit Awards for Examinations
None

Credit Awards for Prior Learning
Transfer credits from accredited, degree-granting institution; portfolio type assessment; department/institutional exams

Description
Business office available to answer questions 8:00 am–5:00 pm Monday–Friday; department director available or will return calls 8:00 am–5:00 pm Monday–Friday; individual instructors available by appointment. Distance education staff other than instruction available 8:00 am–5:00 pm Monday–Friday; after hours calls/appointments can be arranged and some instructors are available by e-mail.

Distance education opportunities include home study (seminar/home study), directed study, directed readings, videotapes, and e-mail.

Access to academic resources via telephone or mail. Medline searches provided upon request for a nominal fee.

The research project may be related to job or community. Through directed studies, students' special interests may be satisfied as an elective course.

Each student is required to communicate their research to the physical therapy profession. This may be as a published article, poster presentation, or a paper at either the annual meeting or combined sections meeting of the American Physical Therapy Association, or some other approved alternative.

Program effectiveness is determined through evaluation and feedback from students via an evaluation form they complete at the end of each course. An assessment of course materials is made and revisions made when deemed necessary from a conclusion of course writers, instructors, and administrators. Certification exams test clinical skills through oral, practical, and written exams. A follow-up survey is conducted after course completion and graduation.

National Institute for Paralegal Arts and Science

Paralegal Specialized Associate's Degree
  Program
164 W. Royal Palm Road
Boca Raton, FL 33432
Phone: 407-368-2522
Fax: 407-368-6827
E-mail: nipas@ix.netcom.com

Degrees Offered
Specialized Associate's degree in Paralegal Studies

Program Mission
To provide paralegal training to busy adults.

Accreditation
Distance Education and Training Council

Admission Requirements
Proof of a high school or GED diploma is a requirement for entrance to the program. Applicants must be 18 years of age or older; minors otherwise qualified must have a cosigner.

Applicants not evidencing prior legal background are required to successfully complete National Institute for Paralegal Arts and Sciences' (NIPAS) Entrance and Legal Aptitude Examination.

Credit Hour Requirements
60 semester hours = 1,440 clock hours

Minimum Campus Time
None

Tuition and Fees
$5900 all-inclusive tuition for the Paralegal Specialized Associate's Degree Program

Credit Awards for Examinations
ACT-PEP: Regents College Examinations Program; CLEP general exams; CLEP subject exams; DANTES subject tests; College Board AP exams; Defense Language Institute proficiency tests; and ACE-evaluated certification exams

Credit Awards for Prior Learning
Transfer credits from accredited, degree-granting institution; ACE military recommendations; ACE/PONSI recommendations; portfolio type assessment

Description
Upon completion of the 1,440 clock hours Paralegal Specialized Associate's Degree (PSAD) Program, students may sit for the Certified Legal Assistant (CLA) Examination, sponsored by the National Association of Legal Assistants (NALA). Students with prior academic or work experience in the legal field are eligible for tuition and transfer credit into the PSAD Program, which consists of 11 foundation level paralegal courses, 4 legal specialty courses, 3 office technology courses, and 3 general knowledge courses.

NIPAS believes that the skills students need to learn to be successful as distance education students are the exact skills needed to be effective paralegals—organization, self-reliance, motivation, the desire to learn, the will to succeed, and the ability to solve problems and make decisions.

The attorney and paralegal instructors are available Monday–Friday 8:30 am–4:30 pm on a toll-free "homework hotline" to assist with lesson help or to provide information on the paralegal profession. NIPAS prides itself on its full-service Student and Exam Services departments. Students may contact the school by phone or in writing with any questions regarding their program work or the paralegal profession.

Placement skills training and counseling services are provided to students and graduates. Projects to assist students in preparing for employment to work for a law firm, on a free-lance basis, or to use their paralegal training in other fields are included. To gain on-the-job experience, students may also participate in optional work-and-learn experiences. Externs work with attorneys, paralegals, and other law office personnel in their local legal communities to gain law office experience that can be added to their résumés.

Students may send their résumés and job search plans to NIPAS at any time during their program. Materials are reviewed and feedback provided for improvement. Students are helped to prepare for job interviews and to have the most efficient plan in place when looking for a new position to grow in their current profession or into a new career with paralegal training.

Independent study by correspondence; toll-free 800 homework hotline for lesson help and information; e-mail and fax availability.

Information is provided on how to access law libraries and other resources in local communities.

Externships provide optional work and learning experiences. Placement skills projects are also included.

Student surveys are conducted to measure program effectiveness.

Nova Southeastern University
Graduate Teacher Education Program

3301 College Avenue
Fort Lauderdale, FL 33314
Phone: 800-986-3223 ext. 1519
Fax: 954-476-4764
E-mail: seldines@fcae.acast.nova.edu

Degrees Offered
Master of Science and Educational Specialist degrees in: Computer Science Education, Educational Media, Education Technology, Elementary Education, Educational Leadership (school administration), English Education, Exceptional Student Education, Mathematics Education, Prekindergarten/Primary Education, Reading, Science Education, Social Studies Education, Teaching English to Speakers of Other Languages

Program Mission
To provide opportunities for teaching and school administration professionals who work full time to earn master's and educational specialist degrees. The curriculum is designed to enable teachers to add certification areas and endorsements, renew current certification areas, and increase their levels of expertise within their fields, and to enable persons who wish to change careers to enter teaching. The focus in all programs is on the improvement of professional practice, the application of current research and theory to the student's professional work, the acquisition and enhancement of leadership capacities, and the achievement of career objectives.

Accreditation
Southern Association of Colleges and Schools

Admission Requirements

Provisional admission: Bachelor's degree with major in education or in any field with teaching certificate, from regionally accredited college or university.

Admission to degree candidacy: between completion of 9 and 18 semester hours; 3.0 GPA in prescribed courses; and passing score on writing assessment procedure.

Credit Hour Requirements

36 semester hours

Minimum Campus Time

None

Tuition and Fees

Tuition $212 per credit; admission fee $40; registration fees $15 each registration; and graduation fee $65

Credit Awards for Examinations

None

Credit Awards for Prior Learning

None

Description

Classes are held at locations and times that make the program accessible to working professionals. The instructional delivery system is designed so that busy professionals can opt to complete the degree program in one year or skip a term if necessary. Instructional teams include practitioners from local school districts who successfully practice what they teach.

Advisors are available at 800-986-3223 ext. 7449, Monday 8:30 am–5:00 pm, Tuesday–Friday 8:30 am–8:00 pm, and Saturday 8:30 am–1:30 pm. Library resources available online and through NSU Distance Library Services.

Classes conducted by compressed video (two-way interactive), audiobridge, voice-print, electronic classroom, etc., in addition to traditional classroom mode.

Through the Distance Library Services Office (DLS), students off campus have access to books, journal articles, Educational Resources Information Center (ERIC) documents, interlibrary loans, database searches, and reference librarians specializing in research services to remote student locations. Students may call DLS to request materials 24 hours a day, using mail, fax, or home computer. To contact DLS by phone, call 800-541-6682 (automated attendant—enter number for "general student services" and follow the menu) or 305-475-7388.

E-mail, telephone, fax, and regular mail are all used for continuous interaction with both local and main campus faculty members. Most delivery systems include group class meetings.

The practicum is a job-related, problem-solving project designed by the student for improving an unsatisfactory educational situation. This systematic process includes the submission of a formal proposal (including problem documentation, operational objectives, and review of the literature), implementation and evaluation of the chosen solution strategy, and submission of a final report that describes the entire process.

Program effectiveness is determined by end-of-course student evaluations of teaching performance and curriculum, and exit program evaluations.

Nova Southeastern University
National EdD Program for Educational Leaders

3301 College Avenue
Fort Lauderdale, FL 33314
Phone: 800-986-3223 ext. 7363

Fax: 954-452-1529
E-mail: borders@fcae.acast.nova.edu

Degrees Offered
Doctorate of Education (EdD) in Educational Leadership

Program Mission
To do the very best job possible in educating school leaders so that K–12 schools improve. The mission is accomplished in the following ways: using renowned professors to deliver instruction in various American and international sites; asking "what is best for our students" in decision-making; risking by constantly improving the program; taking an individual interest in each student; and promoting an international learning community by recruiting international students and professors.

Accreditation
Southern Association of Colleges and Schools

Admission Requirements
Master's degree from regionally accredited institution with at least 3.0 GPA; current employment in a school administrative position; and three letters of recommendation from superiors/colleagues. Candidates must have authority and latitude to conduct an action research practicum designed to improve education in their own local school or schools.

Credit Hour Requirements
66 semester hours

Minimum Campus Time
Two week-long summer institutes during three-year program. Remainder of program conducted at instructional sites.

Tuition and Fees
Tuition $7100 per year (payable quarterly); admission fees $40; registration fee $20 per registration; graduation fee $65; and fourth-year fees $1000 per quarter

Credit Awards for Examinations
None

Credit Awards for Prior Learning
None

Description
Advising is provided by local cluster (student group) coordinators and by main campus program staff at times convenient to the student. E-mail is heavily used in this regard. Library resources available online and through NSU Distance Library Services.

National faculty members travel to cluster locations in turn. All faculty, staff, and students maintain online accounts and these are used to provide a variety of opportunities.

Through the Distance Library Services Office (DLS), students off campus have access to books, journal articles, Educational Resources Information Center (ERIC) documents, interlibrary loans, database searches, and reference librarians specializing in research services to remote student locations. Students may call the DLS to request materials 24 hours a day, using mail, fax, or home computer. To contact DLS by phone, call 800-541-6682 (automated attendant—enter number for "general student services" and follow the menu) or 305-475-7388. The DLS e-mail address is: library@alpha.acast.nova.edu.

E-mail, telephoning, fax, and regular mail are all used for continuous interaction with both national and main campus faculty members.

Students interact with each other at weekend and between meetings via e-mail.

Parallel with the study areas and extending through the three years of doctoral work, a problem-solving project—a practicum—is required of all participants. The practicum is a research-based, problem-solving project executed in a school or school system setting designed to improve some aspect of education.

Program effectiveness is determined by student evaluations of teaching performance and curriculum and exit program evaluations.

Nova Southeastern University
Programs in Education and Technology

3301 College Avenue
Fort Lauderdale, FL 33314
Phone: 800-986-3223
Fax: 954-423-1224
E-mail: flightv@fcae.acast.nova.edu

Degrees Offered
Doctorate of Education (EdD) in Child and Youth Studies; Master of Science and EdD in Instructional Technology and Distance Education (ITDE)

Program Mission
To use modem tools to enhance the professional and leadership skills of individuals whose work influences or determines the quality of life of children, youth, and adults.

Accreditation
Southern Association of Colleges and Schools

Admission Requirements
Child and Youth Studies: A master's degree in education, child development, child care, psychology, counseling, speech-pathology, human services, or a related field from a regionally accredited institution, with a 3.0 GPA. Evidence that the applicant has the academic background to be successful in the program. This judgment, made by the Admissions Committee, will be based upon previous academic records, academic activities since obtaining the master's degree, letters of recommendation, a personal interview, and written responses to questions dealing with the field of child and youth studies. Applicants must occupy a position that requires or allows them work independently and to have direct or indirect impact on children and/or youth. Three years of work experience with children between birth and 18 years of age.

Programs in Instructional Technology and Distance Education: Evidence that the applicant has the academic background to be successful in the program. This judgment, made by the Admissions Committee, will be based upon previous academic records, academic activities since obtaining the previous degree, letters of recommendation, an interview, and written responses to questions dealing with the applicant's field of study. Applicants must occupy a position that requires or allows them to work in their area of study. Three years of work experience in education or training with experience in their field of study. For the master's program: A bachelor's degree from a regionally accredited institution with a 2.5 GPA. For the doctoral program: A master's degree in education, instructional media, technology, training, human resources development, or a related field from a regionally accredited institution with a 3.0 GPA.

Credit Hour Requirements
EdD in Child and Youth Studies (CYS), 66 semester hours; EdD in Instructional Technology and Distance Education, 62 semester hours; MS in Instructional Technology and Distance Education, 36 semester hours

Minimum Campus Time
EdD CYS two week-long summer institutes during three-year program; EdD ITDE one week-long summer institutes and two extended weekend sessions

Tuition and Fees

Tuition $7100 per year; application fee $40; graduation fee $65; extended time fees $1775 per each of two MS six-month extensions; $3550 for all or part of fourth year for CYS students and $1755 for six-month extension beyond fourth year

Credit Awards for Examinations

None

Credit Awards for Prior Learning

None

Description

Advising is provided by local cluster (student group) coordinators and main campus program staff at times convenient to the student. E-mail is heavily used in this regard. Library resources available online and through the NSU Distance Library Services Office (DLS).

National faculty members travel to cluster locations in turn. All faculty and staff, and most students, maintain online accounts that are used to provide a variety of opportunities.

Through the DLS, students off campus have access to books, journal articles, Educational Resources Information Center (ERIC) documents, interlibrary loans, database searches, and reference librarians specializing in research services to remote student locations. Students may call the DLS to request materials 24 hours a day, using mail, fax, or home computer. To contact DLS by phone, call 800-541-6682 (automated attendant—enter number for "general student services" and follow the menu) or 305-475-7388.

E-mail, telephoning, fax, and regular mail are all used for continuous interaction with both national and main campus faculty members.

Clusters meet monthly on weekends and interact then and between meetings via e-mail, etc.

Parallel with the study areas and extending through the three years of doctoral work, problem-solving projects and two practicums are required of all students.

Program effectiveness is determined by end-of-study-area student evaluations of teaching performance and curriculum, and exit program evaluations.

Nova Southeastern University
School of Business and Entrepreneurship

3301 College Avenue
Fort Lauderdale, FL 33314
Phone: 954-475-7690
Fax: 954-476-4865
E-mail: sheinfo@sbe.nova.edu

Degrees Offered

Master's degrees in Business Administration, Health Administration, Human Resource Management, Public Administration, International Business Administration, Accounting, and Medical Management; Doctoral degrees in Business Administration, International Business Administration, and Public Administration

Program Mission

To advance the professional development of individuals in business, government, and nonprofit settings at the managerial and executive levels. The school emphasizes creativity, innovation, and productivity in human enterprise. The educational philosophy of the school is growth through the practical application of theory. The school projects an activist, interventionist strategy in the delivery and design of its program in pursuit of this education philosophy.

Accreditation
Southern Association of Colleges and Schools

Admission Requirements
All programs offered by the school of business require the student to possess a bachelor's degree from an accredited institution for master's admissions, and an approved master's degree for doctoral admissions. The GMAT or GRE is required and a student's undergraduate or graduate grade point average is also considered. A professional portfolio in lieu of the GMAT or GRE; letters of recommendation; and a written essay included in the professional portfolio.

Credit Hour Requirements
All master's programs are 41 credit hours except for the health services and public administration degrees (which are 40 credit hours) and the medical management degree (which is 36 credit hours). All doctoral programs are 60 credit hours.

Minimum Campus Time
All master's students, excluding medical management students may have to attend the campus for a one-week workshop. Medical management students must visit the campus once a month on an extended weekend for the entire two-year program. Doctoral students will attend the main campus in varying durations, depending on program and format.

Tuition and Fees
Master's tuition per credit hour, $395; doctoral tuition per credit hour, $480; application fee, $40; and graduation fee $65

Credit Awards for Examinations
ACT-PEP: Regents College Examinations Program; DANTES subject tests; College Board AP exams; Defense Language Institute proficiency tests; ACE-evaluated certification exams; and NSU Challenge Exam

Credit Awards for Prior Learning
Transfer credits from accredited, degree-granting institution

Description
Students may call the main campus and receive counseling over the phone from 9:00 am–5:00 pm. Also, students may visit the campus during those same hours. All counseling is routed through the student services department at the School of Business. There is a microcomputer lab available to students near the East Campus during the hours of 9:00 am–5:00 pm.

Students lacking certain prerequisite courses necessary for master's level course work may complete a video-format course for undergraduate transfer credit. Classes are offered on campus and off campus. Off-campus classes are taught by faculty as organized classroom activities on location at field-based sites throughout Florida, in other states, and at selected international sites.

All students enrolled at the School of Business must have an online account giving them access to the Internet. Using this resource, students may complete online library searches, as well as communicate with the NSU library department. Students may also request interlibrary loan of a particular article to be sent to them by the NSU campus library.

Students may send e-mail to faculty or communicate with one another via e-mail. Also, students interact during a one-week seminar held at the end of their degree program.

Students are encouraged to use their work environment as a basis for research projects. These projects are intended to give the student a working solution and environment to real-world problems.

Nova Southeastern University
School of Computer and Information Sciences (MS in Management Information Systems)

3100 S.W. 9th Avenue
Fort Lauderdale, FL 33315
Phone: 800-986-2247 ext. 7352
Fax: 954-476-1982
E-mail: liz@scis.nova.edu

Degrees Offered
Master of Science in Management Information Systems

Program Mission
To offer a course of study leading to the Master of Science (MS) in management information systems.

Accreditation
Southern Association of Colleges and Schools

Admission Requirements
An earned bachelor's degree from a regionally accredited college or university. The program is designed for students with undergraduate majors in management information systems, computer information systems, business administration, or a related field, and having knowledge and experience in computer applications. The candidate must have an undergraduate GPA of at least 2.5 and a GPA of 3.0 in a major field. Applicants must provide a score report of the GRE or a comprehensive portfolio of appropriate professional experience and credentials.

Credit Hour Requirements
36 credit hours

Minimum Campus Time
New students must attend a weekend orientation prior to the start of their first term.

Tuition and Fees
Tuition $330 per credit hour; application fee $40; registration fee $30

Credit Awards for Examinations
GRE or comprehensive portfolio

Credit Awards for Prior Learning
Transfer credits from accredited, degree-granting institution

Description
The focus of the program is on the application of information system concepts to the collection, retention, and dissemination of information for management planning and decision making. The program blends theory and practice into a learning experience that develops skills applicable to complex real-world problems. Its formats offer professionals the opportunity to earn the master's degree in 18 months while continuing to work in their current positions.

Advising and support services are provided by the student's program office, which is open 8:30 am–5:00 pm Monday–Friday. Students may communicate with the program office via e-mail or telephone.

Online courses are taken via computer (IBM-compatible PC or Apple/Macintosh) and modem from home, office, or on the road while traveling. The student may participate in courses from anywhere in the United States or outside the United States where Internet access is available. The format involves the use of online interactive learning methods and teleconferencing throughout the instructional sequence. Courses involve a range of online activities that facilitate frequent interaction with faculty, classmates, and colleagues. Teachers and students are able to interact in real time during scheduled electronic classroom sessions that include lectures and discussions. Online activities also include interactive bulletin boards, electronic submission of assignments for review by faculty, electronic mail, the electronic library, and access to the school's computer systems. The Internet is also used extensively for research. Learning and interaction are facilitated by hypertext menuing systems. Costs for online connection and activities are included in the tuition. Students may use any Internet connection available to them or may use a toll-free number that is available from 7:00 pm–6:00 am, plus weekends and holidays.

All faculty members (full-time and adjunct) are accessible online by students and communicate online regularly with students on academic matters. Under normal circumstances, students receive responses to their e-mail within 1–2 business days. Faculty and students also interact via online bulletin boards and also in real time via use of NSU's electronic classroom.

All students are online and are encouraged to communicate with each other via e-mail and bulletin boards. Also, students are able to use NSU's electronic classroom for real-time group meetings without the presence of a faculty member.

In many cases, students complete course projects that apply to both course requirements and job responsibilities.

A student may apply for three credits of independent study under the supervision of a faculty member. Generally, no more than two independent study courses will be approved. The student may also complete a six-credit master's thesis.

Program effectiveness is determined through student course evaluations, student program evaluations, other surveys of students, surveys of employers, and benchmarking.

Nova Southeastern University
School of Computer and Information Sciences (Doctorate in Information Science)

3100 S.W. 9th Avenue
Fort Lauderdale, FL 33315
Phone: 800-986-2247 ext. 7352
Fax: 954-476-1982
E-mail: liz@scis.nova.edu

Degrees Offered
Doctor of Philosophy (PhD) or Doctor of Science (ScD) in Information Science

Program Mission
To offer a course of study leading to a PhD in information science.

Accreditation
Southern Association of Colleges and Schools

Admission Requirements
An earned master's degree from a regionally accredited institution with a GPA of at least 3.25. This program is designed for students with master's degrees in information systems, information science, library science, computer education, or a related area. Applicants must provide a score report of the GRE or a comprehensive portfolio of appropriate professional experience and credentials.

Credit Hour Requirements
64 credit hours

Minimum Campus Time
Students may select one of two formats: cluster or institute. Both include group meetings on the campus and online activities. Students electing the cluster format attend four cluster meetings per year, held quarterly over an extended weekend (Friday, Saturday, and half-day Sunday) at the

university. Cluster terms start in March and September. Cluster weekends take place in March, June, September, and December. Students choosing the institute format attend a week-long institute twice a year at the university. Institutes are held in mid-January and mid-July at the start of each six-month term. Clusters and institutes bring together students, faculty, staff, and nationally recognized lecturers for participation in courses, workshops, discussions, training, and dissertation counseling.

Tuition and Fees
Tuition $3725 per six-month term; application fee $40; registration fee $30

Credit Awards for Examinations
GRE or comprehensive portfolio

Credit Awards for Prior Learning
None

Description
The focus of the program is on information organization and retrieval. Program formats combine traditional and nontraditional instruction to provide professionals the opportunity to obtain the doctorate while continuing to work in their current positions. The program is designed for professionals working in business, government, industry, or education in a library of information center environment. It is intended to provide technology-oriented professionals the knowledge and ability to develop creative solutions to substantive real-world problems. Courses, course-extending projects, and research activities serve as an expanded learning environment. Each student must complete eight courses, four projects, and a dissertation. The program may be completed in three years but students have up to seven years to complete all requirements. In the first two years, students register for 10 credits per term. In the third year, students register for 12 credits per term.

Advising and support services are provided by the student's program office, which is open 8:30 am–5:00 pm Monday–Friday. Students may communicate with the program office via e-mail or telephone.

Between on-campus meetings, students complete assignments, research papers, and/or applied research projects, and participate in various online activities. Online activities facilitate frequent interaction with faculty, classmates, and colleagues. The online component involves NSU's real-time electronic classroom sessions, computer discussions and conferences, electronic submission of assignments for review by faculty, electronic mail, interactive bulletin boards, the electronic library, NSU's distance library services, and use of the Internet. Learning and interaction are facilitated by hypertext menuing systems. Costs for online activities are included in the tuition. Online interaction takes place via computer (IBM-compatible PC or Apple/Macintosh) and modem from home, office, or on the road while traveling. Students may use any Internet connection available to them or may use a toll-free number that is available from 7:00 pm–6:00 am, plus weekends and holidays.

All faculty members (full-time and adjunct) are accessible online by students and communicate online regularly with students on academic matters. Under normal circumstances, students receive responses to their e-mail within 1–2 business days. Faculty and students also interact via online bulletin boards and also in real time via use of NSU's electronic classroom.

All students are online and are encouraged to communicate with each other via e-mail and bulletin boards. Also, students are able to use NSU's electronic classroom for real-time group meetings without the presence of a faculty member.

In many cases, students complete course projects that apply to both course requirements and job responsibilities.

A student may apply for independent study under the supervision of a faculty member. Generally, no more than two independent-study courses will be approved. Each student is expected, with the help and approval of an advisor, to select an appropriate topic of sufficient scope to satisfy the requirements for the dissertation. Dissertation results must, in a significant way, advance knowledge, improve professional practice, and/or contribute to understanding in the field.

Program effectiveness is determined through student course evaluations, student program evaluations, other surveys of students, surveys of employers, and benchmarking.

Nova Southeastern University
School of Computer and Information Sciences (MS in Computer Information Systems)

3100 S.W. 9th Avenue
Fort Lauderdale, FL 33315
Phone: 800-986-2247 ext. 7352
Fax: 954-476-1982
E-mail: liz@scis.nova.edu

Degrees Offered
Master of Science in Computer Information Systems

Program Mission
To offer a course of study leading to a Master of Science degree in computer information systems.

Accreditation
Southern Association of Colleges and Schools

Admission Requirements
An earned bachelor's degree in computer science, computer information systems, engineering, mathematics, or physics from a regionally accredited college or university. The candidate must have an undergraduate GPA of at least 2.5 and a GPA of 3.0 in a major field. Applicants must provide a score report of the GRE or a comprehensive portfolio of appropriate professional experience and credentials. Applicants must have knowledge of data structures, computer hardware and architecture, structured programming, college algebra, and discrete mathematics.

Credit Hour Requirements
36 credit hours

Minimum Campus Time
New students must attend a weekend orientation prior to the start of their first term

Tuition and Fees
$330 per credit hour; application fee $40; and registration fee $30

Credit Awards for Examinations
GRE or comprehensive portfolio

Credit Awards for Prior Learning
None

Description
This program is offered in an online format. It focuses on the technological foundations of computer information systems including areas such as database systems, human-computer interaction, data and computer communications, computer security, computer graphics, system test and evaluation, and object orientation. It is designed to give students a thorough knowledge of the field and to provide an enduring foundation for future professional growth. The

program blends theory and practice into a learning experience that develops skills applicable to complex real-world problems. Its format offers professionals the opportunity to earn the master's degree in 18 months while continuing to work in their current positions. The curriculum is consistent with recommendations for a model curriculum in computer information systems as outlined by the Association of Computing Machinery (ACM).

Advising and support services are provided by the student's program office, which is open 8:30 am–5:00 pm Monday–Friday. Students may communicate with the program office via e-mail or telephone.

Online courses are taken via computer (IBM-compatible PC or Apple/Macintosh) and modem from home, office, or on the road while traveling. The student may participate in courses from anywhere in the United States or outside the United States where Internet access is available. The format involves the use of online interactive learning methods and teleconferencing throughout the instructional sequence. Courses involve a range of online activities that facilitate frequent interaction with faculty, classmates, and colleagues. Teachers and students are able to interact in real time during scheduled electronic classroom sessions that include lectures and discussions. Online activities also include interactive bulletin boards, electronic submission of assignments for review by faculty, electronic mail, the electronic library, and access to the school's computer systems. The Internet is also used extensively for research. Learning and interaction are facilitated by hypertext menuing systems. Costs for online connection and activities are included in the tuition. Students may use any Internet connection available to them or may use a toll-free number that is available from 7:00 pm–6:00 am, plus weekends and holidays.

All faculty members (full-time and adjunct) are accessible online by students and communicate online regularly with students on academic matters. Under normal circumstances, students receive responses to their e-mail within 1–2 business days. Faculty and students also interact via online bulletin boards and also in real time via use of NSU's electronic classroom.

All students are online and are encouraged to communicate with each other via e-mail and bulletin boards. Also, students are able to use NSU's electronic classroom for real-time group meetings without the presence of a faculty member.

In many cases, students complete course projects that apply to both course requirements and job responsibilities.

A student may apply for three credits of independent study under the supervision of a faculty member. Generally, no more than two independent-study courses will be approved. The student may also complete a six-credit master's thesis.

Program effectiveness is determined through student course evaluations, student program evaluations, other surveys of students, surveys of employers, and benchmarking.

Nova Southeastern University
School of Computer and Information Sciences (MS in Computing in Education)

3100 S.W. 9th Avenue
Fort Lauderdale, FL 33315
Phone: 800-986-2247, ext. 7352
Fax: 954-476-1982
E-mail: liz@scis.nova.edu

Degrees Offered
Master of Science in Computing in Education

Program Mission
To offer a course of study leading to a Master of Science degree in computing technology in education.

Accreditation
Southern Association of Colleges and Schools

Admission Requirements
An earned bachelor's degree in a related field from a regionally accredited college or university, and experience using computer applications. The candidate must have an undergraduate GPA of at least 2.5 and a GPA of 3.0 in a major field. Applicants must provide a score of the GRE or a comprehensive portfolio of appropriate professional experience and credentials.

Credit Hour Requirements
36 credit hours

Minimum Campus Time
New students must attend a weekend orientation prior to the start of their first term.

Tuition and Fees
$330 per credit hour; application fee $40; registration fee $30

Credit Awards for Examinations
GRE or comprehensive portfolio

Credit Awards for Prior Learning
Transfer credits from accredited, degree-granting institution

Description
The program is designed to meet the needs of working professionals such as teachers, educational administrators, and trainers working in either the public or the private sector. The program blends educational theory and practice into a learning experience that develops skills applicable to complex real-world problems.

It is designed enhance knowledge of how computers, software, and other forms of high technology can be used to improve learning outcomes. Its format offers professionals the opportunity to earn the master's degree in 18 months while continuing to work in their current positions. Courses in the program have been approved for teacher certification in computer science (grades K–12) or recertification by Florida's Bureau of Teacher Certification. They may be taken as part of the degree program or independently.

Advising and support services are provided by the student's program office, which is open 8:30 am–5:00 pm Monday–Friday. Students may communicate with the program office via e-mail or telephone.

Online courses are taken via computer (IBM-compatible PC or Apple/Macintosh) and modem from home, office, or on the road while traveling. The student may participate in courses from anywhere in the United States or outside the United States where Internet access is available. The format involves the use of online interactive learning methods and teleconferencing throughout the instructional sequence. Courses involve a range of online activities that facilitate frequent interaction with faculty, classmates, and colleagues. Teachers and students are able to interact in real time during scheduled electronic classroom sessions that include lectures and discussions. Online activities also include interactive bulletin boards, electronic submission of assignments for review by faculty, electronic mail, the electronic library, and access to the school's computer systems. The Internet is also used extensively for research. Learning and interaction are facilitated by hypertext menuing systems. Costs for online connection and activities are included in the tuition. Students may use any Internet connection available to them or may use a toll-free number that is available from 7:00 pm–6:00 am, plus weekends and holidays.

All faculty members (full-time and adjunct) are accessible online by students and communicate online regularly with students on academic matters. Under normal circumstances, students receive responses to their e-mail within 1–2 business days. Faculty and students also interact via online bulletin boards and also in real time via use of NSU's electronic classroom.

All students are online and are encouraged to communicate with each other via e-mail and bulletin boards. Also, students are able to use NSU's electronic classroom for real-time group meetings without the presence of a faculty member.

In many cases, students complete course projects that apply to both course requirements and job responsibilities.

A student may apply for three credits of independent study under the supervision of a faculty member. Generally, no more than two independent study courses will be approved. The student may also complete a six-credit master's thesis.

Program effectiveness is determined through student course evaluations, student program evaluations, other surveys of students, surveys of employers, and benchmarking.

Nova Southeastern University
School of Computer and Information Sciences (Doctorates in Computer Information Systems)

3100 S.W. 9th Avenue
Fort Lauderdale, FL 33315
Phone: 800-986-2247 ext. 7352
Fax: 954-476-1982
E-mail: liz@scis.nova.edu

Degrees Offered
Doctor of Philosophy (PhD) or Doctor of Science (ScD) in Computer Information Systems

Program Mission
To offer a course of study leading to a PhD or ScD in computing information systems.

Accreditation
Southern Association of Colleges and Schools

Admission Requirements
An earned master's degree from a regionally accredited institution with a graduate GPA of at least 3.25. This program is designed for the student with a master's degree in computer information systems, computer science, or a related area. The applicant should satisfy graduate prerequisites or have equivalent experience in information systems, programming languages, database systems, systems analysis and design, data communications and networks, and computer architecture. Applicants must provide a score report of the GRE or comprehensive portfolio of appropriate professional experience and credentials.

Credit Hour Requirements
68 credit hours

Minimum Campus Time

Students attend four cluster meetings per year, held quarterly over an extended weekend (Friday, Saturday, and half-day Sunday) at the university. Cluster weekends take place in March, June, September, and December. They bring together students, faculty, staff, and nationally recognized lecturers for participation in courses, workshops, discussions, training, and dissertation counseling.

Tuition and Fees

Tuition $3725 per six-month term; application fee $40; registration fee $30

Credit Awards for Examinations

GRE or comprehensive portfolio

Credit Awards for Prior Learning

None

Description

The program format provides professionals the opportunity to pursue graduate study while continuing to work in their current positions. The program is designed for professionals in business, government, industry, or education who are involved with research, design, implementation, management, evaluation, utilization, or teaching of computer information systems. It is intended to provide technology-oriented professionals with the knowledge and ability to develop creative solutions to substantive real-world problems. Courses, course-extending projects, and research activities serve as an expanded learning environment. Each student must complete eight courses, six projects, and a dissertation. The program may be completed in four years, but students have up to seven years to complete all requirements. During the first three years, students register for seven credits per term. In the fourth year, students register for 13 credits per term.

Advising and support services are provided by the student's program office, which is open 8:30 am–5:00 pm Monday–Friday. Students may communicate with the program office via e-mail or telephone.

Between cluster meetings, students complete assignments, research papers, and/or applied research projects, and participate in various online activities that facilitate frequent interaction with faculty, classmates, and colleagues. This may involve electronic mail communications, computer discussions and conferences, interactive bulletin boards, the electronic mail communications, computer discussions and conferences, the electronic library, NSU's distance library services, and use of the Internet. Costs for online activities are included in the tuition. Online interaction takes place via computer (IBM-compatible PC or Apple/Macintosh) and modem from home, office, or on the road while traveling. Students may use any Internet connection available to them or may use a toll-free number that is available from 7:00 pm–6:00 am, plus weekends and holidays.

All faculty members (full-time and adjunct) are accessible online by students and communicate online regularly with students on academic matters. Under normal circumstances, students receive responses to their e-mail within 1–2 business days. Faculty and students also interact via online bulletin boards and also in real time via use of NSU's electronic classroom.

All students are online and are encouraged to communicate with each other via e-mail and bulletin boards. Also, students are able to use NSU's electronic classroom for real-time group meetings without the presence of a faculty member.

In many cases, students complete course projects that apply to both course requirements and job responsibilities.

A student may apply for independent study under the supervision of a faculty member. Generally, no more than two independent-study courses will be approved. Also, each doctoral student must complete a dissertation, which is the most important requirement for the doctorate. Each student is expected, with the help and approval of an advisor, to select an appropriate topic of sufficient scope to satisfy the requirements for the dissertation. Dissertation results must, in a significant way, advance knowledge, improve professional practice, and/or contribute to understanding in the field.

Program effectiveness is determined through student course evaluations, student program evaluations, other surveys of students, surveys of employers, and benchmarking.

Nova Southeastern University
School of Computer and Information Sciences (Doctorates in Computer Science)

3100 S.W. 9th Avenue
Fort Lauderdale, FL 33315
Phone: 800-986-2247 ext. 7352
Fax: 954-476-1982
E-mail: liz@scis.nova.edu

Degrees Offered
Doctor of Philosophy (PhD) or Doctor of Science (ScD) in Computer Science

Program Mission
To offer a course of study leading to a PhD or ScD in computer science.

Accreditation
Southern Association of Colleges and Schools

Admission Requirements
An earned master's degree from a regionally accredited institution with a graduate GPA of at least 3.25. This program is designed for the student with a master's degree in computer information systems, computer science, or a related area. The applicant should satisfy graduate prerequisites or have equivalent experience in information systems, programming languages, database systems, systems analysis and design, data communications and networks, and computer architecture. Applicants must provide a score report of the GRE or comprehensive portfolio of appropriate professional experience and credentials.

Credit Hour Requirements
68 credit hours

Minimum Campus Time
Students attend four cluster meetings per year, held quarterly over an extended weekend (Friday, Saturday, and half-day Sunday) at the university. Cluster weekends take place in March, June, September, and December. They bring together students, faculty, staff, and nationally recognized lecturers for participation in courses, workshops, discussions, training, and dissertation counseling.

Tuition and Fees
Tuition $3725 per six-month term; application fee $40; registration fee $30

Credit Awards for Examinations
GRE or comprehensive portfolio

Credit Awards for Prior Learning
None

Description
The program format provides professionals the opportunity to pursue graduate study while continuing to work in their current positions. The program is designed for professionals in business, government, industry, or education who are involved with research, design, implementation, management, evaluation, utilization, or teaching of computer information systems. It is in-

tended to provide research-oriented professionals with knowledge in the major areas of computer science and the ability to develop creative solutions to substantive real-world problems. Courses, course-extending projects, and research activities serve as an expanded learning environment. Each student must complete eight courses, six projects, and a dissertation. The program may be completed in four years, but students have up to seven years to complete all requirements. During the first three years, students register for seven credits per term. In the fourth year, students register for 13 credits per term.

Advising and support services are provided by the student's program office, which is open 8:30 am–5:00 pm Monday–Friday. Students may communicate with the program office via e-mail or telephone.

Between cluster meetings, students complete assignments, research papers, and/or applied research projects, and participate in various online activities that facilitate frequent interaction with faculty, classmates, and colleagues. This may involve electronic mail communications, computer discussions and conferences, interactive bulletin boards, the electronic library, NSU's distance library services, and use of the Internet. Costs for online activities are included in the tuition. Online interaction takes place via computer (IBM-compatible PC or Apple/Macintosh) and modem from home, office, or on the road while traveling. Students may use any Internet connection available to them or may use a toll-free number that is available from 7:00 pm–6:00 am, plus weekends and holidays.

All faculty members (full-time and adjunct) are accessible online by students and communicate online regularly with students on academic matters. Under normal circumstances, students receive responses to their e-mail within 1–2 business days. Faculty and students also interact via online bulletin boards and also in real time via use of NSU's electronic classroom.

All students are online and are encouraged to communicate with each other via e-mail and bulletin boards. Also, students are able to use NSU's electronic classroom for real-time group meetings without the presence of a faculty member.

In many cases, students complete course projects that apply to both course requirements and job responsibilities.

A student may apply for independent study under the supervision of a faculty member. Generally, no more than two independent-study courses will be approved. Also, each doctoral student must complete a dissertation, which is the most important requirement for the doctorate. Each student is expected, with the help and approval of an advisor, to select an appropriate topic of sufficient scope to satisfy the requirements for the dissertation. Dissertation results must, in a significant way, advance knowledge, improve professional practice, and/or contribute to understanding in the field.

Program effectiveness is determined through student course evaluations, student program evaluations, other surveys of students, surveys of employers, and benchmarking.

Nova Southeastern University
School of Computer and Information Sciences (Doctorates in Computing Technology in Education)

3100 S.W. 9th Avenue
Fort Lauderdale, FL 33315
Phone: 800-986-2247 ext 7352

Fax: 954-476-1982
E-mail: liz@scis.nova.edu

Degrees Offered
Doctor of Philosophy (PhD), Doctor of Education (EdD), or Doctor of Science (ScD) in Computing Technology in Education

Program Mission
To offer a course of study leading to a PhD, EdD, or ScD in computing technology in education. It addresses: (1) the use of computing technologies to improve cognition; (2) the development, management, and evaluation of computing systems that support the educational process; and (3) the role of computing and other advanced technology in training.

Accreditation
Southern Association of Colleges and Schools

Admission Requirements
An earned master's degree from a regionally accredited institution with a graduate GPA of at least 3.25. This program is designed for the student with a master's degree in education, training and learning, instructional design, information systems, human resources, educational leadership, or an area related to education. Applicants must provide a score report of the GRE or comprehensive portfolio of appropriate professional experience and credentials

Credit Hour Requirements
64 credit hours

Minimum Campus Time
Students may select one of two formats: cluster or institute. Both include group meetings on the campus and online activities. Students electing the cluster format attend four cluster meetings per year, held quarterly over an extended weekend (Friday, Saturday, and half-day Sunday) at the university. Cluster terms start in March and September. Cluster weekends take place in March, June, September, and December. Students choosing the institute format attend a week-long institute twice a year at the university. Institutes are held in mid-January and mid-July at the start of each six-month term. Clusters and institutes bring together students, faculty, staff, and nationally recognized lecturers for participation in courses, workshops, discussions, training, and dissertation counseling. Between meetings, students complete assignments, research papers, and/or applied research projects, and participate in various online activities that facilitate frequent interaction with faculty, classmates, and colleagues.

Tuition and Fees
Tuition $3725 per six-month term; application fee $40; registration fee $30

Credit Awards for Examinations
GRE or comprehensive portfolio

Credit Awards for Prior Learning
None

Description
Program formats combine traditional and nontraditional instruction to provide professionals the opportunity to obtain the doctorate while continuing to work in their current positions. The program is designed for educators, educational administrators, and trainers working in the public or private sector. It is intended to provide technology-oriented professionals with the knowledge and ability to develop creative solutions to substantive real-world problems. Courses, course-extending projects, and research activities serve as an expanded learning environment. Each student must complete eight courses, four projects, and a dissertation. The program may be completed in three years, but students have up to seven years to complete all requirements. In the first two years, students register for 10 credits per term. In the third year, students register for 12 credits per term.

Advising and support services are provided by the student's program office, which is open 8:30 am–5:00 pm Monday–Friday. Students may communicate with the program office via e-mail or telephone.

Between on-campus meetings, students complete assignments, research papers, and/or applied research projects, and participate in various online activities. Online activities facilitate frequent interaction with faculty, classmates, and colleagues. The online component involves NSU's real-time electronic classroom sessions, computer discussions and conferences, electronic submission of assignments for review by faculty, electronic mail, interactive bulletin boards, the electronic library, NSU's distance library services, and use of the Internet. Learning and interaction are facilitated by hypertext menuing systems. Costs for online activities are include in the tuition. Online interaction takes place via computer (IBM-compatible PC or Apple/Macintosh) and modem from home, office, or on the road while traveling. Students may use any Internet connection available to them or may use a toll-free number that is available from 7:00 pm–6:00 am, plus weekends and holidays.

All faculty members (full-time and adjunct) are accessible online and communicate online regularly with students on academic matters. Under normal circumstances, students receive responses to their e-mails within 1–2 business days. Faculty and students also interact via online bulletin boards and also in real time via use of NSU's electronic classroom.

All students are online and are encouraged to communicate with each other via e-mail and bulletin boards. Also, students are able to use NSU's electronic classroom for real-time group meetings without the presence of a faculty member.

In many cases, students complete course projects that apply to both course requirements and job responsibilities.

A student may apply for independent study under the supervision of a faculty member. Generally, no more than two independent-study courses will be approved. Also, each doctoral student must complete a dissertation, which is the most important requirement for the doctorate. Each student is expected, with the help and approval of an advisor, to select an appropriate topic of sufficient scope to satisfy the requirements for the dissertation. Dissertation results must, in a significant way, advance knowledge, improve professional practice, and/or contribute to understanding in the field.

Program effectiveness is determined through student course evaluations, student program evaluations, other surveys of students, surveys of employers, and benchmarking.

Nova Southeastern University
School of Computer and Information Sciences (PhD in Information Systems)

3100 S.W. 9th Avenue
Fort Lauderdale, FL 33315
Phone: 800-986-2247 ext. 7352
Fax: 954-476-1982
E-mail: liz@scis.nova.edu

Degrees Offered
Doctor of Philosophy (PhD) in Information Systems

Program Mission
To offer a course of study leading to a PhD in information systems.

Accreditation
Southern Association of Colleges and Schools

Admission Requirements
An earned master's degree from a regionally accredited institution with a graduate GPA of at least 3.25. This program is designed for the student with a master's degree in information systems, information science, computer science, or a related area. The applicant should satisfy graduate prerequisites or have equivalent experience in information systems, programming languages, database systems, systems analysis and design, data communications and networks, and computer architecture. Applicants must provide a score report of the GRE or comprehensive portfolio of appropriate professional experience and credentials.

Credit Hour Requirements
64 credit hours

Minimum Campus Time
Students may select one of two formats: cluster or institute. Both formats include group meetings on the campus and online activities. Students electing the cluster format attend four cluster meetings per year, held quarterly over an extended weekend (Friday, Saturday, and half-day Sunday) at the university. Cluster terms start in March and September. Cluster weekends take place in March, June, September, and December. Students choosing the institute format attend a week-long institute twice a year at the university. Institutes are held in mid-January and mid-July at the start of each six-month term. Clusters and institutes bring together students, faculty, staff, and nationally recognized lecturers for participation in courses, workshops, discussions, training, and dissertation counseling. Between meetings, students complete assignments, research papers, and/or applied research projects, and participate in

various online activities that facilitate frequent interaction with faculty, classmates, and colleagues.

Tuition and Fees
Tuition $3725 per six-month term; application fee $40; registration fee $30

Credit Awards for Examinations
GRE or comprehensive portfolio

Credit Awards for Prior Learning
None

Description
The program combines traditional and nontraditional instruction to provide professionals working in business, government, industry, or education the opportunity to obtain the doctorate while continuing in their current positions. The program is designed for professionals working in areas such as information system planning, systems analysis and design, project management, information system administration, or software engineering. It is intended to provide technology-oriented professionals with the knowledge and ability to develop creative solutions to substantive real-world problems. Courses, course-extending projects, and research activities serve as an expanded learning environment. Each student must complete eight courses, six projects, and a dissertation. The program may be completed in four years, but students have up to seven years to complete all requirements. During the first three years, students register for seven credits per term. In the fourth year, students register for 12 credits per term.

Advising and support services are provided by the student's program office, which is open 8:30 am–5:00 pm Monday–Friday. Students may communicate with the program office via e-mail or telephone.

Between on-campus meetings, students complete assignments, research papers, and/ or applied research projects, and participate in various online activities. Online activities facilitate frequent interaction with faculty, classmates, and colleagues. The online component involves NSU's real-time electronic classroom sessions, computer discussions and conferences, electronic submission of assignments for review by faculty, electronic mail, interactive bulletin boards, the electronic library, NSU's distance library services, and use of the Internet. Learning and interaction are facilitated by hypertext menuing systems. Costs for online activities are include in the tuition. Online interaction takes place via computer (IBM-compatible PC or Apple/Macintosh) and modem from home, office, or on the road while traveling. Students may use any Internet connection available to them or may use a toll-free number that is available from 7:00 pm–6:00 am, plus weekends and holidays.

All faculty members (full-time and adjunct) are accessible online and communicate online regularly with students on academic matters. Under normal circumstances, students receive responses to their e-mail within 1–2 business days. Faculty and students also interact via online bulletin boards and also in real time via use of NSU's electronic classroom.

All students are online and are encouraged to communicate with each other via e-mail and bulletin boards. Also, students are able to use NSU's electronic classroom for real-time group meetings without the presence of a faculty member.

In many cases, students complete course projects that apply to both course requirements and job responsibilities.

A student may apply for independent study under the supervision of a faculty member. Generally, no more than two independent study courses will be approved. Also, each doctoral student must complete a dissertation, which is the most important require-

ment for the doctorate. Each student is expected, with the help and approval of an advisor, to select an appropriate topic of sufficient scope to satisfy the requirements for the dissertation. Dissertation results must, in a significant way, advance knowledge, improve professional practice, and/or contribute to understanding in the field.

Program effectiveness is determined through student course evaluations, student program evaluations, other surveys of students, surveys of employers, and benchmarking.

Peoples College

233 Academy Drive
Kissimmee, FL 34742-1768
Phone: 407-847-4444
Fax: 407-847-8793
E-mail: peoples@gdi.net

Degrees Offered
Specialized Associate degree in Electronics; Specialized Associate degree in Personal Computer Programming

Program Mission
To provide convenient and cost-effective technical training in order to fulfill the mission of assisting students to develop the demonstrable entry-level ability and skills of technicians and professionals.

Accreditation
Distance Education Training Council

Admission Requirements
High school diploma or GED

Credit Hour Requirements
Personal Computer Programming, 98 quarter hours; Electronics, 108 to 120 quarter hours

Tuition and Fees
Tuition $3995 for each degree program

Credit Awards for Examinations
DANTES subject tests

Credit Awards for Prior Learning
Transfer credits from accredited, degree-granting institution; ACE military recommendations; ACE/PONSI recommendations

Description
The entire program is distance education and independent study with no on-campus time.

Students learning at a distance access academic resources through the Internet, e-mail, and regular mail.

Students and faculty interact over the telephone and through e-mail.

Students may exchange information via e-mail.

All technical training is hands-on. The student must perform within a working environment to successfully complete the courses.

Program effectiveness is measured through the accrediting commission, through advisory staffs, and through student success.

University of Sarasota

Graduate Programs
5250 17th Street
Sarasota, FL 34235
Phone: 800-331-5995
Fax: 941-379-9464
E-mail: 102556.2652@compuserve.com

Degrees Offered
Doctor of Business Administration; Doctor of Education in Educational Leadership, Curriculum and Instruction, Counseling Psychology, or Human Services Administration; Master of Arts in Guidance Counseling, Human Services Administration, Marriage and Family Counseling, or Mental Health Counseling; Master of Arts in Education in Educational Leadership or Curriculum and Instruction

Program Mission
To educate capable, serious, mature, and motivated graduate students with the intent of equipping them to become leaders in their professions.

Accreditation
Southern Association of Colleges and Schools

Admission Requirements
Doctoral programs: 3.0 GPA in master's degree; three professional recommendations. Master's programs: 3.0 GPA during last two years of undergraduate work; three professional recommendations. International students (whose native language is not English) must score above 550 on the TOEFL.

Credit Hour Requirements
Doctoral programs, 60 credits; Master of Arts in Education, 39 credits; Master of Arts, 48 credits

Minimum Campus Time
Doctoral programs require eight courses on campus. Master of Arts in Education requires six courses on campus. Master of Arts require seven courses on campus (courses are offered in one-week sessions scheduled throughout the year).

Tuition and Fees
$317 per credit

Credit Awards for Examination
None

Credit Awards for Prior Learning
Transfer credits from accredited, degree-granting institution

Description
Advising and other support services can be accessed through toll-free phone contact,

Monday-Friday 9:00 am–5:00 pm, or through the electronic mail system.

Distance learning courses (tutorials) offer individual contact with faculty mentors. Contact is maintained through toll-free 800 number, fax, and electronic mail. Tutorial packets and textbooks are shipped to the student upon registration, and a specific faculty member is assigned to the student.

Research and electronic mail capability is offered through CompuServe. On-campus library facilities are available to all students.

Distance learning courses require a minimum of four phone or electronic mail consultations with faculty.

The university facilitates the communication among students through its electronic newsletter and published electronic mail directory.

Directed independent study courses can involve work-related research projects.

As part of the accreditation process, the university conducts a comprehensive self-study to examine various issues relating to program effectiveness. Continual feedback is solicited and encouraged from students in all programs through the course evaluation process.

University of South Florida

Bachelor of Independent Studies (BIS)
 Program
HMS-443
Tampa, FL 33620
Phone: 813-974-4058
Fax: 813-974-5101
E-mail: bis@luna.cas.usf.edu

Degrees Offered
Bachelor of Independent Studies

Program Mission
To serve students who would not be able to earn a college degree in a traditional setting.

Accreditation
Southern Association of Colleges and Schools

Admission Requirements
High school or GED diploma for four curriculum area track. Associate's degree or equivalent for two curriculum area track. Students must be admitted by both the University of South Florida and by the BIS program.

Credit Hour Requirements
120 semester hours for the four curriculum area track; 60 semester hours for the two curriculum area track

Minimum Campus Time
One-day orientation at the beginning of studies; two-week summer seminar for each of three curriculum areas (for four-area track) or two curriculum areas (for two-area track)

Tuition and Fees
In-state tuition $55 per credit hour; out-of-state tuition is approximately $150 per credit hour

Credit Awards for Examinations
CLEP general exams; CLEP subject exams; College Board AP exams

Credit Awards for Prior Learning
Transfer credits from accredited, degree-granting institution

Description
Staff and faculty work with students at any time.

Distance education opportunities include distant tutorial study, normally using e-mail, mail, and telephone.

BIS students use any of the 10 state university libraries, community and junior college libraries, and local libraries. The BIS program also has its own internal lending library.

Interaction between faculty and students occurs through community-based courses, communication, and meetings.

Interaction between students is through informal mentoring of more experienced students with new students.

Academic Profile Examination, retention studies, graduate programs attended, admission to Phi Kappa and Phi Honor Society are measures used to determine program effectiveness.

University of South Florida College of Public Health

13201 Bruce B. Downs Boulevard
Tampa, FL 33612
Phone: 813-474-6666
Fax: 813-974-4718
E-mail: k.blevins@cophadm1.coph.usf.edu

Degrees Offered
Master of Public Health in Public Health Practice; Executive Master of Public Health

Program Mission
To improve the ability of the College of Public Health to respond to Florida's public health needs and to enable and enhance its role in building the capacity of the public health system and the competencies of the public health workforce through the delivery of academic and continuing education programs throughout the state; serving as a resource in the development of public policy; and fostering practice links and service opportunities with state and/or local public health agencies. The primary purpose of the Master of Public Health in

Public Health Practice is to prepare experienced health professionals to assume leadership roles as members of multidisciplinary teams and to be able to effectively develop, implement, and evaluate programs that have an impact on the health of the public.

Accreditation
Southern Association of Colleges and Schools

Admission Requirements
Limited to Florida residents with three years or more experience in public health (or closely related field), computer proficiency, 1000 or higher on the GRE (combined quantitative and verbal)

Credit Hour Requirements
40–51 semester credits

Minimum Campus Time
Approximately 4–6 weeks, in 1- to 2-week blocks.

Tuition and Fees
$115.89 per semester hour credit

Credit Awards for Examinations
None

Credit Awards for Prior Learning
Transfer credits from accredited, degree-granting institution and procedure for waiver of required courses based on prior courses completed elsewhere

Description
Executive MPH is limited to physicians, veterinarians, and dentists.

Student support services are available 8:00 am–5:00 pm Monday–Friday; e-mail and voice mail anytime.

Distance education opportunities include satellite-delivered television (receive-only format with live two-way audio interface); videotaped lectures to a limited number of students. Students access academic resources through the Internet and/or modem access to online databases.

Classes are delivered in a live format; interim communication is through cluster-based, scheduled audio teleconferences, e-mail, phone, and face-to-face if possible.

Students must gather at a downlink site to participate in class together. Plans are in progress to develop computer-based course and program-specific chat rooms and discussion groups. There is an emphasis on communities of learners that are public health–focused and represent a microcosm of the local (or regional) community. Program is structured to enlist student involvement in meeting their own educational needs.

Field experience (1–12 hours) is a required part of the curriculum. This is usually completed in conjunction with a special project.

It is possible to self-design some courses and projects based on student interest and need in areas not covered by the curriculum or other course work on campus, or in some areas when a course is needed by the student but not scheduled that semester by the college. These are contingent upon advisor's prior certification of project of independent study course work.

Program effectiveness is determined through survey evaluations, in-depth interviews, employer feedback, and student feedback, and a combination of qualitative and quantitative measures.

GEORGIA

Georgia Institute of Technology

Video-Based Instruction System
Center for Media-Based Instruction
Atlanta, GA 30332-0385

Phone: 404-894-3378
Fax: 404-894-8924
E-mail: vbis@conted.gatech.edu

Degrees Offered
Master of Science in the following areas: Electrical Engineering; Environmental Engineering; Health Physics, Industrial and Systems Engineering; and Mechanical Engineering

Program Mission
Utilizing a video-based delivery system, Georgia Tech electronically extends its classroom walls to serve students who cannot attend on-campus classes. Busy professionals have the opportunity to earn advanced degrees or simply to take a sequence of courses while still working full-time anywhere in the United States or Puerto Rico.

Accreditation
Southern Association of Colleges and Schools; Accrediting Board for Engineering and Technology (ABET)

Admission Requirements
Requirements vary according to discipline. GRE scores are considered in the admission process.

Credit Hour Requirements
All master's degrees based on quarter hours: Electrical Engineering, 50; Environmental Engineering, 50; Health Physics, 45; Industrial and Systems Engineering, 48; and Mechanical Engineering, 45

Minimum Campus Time
Two health physics courses have required laboratories that meet three times per quarter, on weekends

Tuition and Fees
$212 per quarter credit hour

Credit Awards for Examinations
None

Credit Awards for Prior Learning
Transfer credits from accredited, degree-granting institution; department/institutional exams

Description
Students in the program have the flexibility to view classroom lectures at times that fit their schedules. Video cameras record instructor presentations and student-instructor interactions during regular Georgia Tech graduate classes. The videotape and supporting materials are sent to off-campus students, who participate in classroom activities by watching the taped classes on video monitors at their place of work, their homes, or at a designated location. Class tapes along with supplemental material will reach off-campus students within two to three days.

Each distance learner student is assigned an academic advisor who can be accessed by phone, e-mail, and fax. Access times are generally 8:00 am–5:00 pm. Also, each learner must identify a proctor who must be approved by the Georgia Tech program director to administer tests and exams.

Distance education opportunities include videotaped lectures.

Students learning at a distance can access academic resources through the Georgia Tech Electronic Library and the Georgia Tech computer network via a computer with a modem or via the Internet.

Students are provided at the beginning of each course with the professor's office hours and phone number, fax number, and e-mail address. Some professors set up electronic bulletin boards for student interaction. Students are provided with the names, phone numbers, fax numbers, and e-mail addresses of other distance learners in the class.

Student and faculty evaluation forms are completed at end of quarter, and there is a comparison of aggregate grades for distance learners vs. campus students enrolled in the same classes each quarter.

Other measures used to determine program effectiveness include encouraging student input throughout the quarter via forms provided.

IDAHO

Boise State University

Master of Science Degree in Instructional and Performance Technology
1910 University Drive
Boise, ID 83725
Phone: 208-385-4457
Fax: 208-385-3467
E-mail: bsu-ipt@micron.net
Internet: http://www-cotldbsu.edu/nipt/

Degrees Offered
Master of Science in Instructional and Performance Technology (IPT)

Program Mission
To prepare students for careers in the areas of instructional design, job performance improvement, human resources, training, and training management. The IPT program is designed to equip students with skills needed to identify, analyze, and solve a variety of human performance problems in settings such as industry, business, the military, education, and private consulting.

Accreditation
Northwest Association of Schools and Colleges

Admission Requirements
Undergraduate degree with a 2.75 overall GPA, minimum score of 50 on the MAT, and required computer hardware

Credit Hour Requirements
36 credit hours

Minimum Campus Time
None

Tuition and Fees
$315 per credit hour

Credit Awards for Examinations
None

Credit Awards for Prior Learning
Transfer credits from accredited, degree-granting institution

Description
Technical support and registration advising available via an 800 number Monday–Friday 8:00 am–5:00 pm. Academic advising available via an 800 number during the above business hours; for evening appointments via a direct line.

Distance education is provided through computer conferencing.

Students access academic resources through the Internet, interlibrary loans, and purchasing course materials online from the BSU Bookstore.

Faculty and students are required to check their mail and respond a minimum of three times a week.

A maximum of 17 students are assigned to each course. Logging on a minimum of three times a week allows dialogue between students and faculty.

Discussion questions encourage life and work experiences to be used in learning experiences.

Directed research projects, internships, readings, and conferences provide flexibility for self-designed courses or projects.

Program effectiveness determined through course evaluations, retention, and number of graduates.

ILLINOIS

Western Illinois University

Board of Governors Bachelor of Arts
1 University Circle
5 Horrabin Hall
Macomb, IL 61455
Phone: 309-298-1929
Fax: 309-298-2226
E-mail: np-gog@wiu.edu

Degrees Offered
Bachelor of Arts

Program Mission
To provide adults with an opportunity to gain a high-quality, academically sound baccalaureate degree while permitting sufficient flexibility to allow them to meet their educational goals while maintaining other adult responsibilities related to work and family. To serve individuals with a diversity of educational experiences by facilitating transfer of college level credit from regionally accredited colleges and universities and by awarding appropriate academic credit through an assessment of prior learning. To make it possible for students to bring together many of their previous college-equivalent learning endeavors in a baccalaureate degree program.

Accreditation
North Central Association of Colleges and Schools

Admissions Requirements
None, however a determination is made to ascertain the appropriateness of the degree program to the specific academic needs of the applicant

Credit Hour Requirements
120 semester hours

Minimum Campus Time
None

Tuition and Fees

Transcript fee, $7, a one-time charge billed at the time of admission; individual transcripts are free; tuition, $80 per semester hour; prior learning portfolio submission fee, $30

Credit Awards for Examinations

ACT-PEP: Regents College Examinations Program; CLEP general exams; CLEP subject exams; DANTES subject tests; College Board AP exams; Defense Language Institute proficiency tests; ACE-evaluated certification exams

Credit Awards for Prior Learning

Transfer credits from accredited, degree-granting institution; ACE military recommendations; ACE/PONSI recommendations; portfolio type assessment; department/institutional exams

Description

Each student is assigned an individual advisor who is available from 7:00 am–5:00 pm Monday–Friday.

Distance education opportunities include extension courses (faculty travel up to 150 miles from the WIU campus) and independent study (regular WIU junior/senior level classes available by mail; some include video).

Only courses that can provide academic resources to the student at the local site are offered to distance learners.

Interaction between faculty and students is by telephone during regular office hours and, in some cases, through e-mail. Faculty have office hours to receive phone calls or some use e-mail.

Learning experiences can be related to the contexts of the student's life through traditional independent study cooperatively by the students and appropriate university faculty.

Program effectiveness is determined by alumni survey.

INDIANA

Ball State University

School of Continuing Education and
  Public Service
Carmichael Hall 200
Muncie, IN 47306
Phone: 317-285-1582
Fax: 317-285-5795
E-mail: oojbroepke@bsu.edu

Degrees Offered

Associate of Arts in General Arts; Associate of Arts in Business Administration; Baccalaureate Completion for Registered Nurses; Master in Business Administration

Program Mission

To extend the talent, research, and resources of the university to persons, businesses, and organizations throughout Indiana. In particular, to enhance the quality of life through lifelong education.

Accreditation

North Central Association of Schools and Colleges

Admission Requirements

Regular admission requires official high school transcript (or passing GED scores) and official transcripts from all previous higher education institutions. ACT or SAT scores are required for students under 23 years of age. The admission decision is based upon high school rank, college preparatory test scores, and for transfer students, the GPA from previous institutions.

Credit Hour Requirements

Associate degrees, 63 semester hours; BS completion for RNs varies with background; MBA, 36 semester hours

Minimum Campus Time
None, except in certain AA general studies courses

Tuition and Fees
Undergraduate $115 per credit hour; graduate $121 per credit hour; independent study by correspondence $98 per credit hour

Credit Awards for Examinations
CLEP general exams; CLEP subject exams

Credit Awards for Prior Learning
Transfer credits from accredited, degree-granting institution; ACE military recommendations; ACE/PONSI recommendations; portfolio type assessment; department/institutional exams

Description
Students have access to curricular advisors by phone, walk-in, and appointment. The School of Continuing Education has personnel with designated duties of graduate and undergraduate advising. They act as liaisons between the off-campus students and the network of on-campus curricular and faculty advisors. Off-campus students are encouraged to visit campus and take advantage of the career services center, which provides career counseling and career placement services. In addition, support services for undergraduate admission, registration, payment, text acquisition, etc. for off-campus students are coordinated centrally in the school of continuing education and public service for efficiency in service to the students. All services are available to off-campus students 8:00 am–5:00 pm Monday–Friday with other hours by appointment only. Director, off-campus academic support services, and staff work to assist students with advising and program problem solving.

Distance education opportunities include independent study by correspondence—standard paper mode and videotape lectures. E-mail courses for undergraduate English composition and nursing research.

Students learning at a distance access academic resources, primarily via computer access, but also by phone. Distance education students subscribe to Internet access provider and, with the purchase of software to access the university system, are given a password with registration each semester.

Interaction between faculty and students include one-day video, two-way audio, supplemented by e-mail, fax, phone, and mail.

Assignments in certain courses in MBA and other programs may be work-related.

There are opportunities for self-designed courses only when plan of study calls for independent study projects or thesis designed with and supervised by faculty.

Program effectiveness is determined through such measures as performance by MBA students on national examinations, assessment program that is part of the university-wide assessment, and faculty evaluations.

Indiana University

School of Continuing Studies, General
    Studies Degrees
University-Wide General Studies Degree
Owen Hall 101
Bloomington, IN 47405
Phone: 800-457-4434
Fax: 812-855-8680
E-mail: extend@indiana.edu

Degrees Offered
Associate of General Studies; Associate of Science in Labor Studies; Bachelor of General Studies; Bachelor of Science in Labor Studies

Program Mission

To meet the lifelong educational needs of learners in Indiana and beyond, by providing both academic degrees and quality learning opportunities in a variety of formats and delivery modes. The general studies degree is a flexible program designed to serve those who find it very difficult to pursue a degree in an on-campus environment because of career, family, military service, and/or other personal circumstances. It enables students to complete a degree in general studies at their own pace and from their own residence.

Accreditation

North Central Association of Schools and Colleges

Admission Requirements

High school diploma or GED certificate. Depending on their individual situation, adults 21 or older who do not have a high school diploma or GED may be granted provisional admission pending successful (grades of C or better) completion of 12 semester hours of credit as non-degree students.

Persons with circumstances listed above may also be admitted on a provisional basis if potential for success in the program is indicated.

Credit Hour Requirements

Associate of General Studies, 60 semester hours; Bachelor of General Studies, 120 semester hours

Minimum Campus Time

None

Tuition and Fees

$86 per credit hour

Credit Awards for Examinations

CLEP general exams; CLEP subject exams; DANTES subject tests; College Board AP exams; Defense Language Institute proficiency tests

Credit Awards for Prior Learning

ACE military recommendations; ACE/PONSI recommendations; and portfolio type assessment

Description

Academic advising available via phone/e-mail, Monday–Friday 8:00 am–5:00 pm. Office is open for instructor calls Monday–Friday 8:00 am–9:00 pm.

Distance education opportunities include independent study courses (including several on the World Wide Web), audio/video cassettes, and television courses.

Students can access the university by e-mail/Internet for library and other resource aids.

All faculty teaching independent-study courses maintain office hours during which time they may be contacted by students using the toll-free number provided the students for this purpose. A majority of the faculty also interact with their students via e-mail.

Exit interviews are conducted with tentative graduates as to their success in completing a coherent plan of study for the degree and if their objectives were reached.

Purdue University

Continuing Engineering Education (CEE)
1575 Civil Engineering Building, Room G216
West Lafayette, IN 47907-1575
Phone: 317-494-7015
Fax: 317-496-1196
E-mail: cee@ecn.purdue.edu
Internet: http://fairway.ecn.purdue.edu/cee/

Degrees Offered
Master of Science in Engineering, Electrical Engineering, Industrial Engineering, and Mechanical Engineering

Program Mission
To meet the lifelong learning needs of practicing engineers in Indiana, the nation, and the world by assessing those needs, marshaling the faculty expertise at Purdue and elsewhere to address the needs, and using television and other appropriate instructional media to deliver high-quality credit and noncredit professional development programs to practicing engineers at the most appropriate locations (campus, workplace, or elsewhere).

Accreditation
North Central Association of Colleges and Schools; Accreditation Board for Engineering and Technology (ABET)

Admission Requirements
Bachelor of Science in Engineering or related area. Minimum 3.0 GPA (4.0 scale) and three letters of recommendation.

Credit Hour Requirements
30 semester hours

Minimum Campus Time
None

Tuition and Fees
$176 per credit hour for in-state, $401 per credit hour for out-of-state students, and a $30 application fee for satellite students, video fees are $453 per credit hour minimum billing of two students per site

Credit Awards for Examinations
None

Credit Awards for Prior Learning
Transfer credits from accredited, degree-granting institution

Description
Continuing Engineering Education open 8:00 am–12 noon and 1:00 pm–5:00 pm Monday–Friday to provide academic advising by phone, e-mail, and in person.

Distance education opportunities include live satellite TV; videotape; e-mail as support for video and TV classes; and WWW site.

Students access academic resources through the Purdue Technical Information Service (modest charge) or dial-up interlibrary loans. Computer—dial-up modem to Engineering Computer Network at Purdue.

Interaction between faculty and students occurs through formative and summative surveys, telephone office hours, e-mail, and occasional visits.

Students can design project courses with a professor; these are often work-oriented.

Program effectiveness is determined through student surveys (formative and summative), surveys of site coordinators, industrial advisory board, and site visits by director and associate director.

Vincennes University

Degree Completion Program
1002 N. First Street
Vincennes, IN 47591
Phone: 800-880-7961
Fax: 812-888-5862
E-mail: tyoung@vunet.vinu.edu

Degrees Offered
Associate of Science in General Studies, Law Enforcement Studies option, Behavioral Sciences, Social Science, Business Studies option, Surgical Technology, and Technology Apprenticeship option

Program Mission

To help distance learners—students who are geographically and/or time bound—to fulfill the requirements for graduation with an associate's degree, and to bring the educational services of Vincennes University to students wherever higher education is sought.

Accreditation

North Central Association of Colleges and Schools; National League for Nursing

Admission Requirements

High school transcript, GED scores, SAT or ACT recommended for academic advising and general counseling purposes

Credit Hour Requirements

General Studies minimum 62 semester hours; Law Enforcement 62–63 hours; Behavioral Sciences 62–65 hours; Social Science 62–66 hours; Business Studies 62–66 hours; Surgical Technology 63 hours; Technology Apprenticeship 62–66 hours

Minimum Campus Time

None

Tuition and Fees

3 credit hour courses, $226.80; 4 credit hour courses, $302.40; and processing fee $10 per course

Credit Awards for Examinations

ACT-PEP: Regents College Examinations Program; CLEP general exams; CLEP subject exams; DANTES subject tests; College Board AP exams; Defense Language Institute proficiency tests; and ACE-evaluated certification exams

Credit Awards for Prior Learning

Transfer credits from accredited, degree-granting institution; ACE military recommendations; ACE/PONSI recommendations; portfolio type assessment; and department/institutional exams

Description

Advising is available 8:00 am–4:30 pm Monday–Friday.

Distance education opportunities include independent study, videotaped lectures, e-mail, satellite, one-way video, and broadband video.

Library information may be accessed through the Internet. Materials on learning skills are available through the study skills department via telephone contact.

A toll-free telephone line is available through the study skills department and another toll-free line is available for student access to faculty.

Student satisfaction surveys and analysis of student achievement are measures used to determine program effectiveness.

IOWA

Upper Iowa University

External Degree Program
P.O. Box 1861
Fayette, IA 52142
Phone: 800-553-4150
Fax: 319-425-5353
E-mail: extdegree@uiu.edu

Degrees Offered

Associate of Arts in Liberal Arts and General Business concentration; Bachelor of Science in Accounting, Business, Management, Marketing, Public Administration, Public Administration with Law Enforcement or Fire Science emphasis, Human Resources Management, Human Services, and Social Science

Program Mission

To provide postsecondary education to a widely diverse student clientele, including both recent high school graduates and mature learners. Since the educational needs of the university's constituency vary significantly, the university is committed to maintaining curricular flexibility to provide for these diverse needs and to encourage lifelong learning.

Accreditation
North Central Association of Colleges and Schools

Admission Requirements
Anyone may apply for admission to the external degree program. Those who have graduated from an accredited public or private high school, or who have passed the GED test (high school equivalency), are almost always granted admission. Admission is also normally granted to those individuals transferring a 2.0 cumulative GPA of work completed at other colleges. Students may be admitted with less than a 2.0 cumulative GPA with special permission.

Credit Hour Requirements
AA, 60 semester hours; BS, 120 semester hours

Minimum Campus Time
None

Tuition and Fees
Independent study $135 per semester hour; summer session $160 per semester hour

Credit Awards for Examinations
ACT-PEP: Regents College Examinations Program; CLEP general exams; CLEP subject exams; DANTES subject tests; Defense Language Institute proficiency tests

Credit Awards for Prior Learning
Transfer credits from accredited, degree-granting institution; ACE military recommendations; ACE/PONSI recommendations; portfolio type assessment

Description
Advising and administration: external degree office, financial aid office, and business office are open 8:00 am–5:00 pm; access to instructors' time varies; messages can be left 24 hours a day using voice mail or e-mail.

Distance education opportunities include independent study courses and videotape supplements to courses.

Students learning at a distance access academic resources through toll-free access to advisors in the external degree office; mail check-out from on-campus library. Most students access local libraries and resources.

At present there are no processes to ensure interaction with instructors, but students are encouraged to contact instructors if they are having problems with courses. The program is working on pilot courses involving e-mail communication with instructors, which should increase interaction between student and instructor.

The independent study project in Human Services can be designed to relate to the student's current job. Other research or special projects can be designed to relate to current job or future field of employment.

Program effectiveness is determined through such measures as student evaluations relating to course content, support materials, instructor support, and administrative support, and informal ongoing self-assessment based on student feedback and instructor recommendation.

KANSAS

Kansas State University

Non-Traditional Study (NTS) Program
Division of Continuing Education
221 College Court
Manhattan, KS 66506
Phone: 913-532-5687
Fax: 913-532-5637
E-mail: academic/services@dce.ksu.edu

Degrees Offered

Bachelor of Science in Interdisciplinary Social Sciences; Bachelor of Science in Agriculture, Animal Sciences and Industry, Animal Products option

Program Mission

To help people complete the last two years of a bachelor of science degree in interdisciplinary social science or in animal sciences and industry. It is designed to meet the needs of mature students who are self-directed and certain of their educational objectives. It strives to provide students with access to a broadened learning environment; a new kind of relationship with academic faculty; and a personalized approach to study, tailored to fit their situations and learning styles.

Accreditation

North Central Association of Colleges and Schools

Admission Requirements

60 semester hours of college credit already earned and a 2.0 GPA (overall) on previous college work. Students who have already earned a bachelor's degree may not apply to the social sciences degree program.

Credit Hour Requirements

Interdisciplinary Social Sciences, 120 semester hours; Agriculture, Animal Sciences and Industry, 127 semester hours

Minimum Campus Time

None

Tuition and Fees

$80 per semester credit hour; tape rental and telecourse fees are in addition to tuition

Credit Awards for Examinations

ACT-PEP: Regents College Examinations Program; CLEP subject exams; CLEP general exams; DANTES subject tests; department/institutional exams; and speech quiz out

Credit Awards for Prior Learning

Transfer credits from accredited, degree-granting institution; credit-by-exam; ACE military recommendations; and portfolio type assessment

Description

Academic advising; library services; NTS student handbook; financial aid; bookstore ordering; NTS newsbrief; and career employment services available 8:00 am–noon and 1:00 pm–5:00 am Monday–Friday.

Each person in the NTS program receives individual advising. A program of study is developed to meet the specific needs of each student.

Distance learning opportunities include: e-mail, audioteleconferences, video lectures, guided study, Web-based courses, and audiocourses.

Most courses follow the regular fall, spring, and summer semester dates. However, some courses are available on a nine-month term.

Information on accessing academic resources at a distance is provided by advisors, the NTS student handbook, and the Library Services Handbook.

Interaction between students and faculty occurs in courses that include regular audioteleconferences with the whole class and the instructor; courses that require listservs; and some that are Web-based and have interaction through Web mail. Instructors are also available by telephone.

Students are sometimes assigned group projects that require student interaction.

Students can select issues of personal interest for class papers or reports. Students sometimes research the community for paper assignments.

There is one self-designed course involving independent study in Women's Studies, where students work with a faculty member to design their own study or projects.

Program effectiveness is determined through course evaluations.

LOUISIANA

The American College of Prehospital Medicine

365 Canal Street, Suite 2300
New Orleans, LA 70130
Phone: 504-561-6543
Fax: 504-561-6585
Internet: http://www.acpm.edu

Degrees Offered
Associate of Science in Emergency Medical Services; Associate of Science in Hazardous Materials Technology; Bachelor of Science in Emergency Medical Services

Program Mission
To enable those involved in the emergency medical services profession an opportunity to complete college education utilizing distance learning. The emergency medical services professional usually works unusual shifts that preclude participation in traditional education schedules.

Accreditation
Distance Education and Training Council

Admission Requirements
Applicants must possess a high school diploma or GED and submit evidence of training at the level of an emergency medical technician or its equivalent, as a minimum. Degree programs are open only to those who are certified as an emergency medical technician or its equivalent, as a minimum. Emergency medical technicians, paramedics, registered nurses, and military medical

personnel with training equivalent to that of a paramedic are typically admitted.

Credit Hour Requirements
Associate of Science in Emergency Medical Services, minimum 70 semester hours; Associate of Science in Hazardous Materials Technology, minimum 70 semester hours; Bachelor of Science in Emergency Medical Services, minimum 130 semester hours

Minimum Campus Time
None

Tuition and Fees
AS in Emergency Medical Services, $4150; AS in Hazardous Materials Technology, $4850; BS in Emergency Medical Services, $6850. These costs are all-inclusive and include not only basic tuition and registration but all of the students' course materials and texts. Students not completing their degree within the prescribed time limit may purchase up to two additional semesters in which to do so. For the AS in Emergency Medical Services and AS in Hazardous Materials Technology degrees the cost per extra semester is $1000. For the BS in Medical Services the cost per extra semester is $1150.

Credit Awards for Examinations
CLEP subject exams; DANTES subject tests

Credit Awards for Prior Learning
Transfer credits from accredited, degree-granting institution; ACE military recommendations; ACE/PONSI recommendations; fire services and emergency medical services educational programs that are documented according to contact hours of lecture, clinical education, and/or field internship

Description
Students can access the college office utilizing the college's toll-free number pro-

vided to students and faculty 8:30 am–5:00 pm Monday–Friday. The student taking a particular course is provided with toll-free number to directly access the faculty person assigned to him/her for that course. Students are provided toll-free access to the college-maintained computer bulletin board service for purposes of communicating with the college office, faculty members, or other students. The college maintains an Internet home page with e-mail links to most of the college's faculty. College policy dictates that the student taking a specific course and the assigned faculty person are to establish a telephone dialogue within 72 hours of the student's receipt of his/her course materials.

ACPM utilizes the mails, bidirectional audiotape submissions, videotape course supplemental materials, and submission of course work via either e-mail or fax. The terminal course leading to the award of the Bachelor of Science in Emergency Medical Services involves an empirical research project that must be completed independently and in cooperation with a physician in the student's community.

ACPM maintains a small library, approximately 700 volumes, primarily focusing on medicine and the emergency medical services. In addition to the volumes maintained, the college maintains a library of approximately 2,500 topical articles in the emergency medical services field. Students are free to request the loan of this material at any time. In addition, most of our faculty maintain substantial personal libraries from which they have generously shared information with students. Finally, we are constantly expanding the services and resources available both on our computer bulletin board and our Internet home page.

As stated above, the college dictates that the student and faculty person establish a telephone dialogue within 72 hours of the

student's receipt of the course materials. Since we maintain the toll-free number linking all of our faculty, the student incurs no additional costs to establish this dialogue. Likewise, we provide all of our faculty with telephone calling cards so they may place calls to students anywhere in the world and incur no personal costs in doing so. For international students, we utilize international air courier services to ship materials to them. Generally, our overseas students receive their course materials within four days of its departure from New Orleans. We monitor this dialogue by encouraging students to contact the college office if they have difficulty getting in touch with their assigned faculty person and retrospectively monitor student satisfaction with a course evaluation questionnaire that is completed by every student at the conclusion of every course. The key question relative to faculty-student dialogue asks to what degree "the faculty member was reasonably accessible."

With the students having toll-free access to the college's computer bulletin board, ACPM provides an opportunity for students to freely dialogue via e-mail, and several of our students have established telephone dialogues subsequent to these initial e-mail contacts.

Candidates for the Bachelor of Science in Emergency Medical Services must complete an original empirical research project as their terminal course. The project concept and design is totally at the discretion of the student with the guidance of the ACPM faculty. Faculty direction focuses on appropriate research methodologies and project structure so the student is free to relate that project to any aspect of his/her professional environment that warrants original, empirical investigation.

The first step in the assessment is the separate evaluation for every course completed by every student. Incorporated within this questionnaire is the student's assessment of the query, "this course expanded my knowledge in the subject area," for which the student provides a quantified response. At the conclusion of the student's degree program, another questionnaire completed by every graduate incorporates a series of questions designed to learn whether or not the student felt the education provided was professionally and personally relevant. ACPM periodically submits questionnaires to students' employers to determine if, in the employer's opinion, the education provided by the college is providing to the student the type of education felt to be useful by the employer. Due to the institution's "youth" we have not as yet done so, but we will be querying all individuals who have graduated in the past on an annual basis to determine their out-year assessment of the value of the education they received from the college. Effectiveness of our program is inextricably tied to learning outcomes.

ACPM is extremely open to the recommendations and suggestions of its students. An ongoing questionnaire on our computer bulletin board is responded to by those exploring educational opportunities with the college and our current students. The responses to those questions and subsequent similar polls have already caused the college to modify some policies and courses. Other responses are responsible for courses and outreach programs that are now under development.

Loyola University New Orleans

Off-Campus Learning Program (OCLP)
Box 14
New Orleans, LA 70118

Phone: 800-488-OCLP (6257)
Fax: 504-865-3883
E-mail: ccnoel@beta.loyno.edu

Degrees Offered
Bachelor of Science in Nursing; Bachelor of Criminal Justice

Program Mission
To provide university access for adults in Louisiana who, because of their work schedules or distance from campus, cannot attend on-campus class meetings.

Accreditation
Southern Association of Colleges and Schools

Admission Requirements
High school diploma or GED

Credit Hour Requirement
129 credit hours each

Minimum Campus Time
One-day orientation each fall for new students. For the BSN, one three-hour nursing course (required) is not available in the OCLP format, so students must travel to campus for the course (taught in intensive weekend format).

Tuition and Fees
$180 per credit hour

Credit Awards for Examinations
ACT-PEP: Regents College Examinations Program; CLEP general exams; CLEP subject exams; DANTES subject tests; College Board AP exams; ACE-evaluated certification exams

Credit Awards for Prior Learning
Transfer credits from accredited, degree-granting institution; ACE military recommendations; department/institutional exam

Description
Off-campus group meets regularly to view classes on videotape. Classes taped are regu-

lar classes—lectures, class discussions, visual presentations, and students' responses are all captured. The course lectures as well as the classroom ambiance are recorded for the OCLP students so that they are not just watching an edited program but are involved in the real dynamics of the university classroom. Assignments, exams, and papers correspond exactly to those of the students on campus.

Currently the OCLP employs an extension librarian available via toll-free number during the week (hours vary each semester). Students may utilize the Writing Across the Curriculum services for writing/composition support and peer tutoring, also available via toll-free number and fax. Each semester, OCLP faculty schedule office hours to receive OCLP students phone calls.

Loyola faculty and staff are available via electronic mail. Students may utilize the new campus mainframe without charge; however, for those students "long distance" from New Orleans, the cost of a toll call will appear on the student's telephone bill. Lectures are available prerecorded on VHS videotape.

Several faculty incorporate audio conferences into course requirements.

Students enrolled in a particular course are encouraged to view videotapes in a group at the OCLP site. This allows for interaction that replicates that of the on-campus class meetings.

Program effectiveness is determined through such measures as ongoing evaluation: surveys and interviews.

MAINE

Saint Joseph's College

Distance Education Program
278 Whites Bridge Road
Standish, ME 04084-5263
Phone: 800-752-4723
Fax: 207-892-7480
Internet: http://www.sjcme.edu

Degrees Offered
Master in Health Services Administration (MHSA); Bachelor of Science in Health Care Administration, Long-Term Care Administration, with Professional Arts (BSPA), Radiologic Science (BSRS), Respiratory Care (BSRC), and Business Administration with concentrations in Management and Banking; Bachelor of Arts in Liberal Studies with concentrations in Christian Tradition, Women's Studies, and American Studies; Associate of Science in Management; Master of Science in Nursing (MS); and Bachelor of Science in Nursing (BSN)

Program Mission
To provide educational opportunities for traditional and nontraditional students with diverse academic needs. Saint Joseph's College offers the adult learner an opportunity to integrate formal education in the liberal arts with professional experience. Saint Joseph's College is committed to the development of every student through a process of lifelong learning.

Accreditation
New England Association of Schools and Colleges; National League for Nursing

Admission Requirements
Undergraduate: High school diploma or GED equivalent. Graduate: baccalaureate degree from accredited institution. BSPA students must be licensed healthcare professionals. BSRS and BSRC students must have graduated from accredited certificate or associate degree programs, passed the national registry examination in their fields, and be currently in good standing with their national certifying body. MHSA students must have a minimum of three years of relevant experience in a health-related

field. BSN applicants must be licensed RNs. MS applicants must be licensed RNs with at least two years experience in nursing (GREs or MATs also required).

Applicants from non-English speaking countries who have not graduated from an English-speaking school at the secondary level must submit TOEFL examination results. Undergraduate students must score 485 or higher; graduate students must score 500 or higher.

Minnesota residents may become students in the Bachelor of Science in Business Administration (BSBA) and the Bachelor of Science in Professional Arts (BSPA) only.

Credit Hour Requirements
Baccalaureate degree, 128 semester hours; BSN degree, 129 semester hours; Associate degree, 66 semester hours; MHSA degree, 48 semester hours; MS in Nursing, 42 semester hours

Minimum Campus Time
Baccalaureate, Associate, and MS in Nursing degrees, one two-week summer residency; BSN degree, one one-week and one two-week summer residency; MHSA degree, two two-week summer residencies

Tuition and Fees
Undergraduate, $175 per credit hour; graduate, $215 per credit hour; application fee for degree programs $50; and application fee for certificates and continuing education $25

Credit Awards for Examinations
ACT-PEP: Regents College Examinations Program; CLEP general exams; CLEP subject exams; DANTES subject tests; Defense Language Institute proficiency tests; and ACE/PONSI-approved credit

Credit Awards for Prior Learning
Transfer credits from accredited, degree-granting institution; ACE military recommendations; ACE/PONSI recommendations; portfolio type assessment (undergraduate only)

Description
Student support services are available through an academic advisor who is assigned to each student to provide ongoing support throughout the student's studies. Academic advisors are available at 800-343-5498, Monday–Friday 8:00 am–5:00 pm, and voice mail is available at all other times. Telephone conferences with faculty are arranged through the student's academic advisor. A free writing skills tutor is provided for students requesting assistance or who demonstrate need. The first course for undergraduate degree students is a one-credit, tuition-free preparation for independent study in a liberal arts institution.

Distance education opportunities are available through faculty-directed independent study; a few courses have video, audio, slides, or computer components.

The college provides a useful supplement to local or interlibrary borrowing systems. Requests must be made in writing to the college librarian. The library Web site describes all of the services available to distance education students (www.sjcme.edu/wellehan/home.htm). A writing skills tutorial program with assistance in basic aspects of writing is available. The tutor and student work together to evaluate needs and plan appropriate actions. The service is free except for rare occasions when additional texts or materials may be required.

Faculty work with students in a one-on-one tutorial mode. The academic advisor is the student's link to faculty members. Students are encouraged to contact their advisors to arrange telephone conferences with their instructors.

The residency required in all degree programs provides networking and group experiences, which students report to be one of the most rewarding components of their programs. Students from all over the world come to Maine for any of three two-week sessions each summer. Many students return after their required residency to attend optional sessions. At the request of one student, and with the consent of both students, advisors may put two students in contact with one another.

Tuition guarantee plan allows students to lock their tuition rate for the duration of study by successfully completing a full enrollment every six months. The tuition installment plan allows students to extend their tuition payments over the period of enrollment.

There is a student evaluation for each course completed, which includes an evaluation of the instructor. There is also a student evaluation of the summer residency program. Alumni surveys including graduate programs attended, promotions, etc. are used to assess effectiveness.

University of New England

Master of Science in Education Program
11 Hills Beach Road
Biddeford, ME 04005
Phone: 207-283-0171
Fax: 207-282-6379
E-mail: msed@mailbox.une.edu

Degrees Offered
Master of Science in Education

Program Mission
To provide the experienced educator with theory and practice in instructional strategies, effective classroom management, curriculum and evaluation, and working with diverse populations. Learners apply newly acquired knowledge and skills to their daily classroom experiences, develop teaching portfolios containing relevant materials from course assignments, and design and complete collaborative action research projects derived from field-based concerns and interests. Each learner is a member of a collegial study team and interacts with other students in the program through school or home-site meetings, e-mail, telephone, and fax.

Accreditation
New England Association of Schools and Colleges

Admission Requirements
Bachelor's degree from an accredited institution; minimum of two years teaching experience and either be presently employed or be certified as a teacher

Credit Hour Requirements
33 credit hours

Minimum Campus Time
One-week summer seminar

Tuition and Fees
$765 per three-credit course

Credit Awards for Examinations
None

Credit Awards for Prior Learning
Transfer credits from accredited, degree-granting institution

Description
The program is offered to learners throughout New England and New York State.

Course delivery is through prerecorded video and printed instructional texts. Videos and materials have been produced by Canter Educational Productions, Inc., in consultation with University of New England faculty. Curriculum development is ongoing and designed to blend current research with practical application.

General advising is available 9:00 am–5:00 pm Monday–Friday.

Interaction between faculty and students is provided through toll-free telephone, voice mail, e-mail, and fax.

Courses require 3–4 submissions per term. All faculty contact learners by telephone within the first two weeks of the term. Students are encouraged to call faculty/mentors during office hours or to leave messages on voice mail.

Interaction between students is available through a monthly newsletter; on-campus summer seminar; and orientation sessions in home location, listserv, and World Wide Web connections.

The entire program is designed for the working teacher to be able to integrate course goals with classroom activities.

Program effectiveness is determined through such measures as course evaluation forms and exit interviews.

MARYLAND

Goucher College

Center for Graduate and Continuing
  Studies
1021 Dulaney Valley Road
Baltimore, MD 21204
Phone: 410-337-6200
Fax: 410-337-6085
E-mail: center@goucher.edu

Degrees Offered
Master of Arts in Historic Preservation

Program Mission
To provide a program for self-dedicated students who find it inconvenient to attend a traditional on-campus graduate program in historic preservation.

Accreditation
Middle States Association of Colleges and Schools

Admission Requirements
Bachelor of Arts; minimum of two years paid or volunteer postbaccalaureate work experience; academic and personal qualifications that give promise of success in self-directed graduate study.

Credit Hour Requirements
36 semester hours

Minimum Campus Time
Three two-week residencies

Tuition and Fees
$1350 per course regardless of credit count, $500 comprehensive exam, $200 thesis, and $250 room and board per week

Credit Awards for Examinations
None

Credit Awards for Prior Learning
Transfer credits from accredited, degree-granting institution

Description
The program combines intensive summer courses with tutorials conducted through the mail, telephone, or other electronic means, providing students with maximum flexibility of time and place of learning.

The curriculum is designed to provide students with the opportunity to concentrate in specific areas of historic preservation through the selection of elective courses, independent study, and a thesis topic. Depending on the course load selected, the program may be completed within three years.

Advising and support services are available Monday–Friday 9:00 am–5:00 pm.

Students may access the Goucher Library through Goucher's Internet server.

Students interact with faculty and each other through mail, e-mail, telephone, and at summer residencies. There is also a newsletter for student-only interaction.

Program effectiveness is determined by student evaluations of courses and programs and program director's evaluation of instructors.

Home Study International/ Griggs University

Bachelor of Arts Degree Programs
P.O. Box 4437
Silver Spring, MD 20914-4437
Phone: 301-680-6570
Fax: 301-680-6577
E-mail: 74617.2474@Compuserve.com

Degrees Offered

Bachelor of Arts in Religion and Theological Studies; Associate of Arts in Personal Ministries

Program Mission

To provide students with a well-balanced education that will enrich the quality of their lives and their ability to serve others, as well as give them the tools to serve their church as ministers, religious workers, and lay church leaders.

Accreditation

Distance Education and Training Council

Admission Requirements

Recognized/accredited high school diploma (2.0 GPA), GED (total score 225, no score below 40), TOEFL 550 or above

Credit Hour Requirements

BA in Religion 120 semester hours; BA in Theological Studies 120 semester hours; and AA in Personal Ministries 60 semester hours

Minimum Campus Time

None

Tuition and Fees

$30 degree application fee, $60 enrollment fee (when courses are requested), $150 per semester hour tuition, and $50 graduate fee

Credit Awards for Examinations

ACT-PEP: Regents College Examinations Program; CLEP general exams; CLEP subject exams; College Board AP exams; ACE-evaluated certification exams

Credit Awards for Prior Learning

Transfer credits from accredited, degree-granting institution; ACE military recommendations; ACE/PONSI recommendations; portfolio type assessment; department/institutional exams

Description

An advisor is available to students from 9:00 am–5:00 pm Monday–Thursday, and 9:00 am-12:00 pm Friday. Students may also write or e-mail advisors.

Distance education opportunities include independent study courses, e-mail, voice mail, and online intensive courses.

Each course is self-sufficient; all instructional materials are available to students as part of course costs. Students may also take advantage of library and research materials available through the worldwide network of Seventh Day Adventist colleges and schools. The Griggs University library participates in resource networks.

All students and faculty are assigned voice mail boxes. Students may contact faculty and each other via e-mail.

Assignments in writing courses allow students to create presentations, report on research, and explore solutions to work-related topics. Business courses encourage students to apply concepts learned to their own work experiences. Course assignments are written in a manner that allows students to make personal applications.

Program effectiveness is determined through such measures as peer reviews of professor/course, student evaluations, student performances on standardized tests, and follow-up studies of graduates.

Howard Community College

Going the Distance
10901 Little Patuxent Parkway
Columbia, MD 21044
Phone: 410-964-4974
Fax: 410-964-4986
E-mail: jhawkins@ccm.howardcc.edu

Degrees Offered
Associate of Arts in General Studies, Liberal Arts, and Business Administration

Program Mission
To enable students to earn an associate's degree through the national project called Going the Distance, sponsored by the Public Broadcasting Corporation.

Accreditation
Middle States Association of Colleges and Schools

Admission Requirements
Open admissions and completion of course prerequisites

Credit Hour Requirements
General Studies, 60 semester credits

Minimum Campus Time
None

Tuition and Fees
In-county tuition, $73 per credit; application fee, $10. Out of county, $123; out of state, $175.

Credit Awards for Examinations
CLEP general exams; CLEP subject exams, DANTES subject tests; College Board AP exams; Defense Language Institute proficiency tests; ACE-evaluated certification exams

Credit Awards for Prior Learning
Transfer credits from accredited, degree-granting institution; ACE military recommendations; ACE/PONSI recommendations; portfolio type assessment; department/institutional exams

Description
This program reflects the needs of those students who have professional or family responsibilities that limit their availability for traditional on-campus classes. By combining telecourses, weekend courses, and new online classes taught via the Internet, students can complete an associate of arts degree and design their own schedule.

Student support services include admissions counseling Monday–Friday 9:00 am–4:00 pm by appointment; academic advising Monday–Thursday 9:00 am–8:00 pm, Friday 9:00 am–3:00 pm; services for students with disabilities Monday–Friday 9:00 am–4:00 pm; financial aid Monday–Thursday day and evening; library 7:45 am–11:00 pm; learning assistance center Monday–Friday 9:00 am–4:00 pm; other grant programs for selected programs; and career counseling, day and evening.

Distance education opportunities include interactive television, online courses, and telecourses.

Interaction between faculty and students is through Internet, telephone, e-mail, and fax.

Program effectiveness is determined by an annual institutional survey and biannual state surveys.

University of Maryland University College

Open Learning/Bachelor's Degree at a
Distance
University Boulevard at Adelphi Road

College Park, MD 20742
Phone: 800-283-6832
Fax: 301-985-4615
E-mail: open-learning@info.umuc.edu

Degrees Offered

Bachelor of Arts or Bachelor of Science in Behavioral and Social Sciences (BEHS), Communication studies (COMM), Computer and Information Science (CMIS), Fire Science (FSCN), Humanities (HUMN), Management (MGMT), Management Studies (MGST), Paralegal Studies (PLGL), and Technology and Management (TMGT)

Program Mission

To serve the educational needs of adult part-time students.

Accreditation

Middle States Association of Colleges and Schools

Admission Requirements

High school or GED diploma. Cumulative GPA must be 2.0 or higher on college-level work completed at other regionally accredited colleges.

Credit Hour Requirements

120 semester hours

Minimum Campus Time

None

Tuition and Fees

In-state or military, $176 per semester credit; out-of-state $203 per credit

Credit Awards for Examinations

ACT-PEP: Regents College Examinations Program; CLEP general exams; CLEP subject exams; DANTES subject tests; College Board AP exams; Defense Language Institute proficiency tests; and ACE-evaluated certification exams

Credit Awards for Prior Learning

Transfer credits from accredited, degree-granting institution; ACE military recommendations; ACE/PONSI recommendations; portfolio type assessment; cooperative education; department/institutional exams

Description

Course formats emphasize student/faculty interaction and a learner-centered environment. Enrollment is limited to students in the United States and Canada. Plans are being made to expand enrollment internationally by 1998.

Advising available by letter, phone (toll-free), or e-mail 8:00 am–7:00 pm Monday–Friday. Voice mail 24 hours a day. E-mail can be used to correspond with to academic counselors: distance@nova.umuc.edu.

Courses are available through voice mail conferencing and computer conferencing. Many courses have videotapes, some have audiotapes, and some faculty use occasional, live phone conferences. All students receive a comprehensive course guide and a detailed course syllabus. Students receive direct feedback on papers and projects throughout the semester.

Via Tyche (computer conferencing software) and VICTOR provide information on books located at the libraries of the University of Maryland system and provides access to journal database. Some courses allow access to LEXIS-NEXIS. Interlibrary loan is also facilitated by VICTOR. Online tutoring for writing skills is also available.

Both computer conferencing and voice mail conferencing support faculty-student interaction. Faculty are provided with training to make courses interactive; course design requires interaction.

Both computer conferencing and voice mail conferencing formats support student-to-student interaction through courses designed to encourage group activity. Both formats allow for formal and informal group activities.

Cooperative education (COOP) is available to distance students, allowing integration of classroom theory with on-the-job application. Monitoring faculty are assigned to each COOP student.

Program effectiveness is determined through evaluation of course and program completion rates, course/faculty evaluations, and postgraduation surveys.

MASSACHUSETTS

Atlantic Union College

Adult Degree Program
P.O. Box 1000
South Lancaster, MA 01561
Phone: 508-368-2300
Fax: 508-368-2015
E-mail: ibothwell@atlanticuc.edu

Degrees Offered
Bachelor of Arts in Communication, English, History, Modern Language, Philosophy, Religion, Theology, Business Administration, Women's Studies, General Science, Minor Secondary Education, Humanities, and Social Science; Bachelor of Science in Behavioral Science, Computer Science, Elementary Education, Early Childhood Education, Personal Ministries, Human Movement, and Psychology

Program Mission
The program is based on two beliefs held by the faculty: that many adults whose college work has been interrupted by marriage, work, military service, or other circumstances should have the opportunity to complete their degrees, and that there are many ways of doing reputable academic work other than being enrolled in on-campus courses.

Accreditation
New England Association of Schools and Colleges

Admission Requirements
The program is open to anyone 25 or older who has a high school diploma or the equivalent or a GED certificate with no score below 50 in any subtest. Applicants whose native language is not English must present a score of 550 on the TOEFL.

Credit Hour Requirements
128 semester hours for all programs

Minimum Campus Time
Enrollment in a seminar course every six months for a period of 8–10 days

Tuition and Fees
$3150 per semester, $40 fees per semester

Credit Awards for Examinations
ACT-PEP: Regents College Examinations Program; CLEP general exams; CLEP subject exams; DANTES subject tests; College Board AP exams; Defense Language Institute proficiency tests; ACE-evaluated certification exams; institutional exams

Credit Awards for Prior Learning
Transfer credits from accredited, degree-granting institution; ACE military recommendations; ACE/PONSI recommendations; portfolio type assessment; department/institutional exams

Description
Adult degree program office staff available 8:00 am–12:00 pm Monday–Friday for academic and career advising.

Distance education opportunities include limited e-mail and videotaped lectures.

In accessing academic resources, students typically use libraries near their home towns.

All students are required to do extensive journaling and submit to assigned faculty member.

All study is self-designed in consultation with a faculty mentor.

Students are asked to do written evaluations of the program each six months. All study program proposals are reviewed by a faculty committee.

Bunker Hill Community College

Center for Self-Directed Learning
250 New Rutherford Avenue
Boston, MA 02129
Phone: 617-228-2350
Fax: 617-228-2082

Degrees Offered
Associate of Arts in General Concentration

Program Mission
To provide a full range of options to students who may wish to complete degree requirements.

Accreditation
New England Association of Schools and Colleges

Admission Requirements
High school or GED diploma

Credit Hour Requirements
60 semester hours

Minimum Campus Time
Approximately 12 semester hours

Tuition and Fees
$80 per credit

Credit Awards for Examinations
ACT-PEP: Regents College Examinations Program; CLEP general exams; CLEP subject exams; DANTES subject tests; ACE-evaluated certification exams

Credit Awards for Prior Learning
Transfer credits from accredited, degree-granting institution; portfolio type assessment; and department/institutional exams

Description
The college offers a complete distance learning degree program through a combination of instruction through telecommunications technology, home study by mail, independent study courses, and community-based courses. Interaction with faculty is by phone, voice mail, and drop-in during faculty office hours.

The advising/counseling staff and faculty/staff advisors are available to all students during the hours the college is open.

Students may access academic resources through library and computer equipment/software.

Baker College

1050 W. Bristol Road
Flint, MI 48507
Phone: 800-469-3165
Fax: 810-766-4399
Internet: http://www.baker.edu

Degrees Offered
Executive Master of Business Administration (MBA); Bachelor of Business Leadership (BBL); Bachelor of Business Administration (BBA)

Program Mission
To provide quality higher education that enables graduates to be successful throughout challenging and rewarding careers.

Accreditation
North Central Association of Colleges and Schools

Admission Requirements
BBL and BBA, high school transcript or GED; MBA, three years work experience,

2.5 GPA in undergraduate degree, three letters of recommendation, and a writing sample

Credit Hour Requirements
MBA 50 quarter hours; BBA/BBL 193 quarter hours

Minimum Campus Time
Students may complete requirements 100% online or may attend campus

Tuition and Fees
MBA $195 per quarter hours and BBA/BBL $125 per quarter hour

Credit Awards for Examinations
Undergraduate only: CLEP general exams; CLEP subject exams; DANTES subject tests; and College Board AP exams

Credit Awards for Prior Learning
Transfer credits from accredited, degree-granting institution; ACE military recommendations; ACE/PONSI recommendations; portfolio-type assessment; and department/institutional exams

Description
Full collegiate services are available from 7:00 am–10:00 pm Monday–Thursday, 7:00 am–5:00 pm Friday. Students can contact college personnel via e-mail.

Distance education opportunities include online classrooms.

Students can access library services via the Baker College Web site.

Students interact with faculty and each other online in the virtual classroom.

Projects and assignments in class always relate to the student's work situation.

Programs and curriculum are continually assessed by students, faculty, area employers, and advisory boards.

MICHIGAN

Michigan Technological University
Surveying

1400 Townsend Drive
Houghton, MI 49931
Phone: 906-487-3170
Fax: 906-487-2453
E-mail: jschultz@mtu.edu

Degrees Offered
Bachelor of Science in Surveying

Program Mission
To provide a laboratory, surveying technologies program, including an intensive, one-summer session covering many field procedures.

Accreditation
North Central Association of Colleges and Schools; Accreditation Board for Engineering Technologies

Admission Requirements
High school diploma with at least 15 acceptable entrance credits including basic algebra (1 unit), intermediate algebra (0.5 units), geometry (1 unit), trigonometry (0.5 unit), chemistry or physics (1 unit), and English (3 units). Copies of high school and/or college transcripts need to be sent to Extended University Programs.

Credit Hour Requirements
A minimum of 207 quarter credit hours for graduation

Minimum Campus Time
Two surveying courses, L5251 and L5252, are given as five-week fast-track courses back to back in the summer

Tuition and Fees

The cost is $200 per quarter credit hour (which includes fees), plus books and supplies

Credit Awards for Examinations

CLEP subject exams; DANTES subject tests; College Board AP exams

Credit Awards for Prior Learning

Transfer credits from accredited, degree-granting institution; portfolio type assessment; department/institutional exams

Description

Student support is available from: Distance Education staff, degree program advisor, library, financial aid, bookstore, career center, admissions and registration, dean of students/student affairs, faculty, affirmative action, mathematics learning center, chemistry learning center, MTU Writing Center, transfer admissions, and transcripts office.

Students are educated primarily by tape-delayed video. They have access to program information via phone, fax, e-mail, and regular mail. Video conferencing capabilities are also available.

A student handbook that summarizes how students may obtain access to university resources is provided. A toll-free phone number is available to contact the Distance Education Department.

Interaction between faculty and students is through e-mail lists, phone, and fax. Faculty also make site visits.

Students are required to meet in groups at a common site; many classes have labs that permit students to interact personally and professionally. Some e-mail may be shared between all students.

Surveying courses provide many "real life" experiences for students. Examples include: "GPS Satellite Surveying," which teaches the newest technologies for surveyors; "Construction Surveying," a nuts-and-bolts course for constructing bridges and buildings; and "Tree Identification," which educates individuals to deal effectively and efficiently with our urban and rural forests.

Program effectiveness is determined through "How's It Going" questionnaires, program evaluations, faculty evaluations, student and faculty daily feedback, and charting of evaluations.

Michigan Technological University
Engineering

1400 Townsend Drive
Houghton, MI 49931
Phone: 906-487-3170
Fax: 906-487-2463
E-mail: jschultz@mtu.edu

Degrees Offered

Bachelor of Science in Engineering

Program Mission

To offer a program that emphasizes mechanical design and strong computer and laboratory experience.

Accreditation

North Central Association of Colleges and Schools; Accreditation Board for Engineering and Technology

Admission Requirements

Accumulate at least 100 quarter credits that are applicable to the BSE degree with a GPA of at least 2.0 for these credits. Early Admission: 15 quarter credits of calculus, 10 quarter credits of chemistry, and 10 quarter credits of physics with a 2.5 GPA.

Credit Hour Requirements

196 quarter hours

Minimum Campus Time
None

Tuition and Fees
$175 per quarter credit for courses without labs; $225 per quarter credit for courses with labs, plus books and supplies

Credit Awards for Examinations
CLEP subject exams; DANTES subject tests; College Board AP exams

Credit Awards for Prior Learning
Transfer credits from accredited, degree-granting institution; portfolio-type assessment; department/institutional exams

Description
Student support services are available from: distance education staff, library, financial aid, bookstore, career center, admissions and registration, dean of student/student affairs, faculty, affirmative action, mathematics learning center, chemistry learning center, writing center, transfer admissions, and transcripts. Advising is available via e-mail (anytime), open office hours via telephone (Monday–Friday, 7:30 am–12:00 pm and 12:30 pm–4:00 pm), and video teleconferencing (on demand).

Students are educated primarily by tape-delayed video. They have access to program information via phone, fax, e-mail, and regular mail. There are also video conferencing capabilities.

Each student is provided a student handbook that summarizes how students may obtain access to university resources. There is also a toll-free phone number they may use to contact the Distance Education Department.

Interaction between faculty and students includes e-mail, phone, and fax. Faculty also make site visits.

Interaction between students is provided by requiring groups of students to meet at a common site, and many classes have labs that permit students to interact personally and professionally. Some e-mail may be shared between all students.

Two required senior projects may be job-related. Other small design projects/problems associated with other courses may also be job-related (i.e., heat transfer, mechanical elements, finite elements, finite elements analysis).

Program effectiveness is determined through such measures as "How's It Going" questionnaires, program evaluations, faculty evaluations, student and faculty daily feedback, charting of evaluations, and retention rates.

Northwood University

University College
3225 Cock Road
Midland, MI 48640
Phone: 517-837-4411
Fax: 517-837-4457
E-mail: uc@northwood.edu

Degrees Offered
Associate of Arts in Accounting, Advertising, Automotive Management, Automotive Marketing, Business Management, and Sales Management; Bachelor of Business Administration in Automotive Marketing/Management, Computer Information Management, and Marketing/Management; Bachelor of Business Administration in Accounting and in Management

Program Mission
To prepare aspiring students of any age or station with the tools, skills, and intellectual capacities for a productive leadership career in an economic system of free markets and private enterprise. The university delivers—to traditional and nontraditional clientele—college-level course work con-

sisting of general education and specialty disciplines to prepare people for management careers with an emphasis on understanding the dynamics of a free enterprise society in which management and entrepreneurial skills predominate and where individuals can take risk for individual and common good and gain; the aesthetic, creative, and spiritual elements of life and their relative importance to living in the fullest sense; and the global nature of enterprise.

Accreditation
North Central Association of Colleges and Schools

Admission Requirements
Age 25 or older, GPA of 2.0 or better on all prior academic work, evidence of good writing and speaking skills, work experience in the business world, and official high school and all previous college transcripts

Credit Hour Requirements
Minimum of 90 quarter hours for AA degree; minimum of 180 quarter hours for the BBA degree

Minimum Campus Time
Most plans require two three-day seminars and an oral/written examination with a faculty panel

Tuition and Fees
Application fee $15 (nonrefundable); tuition varies depending on course delivery method: range $50 per quarter hour to $215 per quarter hour; graduation fee $25

Credit Awards for Examinations
ACT-PEP: Regents College Examinations Program; CLEP general exams; CLEP subject exams; DANTES subject tests; College Board AP exams; Defense Language Institute proficiency tests; ACE-evaluated certification exams

Credit Awards for Prior Learning
Transfer credits from accredited, degree-granting institution; ACE military recommendations; ACE/PONSI recommendations; portfolio type assessment

Description
Counselors and administrative support available at all extension and outreach centers during the hours of 9:00 am–5:00 pm Monday–Friday. Voice mail is available to leave messages 24 hours a day, seven days per week.

Distance education opportunities include independent study courses and limited closed-circuit TV course delivery.

Students learning at a distance access academic resources at extension and at outreach centers and may also contact library services via telephone, mail, or e-mail.

All independent study courses are written, administered, and graded by full-time, on-campus faculty. Contact with faculty is available via telephone (including voice mail), mail, or e-mail.

For students involved in extension center/ outreach center programs, students meet regularly in classroom settings. Classroom settings are located in over 30 sites nationwide. For students not able to participate in Northwood classroom instruction and choosing to pursue their degree exclusively through independent study, a comprehensive oral/written examination with a panel of campus faculty is required in conjunction with two required on-campus seminars.

Seminar courses require topics covered by presenters to be summarized, and then applied to the individual student's workplace, career, or an aspect of his or her job description.

Some degree requirements may be met through new self-designed courses or projects when specifically arranged with a faculty member. Project must meet course goals and objectives.

Program effectiveness is determined through such measures as continuing contact with graduates and with business and industry entities employing graduates. Individual contact and correspondence as well as comprehensive surveys are also used. Program effectiveness is measured primarily by the success experienced by graduates, both in their careers and in their impact on their chosen fields and their communities.

MINNESOTA

The College of St. Scholastica

Master of Education via Distance
    Learning Program
1200 Kenwood Avenue
Duluth, MN 55811
Phone: 800-888-8796
Fax: 218-723-6709
E-mail: mfoss@facl.css.edu

Degrees Offered
Master of Education

Program Mission
To provide teachers with the opportunity to reflect on their current practice and on the theoretical underpinnings of educational innovation and thought, in order to better provide educational opportunities for their students.

Accreditation
North Central Association of Colleges and Schools. The Master of Education via Distance Learning has been accredited to serve students in five states: Minnesota, North Dakota, South Dakota, Iowa, and Wisconsin.

Admission Requirements
A bachelor's degree from an accredited institution, preferred undergraduate GPA of 2.8 or higher, and minimum of two years teaching experience, application essay, official transcripts of all undergraduate and graduate work, and two letters of recommendation from academic or supervisory individuals.

Credit Hour Requirements
48 quarter credit (40 core, two orientation, two capstone, and four elective courses)

Minimum Campus Time
Two on-site courses offered at various locations

Tuition and Fees
$138 per credit, $68 per course fee for books and instructional materials

Credit Awards for Examinations
None

Credit Awards for Prior Learning
Transfer credits from accredited, degree-granting institution

Description
The opportunity for reflection is introduced to participants in the initial seminar, where the definition and process of reflection are explored. Further opportunities to think about the practice of education are provided. Participants will be asked to review and summarize their reflections over the course of the program, which provides the penultimate experience in reflection. Participants conclude the program by thoughtfully examining their personal and professional growth through the entire experience.

On-campus services provided for students 9:00 am–4:30 pm Monday–Friday. Tutoring for remedial math, remedial writing, and most subjects, to individuals and small groups. Academic counseling services offered to minority, veteran, and older students. In addition, there is counseling for relationships, career, personal, academic, psychological, religious, etc. Services for career placement include: career classes, interest inventory, on-campus job interviews, résumé assistance, alumni services, credentials, job search assistance, job fairs, job boards, mentorships, and internships. Students are not required to register for career services but must go through an orientation to career resources and services interview with one of the counselors when requesting career services.

Faculty advisement is available by telephone (800 number), fax, or mail, 24 hours a day. Students may call or contact faculty advisors via voice mail at any time. Calls are returned at the earliest convenience.

The Master of Education via Distance Learning program incorporates various modes of instruction and interaction. Each course involves tests, journal articles, and videotaped lectures/presentations, all of which are shipped directly to the student. Students interact with instructors and peers through telephone, mail, e-mail, and fax.

Students are provided with a library card and manual to enable them to make full use of all available library resources. The CSS library belongs to the statewide MINITEX system, which includes interlibrary loan service. A CSS library card is accepted at any MINITEX library, so students need not come to campus to make use of the library resources. In addition, the CSS library is a participating member of the MSUS/PALS online networking system.

Because students in the program are practicing teachers, many have access to computer equipment/software through their schools. In addition, many students have a computer at home. The faculty encourage students to access computer resources whenever possible and offer assistance when necessary.

For each course in which a student is enrolled, he/she receives an introductory letter and syllabus from the instructor in addition to other course materials. The letter and syllabus provide students with information about the instructor, the course, office hours, and the various modes of communication available. The student is provided with an 800 number, fax number, post office address, and e-mail address for each instructor. Students are encouraged to use any/all of these media to submit assignments, discuss course content, ask questions, address concerns, and evaluate progress.

Faculty are encouraged to contact their students by mail or by telephone every other week. This often results in a mentoring relationship with the students. Instructors respond to and return written assignments in a timely fashion (in most cases, within a week of receipt). This provides students with immediate and ongoing feedback regarding their progress in the course.

Students in the program are encouraged to form peer groups with fellow students in their building, district, or geographic area. Formulation of these peer groups is facilitated at the on-site orientation seminar. When face-to-face interaction is not possible (some students are located in isolated, rural areas), students interact with each other via phone, mail, and e-mail. Some courses require students to contact fellow students and hold a discussion or collaborate on a project. Many students take advantage of the opportunity to network with other teachers of their discipline or grade level, which promotes collegiality and support to all involved.

Each quarter, students in the program are provided with a comprehensive student directory that organizes students by geographic area and provides the grade level/ subject area in which each student currently teaches.

The program is designed to help teachers learn about their surrounding world, about how they think about the world, and how the world affects their teaching. Learning experiences are specifically designed to be practical and applicable within the context of the teacher's school and community environments. The program also prepares teachers to conduct action research; that is, research conducted about and in their own classrooms.

At the end of each quarter, students are sent a course evaluation form for each course in which they are currently enrolled. The evaluation form allows students to rate various aspects of the course, instructor, and program. It also encourages narrative feedback. The evaluation data are summarized and analyzed periodically.

Faculty feedback is solicited in both quantitative and qualitative forms, through time sheets for each course and anecdotal evidence about their role and program features. Regular meetings of faculty to discuss program design are held.

In addition to formal evaluation, program effectiveness is determined by the quality of student work and by informal written and verbal feedback received by participating students throughout the program. Some student work for each quarter is maintained and will be evaluated by an independent agent for longitudinal change on an annual basis.

North Central Bible College

Carlson Institute for Church Leadership
800 S. 10th Street
Minneapolis, MN 55404
Phone: 612-343-4430

Fax: 612-343-4435
E-mail: carlinst@ncbc.edu

Degrees Offered
Bachelor of Arts or Bachelor of Science in Church Ministries, Christian Education, and Christian Studies; Associate of Arts in Bible/Theology and Christian Education

Program Mission
To provide nontraditional programs of adult education with a Christian worldview for those who cannot participate in the traditional programs offered on the main campus. This is accomplished chiefly through independent study and learning centers established in churches.

Accreditation
North Central Association of Colleges and Schools

Admission Requirements
High school or GED diploma, for individual courses. Entrance to degree program requires in addition a minimum of a "C" average in high school or other college work, and references.

Credit Hour Requirements
BA/BS in Church Ministries, 130 semester hours; BA/BS in Christian Education, 130; AA in Church Ministries, 65; BA/BS in Christian Studies, 128; AA in Christian Education, 65

Minimum Campus Time
None

Tuition and Fees
$79 per credit hour plus materials, $10 processing fee, and $30 application/transcript analysis fee for degree enrollment

Credit Awards for Examinations
CLEP general exams; CLEP subject exams

Credit Awards for Prior Learning
Transfer credits from accredited, degree-granting institution; ACE military recom-

mendations; ACE/PONSI recommendations; portfolio type assessment

Description

General information and advising available
8:00 am–5:00 pm Monday–Friday.

Distance education opportunities include
independent study courses and study in
learning centers using independent study
materials in a group setting. Some courses
include videotaped lectures and audiotapes.

Students have access to the on-campus
library through direct or interlibrary loan.
Student ID cards are provided to assist in
accessing local college libraries.

Interaction between faculty and students is
monitored through the Carlson Institute.
Contact with faculty may be made by telephone, fax, or e-mail.

Interaction between students occurs in the
learning center environment where groups
of students study together with the help of
a small-group facilitator.

Most students have regular responsibilities
in their church related to their studies.

Program effectiveness is determined by such
measures as student surveys, surveys of
learning center directors, informal telephone or personal conversation with pastors of the students, and course evaluation
forms for each course taken.

MISSOURI

Berean University

Berean School of the Bible, Berean
  College, and Master's Program
1445 Boonville Avenue
Springfield, MO 65802
Phone: 417-862-2781
Fax: 417-862-5318
E-mail: berean@ag.org

Degrees Offered

Master of Arts in Christian Counseling;
Bachelor of Arts in Bible/Theology, Pasto-
ral Ministries, Christian Education, Christian Counselor, and Missions; Associate of
Arts in Church Ministries, Ministerial Studies, Bible/Theology

Program Mission

To provide for ministers and lay persons
accredited distance education, based on a
Christian worldview, utilizing current technologies to facilitate the evangelization of
the world, the nurturing of the Church,
and the well-being and improvement of
society.

Accreditation

Distance Education and Training Council

Admission Requirements

Student must be 20 years of age and have a
GED or high school diploma to enter college-level studies. Must have a recognized
BA to enter master's-level studies; letters
of reference and a short essay to enter
master's-level studies.

Credit Hour Requirements

AA, 64–68 semester hours; BA, 128 semester hours; MA, 3–42 semester hours

Minimum Campus Time

For the MA in Christian Counseling, three
one-week practicums are required on campus.

Tuition and Fees

Undergraduate $138–$207 per semester
hour, plus fees; master's degree $387 per
semester hour, plus fees

Credit Awards for Examinations

CLEP general exams; CLEP subject exams;
DANTES subject tests

Credit Awards for Prior Learning

Transfer credits from accredited, degree-
granting institution; ACE military recommendations; ACE/PONSI recommenda-

tions; portfolio type assessment; and department/institutional exams

Description
Student services representatives can be contacted from 8:00 am–4:30 pm on Monday, Wednesday, Thursday, and Friday; and 9:00 am–4:30 pm on Tuesday. The Dean of Instruction can be contacted by phone at the same times or through correspondence. Students may be referred to a faculty content specialist (adjunct faculty) when appropriate.

Distance education opportunities include independent study courses and study centers; students may interact with Berean University by e-mail (berean@ag.org) and the World Wide Web page. In study center all students study the same course at the same time under an instructor. Peer networking via computer and audioconferencing is a planned option.

There are forms designed to address students' questions; these are responded to and mailed back to the student.

Program effectiveness is determined by unit progress evaluations at the end of each unit of study, end of course evaluations, and surveys of student satisfaction.

Graceland College

Outreach Program
221 W. Lexington
Independence, MO 64050
Phone: 816-833-0524
Fax: 816-833-2990

Degrees Offered
Bachelor of Science in Nursing (BSN); Bachelor of Arts in Liberal Studies (BA-Liberal Studies); Bachelor of Science in Addiction Studies; and Master of Science in Nursing (MSN)

Program Mission
To educate students for advanced study, for productive careers, and for rich lives. Its student body is a targeted, yet diverse group that includes persons of different ages, backgrounds, and national origins who share a commitment to learning. Its curriculum, firmly rooted in the liberal arts tradition and enhanced by career-oriented practical experiences, affirms different styles of learning and prepares students to become competent professionals. Graceland offers a learning environment for the residential as well as the nonresidential student that nurtures personal growth. Its challenging academic program stresses the joy of lifelong learning, the rigor of intellectual discipline, and the relationship of both to a satisfying professional and personal life.

Accreditation
North Central Association of Colleges and Schools; National League for Nursing (NLN)

Admission Requirements
Varies for each program: 2.5 GPA for Bachelor of Science in Nursing program; 3.0 GPA for Master of Science in Nursing program and graduate of NLN Bachelor of Science in Nursing program; and 2.0 GPA for addiction studies. Reference letters and student's own statement of goals are also considered.

Credit Hour Requirements
128 semester hours for bachelor's degrees and 45 semester hours for MSN program

Minimum Campus Time
BSN, 2 two-week residencies; BA-Liberal Studies, 1 two-week residency; BS-Addiction Studies, 2 two-week residencies; MSN, 3 two- or three-week residencies

Tuition and Fees
BS-Addiction Studies, $195 per semester hour; BSN and BA-LS, $240 for indepen-

dent study and $300 for residency courses per semester hour; MSN, $300 per semester hour for independent study and $375 for residency courses per semester hour

Credit Awards for Examinations
ACT-PEP: Regents College Examinations Program; CLEP general exams; CLEP subject exams; DANTES subject tests; College Board AP exams; ACE-evaluated certification exams; International Baccalaureate

Credit Awards for Prior Learning
Transfer credits from accredited, degree-granting institution, ACE military recommendations, ACE/PONSI recommendations, portfolio type assessment, department/institutional exams, International Baccalaureate

Description
Students may call a toll-free number 8:00 am–5:00 pm to access any of the college offices or services. Students may call the toll-free student information number to speak to a counselor 8:30 am–5:30 pm. Students may call using the toll-free number from most foreign countries. Access to faculty members is provided via voice mail, 800 number, and mail.

Distance education opportunities include directed independent study courses; videotaped mini-lectures and clinical practicums contracted in the student's own community. Students who have computer access available can connect online with library services. Students may also fax or phone-in requests to receive books or photocopied materials by mail. Students have immediate access to all services when they are on campus.

Faculty guide students through each step of each course. Extensive and detailed learning guides supplemented by videotapes assist students through reading assignments as well as examinations. Students receive feedback on each assignment submitted and are encouraged to call faculty members and request assistance if they are having difficulty or have questions.

Extensive networking occurs while students are on campus. Students study together in the residence hall and develop friendships that are pursued throughout the program. A directory of names of students willing to be contacted by new or prospective students is available and utilized by geographical area.

Nurses can obtain practical clinical experiences in pertinent areas. Addiction studies students also help design their practicum experience.

Program and course evaluations are conducted on an ongoing basis. Student satisfaction is assessed regularly. Admittance into graduate school is seen as one measure of success for undergraduates.

Stephens College

School of Continuing Education
Campus Box 2083
Columbia, MO 65215
Phone: 800-388-7579
Fax: 573-876-7248
E-mail: sce@womenscol.stephens.edu

Degrees Offered
Bachelor of Arts in Business Administration, Psychology, Philosophy, Law and Rhetoric, English, Health Care, and Health Science; Bachelor of Science in Health Information Management, Early Childhood, and Elementary Education Certification

Program Mission
To support lifelong learning and to provide quality education designed to meet the needs of women and men 23 years of age and older. With a curriculum that emphasizes issues of concern to women and eth-

nic minorities, the program strives to promote and enhance personal and professional development, personal empowerment, and leadership skills.

Accreditation
North Central Association of Colleges and Schools; Commission on Accreditation of Allied Health Education Programs; American Health Information Management Association

Admission Requirements
High school diploma or GED certificate; passage of the introductory course, "The Changing Human Image," with a grade of "C" or better; 23 years of age or older. TOEFL score of 550 or higher for students for whom English is a second language; completed application form and receipt of $50 application fee; receipt of official transcripts from other schools, professional programs and standardized exams.

Health care and a second curriculum area is a major for students who have an associate degree in registered nursing or a hospital diploma in registered nursing. Health science and a second curriculum area is a major for students who have graduated from an accredited allied health program.

Credit Hour Requirements
A minimum of 120 semester hours and completion of all degree requirements

Minimum Campus Time
Completion of the on-campus introductory course, which is scheduled in a seven-day format or in a double weekend format (total of six days). Several are scheduled throughout the year.

Tuition and Fees
$217 per semester hour; application fee $50; introductory course deposit $150 (will be applied to tuition for first course if registered within one year of introductory course reservation date); and optional pre-advis-ing fee of $150 (will be applied to tuition for first course if registered within one year of pre-advising date)

Credit Awards for Examinations
ACT-PEP: Regents College Examinations Program; CLEP general exams; CLEP subject exams; DANTES subject tests; College Board AP exams; ACE-evaluated certification exams

Credit Awards for Prior Learning
Transfer credits from accredited, degree-granting institution; ACE military recommendations; ACE/PONSI recommendations; portfolio-type assessment; department/institutional exams

Description
Advising services are available to students at their convenience. Students are assigned one advisor and remain with that person during the progression of their studies. Students maintain dialogue with faculty who have e-mail capabilities.

Students receive letter of introduction from Stephens librarian that can be used at local library. Stephens librarian will assist students with interlibrary loan and will mail books, references, etc. to students. Students may apply for a Stephens computer account to access the Internet for e-mail, etc. Students attend workshops on study skills, library skills, time management, writing research papers during the introductory course. Counselor works with students by mail and phone to meet career services needs.

Students work one-on-one with faculty as they work on each course. Students submit course work in units and receive feedback from instructor prior to proceeding to next unit in the course. Interaction occurs by mail, telephone, and e-mail.

Interaction between students occurs informally, as students meet during the introductory course or when they have a fellow student in their geographic area.

The student may work with an instructor to develop an individualized course. The student and instructor will decide on reading materials, course content, methods of evaluation, etc. The course is referred to as a contract study.

Students are asked to complete an evaluation for each course in which they enroll. After a grade is submitted by the instructor, a copy of the evaluation is sent to the instructor. Students who withdraw from the program are asked to complete an exit questionnaire. Graduates complete a survey at the time of graduation.

MONTANA

University of Montana

External Graduate Programs
Center for Continuing Education
Missoula, MT 59812
Phone: 406-243-6430
Fax: 406-243-2047
E-mail: peletier@selway.umt.edu

Degrees Offered
Master of Business Administration; Master of Education; Educational Doctorate

Program Mission
To provide fully accredited graduate degree programs in several disciplines in selected sites. These programs are designed for full-time working professionals and delivered via electronic delivery systems to selected classroom sites throughout Montana. Teleconferencing equipment, e-mail, electronic bulletin boards, interactive computer interface, and instantaneous two-way telecommunications systems are utilized for the best interests of the students.

Accreditation
Northwest Association of Schools and Colleges; National Council for Accreditation of Teacher Education

Admission Requirements
Master of Education and Educational Doctorate, transcripts, GRE scores, admission application, letters of reference, and GPA; Master of Business Administration, transcripts, GRE scores, admission application, letters of reference, GPA, and GMAT scores. Employment history may be a factor.

Credit Hour Requirements
MBA, 36 semester hours; MEd, 37 semester hours; and EdD, 90 semester hours or master's degree plus 52

Minimum Campus Time
EdD several weekends per semester

Tuition and Fees
MBA, $250 per credit; MEd, $225 per credit; EdD $215 per credit. Classes are currently delivered to specific designated classroom sites via electronic delivery systems. Courses and programs are being developed for delivery on the Internet.

Credit Awards for Examinations
None

Credit Awards for Prior Learning
Transfer credits from accredited, degree-granting institution; portfolio type assessment; department/institutional exams

Description
Academic advisors available by phone, e-mail, fax, or in person. Library support via the Internet, phone, or walk-in. Free e-mail accounts available in some areas to students.

Interaction between faculty and students include e-mail, electronic bulletin boards, two-way interactive video, teleconferencing, and multimedia and software exchanges.

Access to library resources are available through the Internet and other networks available through the University of Montana campus and extended campus.

Audio and video two-way interaction in Montana is available at selected sites. MBA courses are conducted live with three sites online simultaneously from different parts of the state. PictureTel and ProShare Video-Conferencing systems are employed for increased interaction of audio, video, and software exchanges and presentations. Multimedia shareware, Hyper Studio, and the latest Powerpoint software are utilized for optimum technological presentations.

Teachers in the MEd program apply course work directly to their own students and classes. MBA students apply course work directly to business plans, new business expansions, and new positions in management.

Program effectiveness is determined through e-mail contacts with students; their comprehension of presented material via tests, papers, presentations, and creative projects, utilizing the latest technology and latest developments of course materials.

NEBRASKA

Central Community College

Extended Learning
P.O. Box 4903
Grand Island, NE 68802-4903
Phone: 308-389-6387
Fax: 308-389-6398
E-mail: cungacc@cccadm.cccneb.edu

Degrees Offered
Associate of Applied Science in Business Administration, Accounting, and Information Technology

Program Mission
To be responsive to central Nebraska higher education needs by providing low-cost tuition, financial aid, and other support services in a manner to assure timely student completion of educational goals no matter where the student may reside.

Accreditation
North Central Association of Colleges and Schools

Admission Requirements
High school diploma or GED

Credit Hour Requirements
64-72 credit hours

Minimum Campus Time
None

Tuition and Fees
$38.50 per credit hour in-state tuition; $42.50 per credit hour out-of-state tuition

Credit Awards for Examinations
CLEP general exams

Credit Awards for Prior Learning
Transfer credits from accredited, degree-granting institution; portfolio type assessment; department/institutional exams

Description
Normal business hours for advising, financial aid services, and student accounts are 9:00 am–7:00 pm. Faculty members are generally available one evening per week.

Distance education opportunities include print-based materials, e-mail, computer-assisted instruction, interactive satellite, and videotaped lectures.

Students can access libraries and other resources via computer. Computer access provided by the college is limited to six sites within central Nebraska. It is the responsibility of students outside this area to provide their own access.

Every course completed at a distance is assigned an instructor who has been trained to provide adequate interaction to meet the objective of the course. This may be through feedback of assignments, e-mail correspondence, and telephone calls.

The distance learning coordinator works with the student throughout the semester to insure the student remains focused.

In cooperation with the employer, a student can develop learner-centered offerings, which must meet the goals and objectives of the program. Amount of credits generated by this method will be determined by the advisor.

Program effectiveness is determined through student completion rates, as well as by survey results.

University of Nebraska–Lincoln

Department of Academic Telecommunications
Division of Continuing Studies
Clifford Hardin Nebraska Center for
   Continuing Education, Room 334
P.O. Box 839805
Lincoln, NE 68583-9805
Phone: 402-472-0400
Fax: 402-472-1901
E-mail: atc@unlinfo.unl.edu

Degrees Offered
Master's degree in Business Administration, Electrical Engineering, Human Resources and Family Sciences, Industrial and Management Systems Engineering, Journalism and Mass Communications, Manufacturing Systems Engineering, and Mechanical Engineering; Doctor of Education (EdD) in Administrative Curriculum and Instruction

Program Mission
To extend the resources of the university by providing educational outreach through innovative technologies.

Accreditation
North Central Association of Colleges and Schools; Accreditation Board for Engineering and Technology

Admission Requirements
Admission to programs is the same as for on-campus graduate degree programs. All master's degree programs require at least a bachelor's degree; for the EdD, a master's degree is required. More specific requirements may be obtained from the program of interest.

Credit Hour Requirements
Most master's degrees 36 semester hours; MBA 48 semester hours; EdD 96 semester hours

Minimum Campus Time
Doctoral program requires one five-week summer session on campus in each of the two consecutive years.

Tuition and Fees
$75 per credit hour for undergraduate resident; $99.25 per credit hour for graduate resident; $135 per credit hour for undergraduate engineering; $160.25 graduate engineering; $204 per credit hour for undergraduate nonresident; and $245.25 per credit hour graduate nonresident

Credit Awards for Examinations
CLEP general exams; DANTES subject tests; College Board AP exams; and Defense Language Institute proficiency test

Credit Awards for Prior Learning
Transfer credits from accredited, degree-granting institution; and ACE military recommendations

Description

All master's degree programs are limited to Nebraska residents.

The following support services are provided to students off campus: advising (done by two-way video as well as phone), library support, library cards, special e-mail requests, computer accounts, assistance with graduate admissions registration, and book orders.

Distance education opportunities include two-way compressed video, one-way video, two-way audio, videotape, audio conferencing, Internet, e-mail, fax, and phone.

The EdD program is available through Lotus Notes, an online computer program.

There is a coordinator for distant learning services at the university library. Students access the library catalog by computer, and can e-mail or fax requests for photocopied articles or books. Students may access numerous databanks and resources.

Most of classes are live-interaction classes. Students receive e-mail accounts. Faculty use e-mail for information dissemination and discussion groups. Audio conferencing and videotape provide interaction. Separate faculty and student orientations are provided by the department.

Students often do projects with other students at different locations. Students communicate with each other via e-mail and phone.

Coursework generally involves projects that are applied to work/professional life. Often professors and students engage in joint research projects utilizing student work situations. Graduate seminars in Teachers College involve self-designed projects/research.

Program effectiveness is determined through such measures as evaluations by students, faculty studies of institutional practices, and studies conducted by the university's Center for the Study of Effectiveness of Technologies in Instruction.

NEW JERSEY

Burlington County College

Going the Distance
Route 530
Pemberton, NJ 08068
Phone: 609-894-9311
Fax: 609-894-4189

Degrees Offered

Associate in Arts in Liberal Arts; Associate in Science in Business Administration

Program Mission

To provide an associate's degree via distance learning.

Accreditation

Middle States Association of Colleges and Schools

Admission Requirements

High school or GED diploma, completion of basic skills requirements

Credit Hour Requirements

64 credits

Minimum Campus Time

Occasional testing, some seminars, an orientation seminar and some lab time

Tuition and Fees

In-county tuition is $55.50 per credit. Out-of-county tuition is $63.50 per credit. Out-of-state tuition is $125.50 per credit. Each course requires a $25 license fee. There is a $20 application fee. Books and video rental are in addition to these fees. Tuition is higher for out-of-county students and much higher for out-of-state students.

Credit Awards for Examinations
CLEP general exams; CLEP subject exams; DANTES subject tests

Credit Awards for Prior Learning
Transfer credits from accredited, degree-granting institution; ACE/PONSI recommendations; department/institutional exams

Description
Support services include counseling and academic advising available by appointment.

Distance education opportunities include telecourses, videotaped courses, and audiotapes.

A faculty member is assigned for each class. The student may interact by phone or come to campus to meet with faculty.

Students are encouraged to exchange phone numbers at an orientation seminar so that they can study together. Some students share videotapes or view them together.

Program effectiveness is determined through such measures as a student survey questionnaire.

New Jersey Institute of Technology

ACCESS/NJIT
University Heights
Newark, NJ 09102
Phone: 201-596-3177
Fax: 201-596-3203
E-mail: dl@njit.edu
Internet: http://www.njit.edu/DL

Degrees Offered
Bachelor of Arts in Information Systems (BAIS); Bachelor of Science in Computer Science (BSCS); Master of Science in Information Systems (MS/IS); Master of Science in Engineering Management (MS/EM)

Program Mission
To help adult men and women attain educational goals.

Accreditation
Middle States Association of Colleges and Schools; Computer Sciences Accreditation Board; Accreditation Board for Engineering Technology

Admission Requirements
Bachelor's degree with GPA that meets academic department standards for graduate admission; high school or equivalent diploma for undergraduate admissions; appropriate math background to be successful in quantitative disciplines; transcripts of previous academic work.

Most of the courses offered require students to have access to a PC and modem for online discussions; it is recommended that students subscribe to a local Internet provider.

Credit Hour Requirements
BAIS, 129 credits; BSCS, 130 credits; MS/IS, 36 graduate credits; MS/EM, 30 graduate credits

Minimum Campus Time
For master's level, a one-day presentation may be required at the discretion of department.

Tuition and Fees
Undergraduate in-state $200 per credit; out-of-state $314; graduate in-state $354; graduate out-of-state $477; per semester fees $140; tape rental fees: undergraduate $55 plus shipping and handling, graduate $150 plus shipping and handling

Credit Awards for Examinations
CLEP subject exams

Credit Awards for Prior Learning

Transfer credits from accredited, degree-granting institution; department/institutional exams

Description

E-mail advisement with faculty and with ACCESS/NJIT staff at any time; phone access to counselors on appointment; online application, registration, and computer account procedures, and computer support help line available weekdays 10:00 am–8:00 pm Monday–Thursday and 10:00 am–6:00 pm Friday.

Distance learning opportunities include videotaped lectures, the "Virtual Classroom" (asynchronous learning network) for online discussion and faculty/student and student/student collaboration, fax communication, and e-mail.

Access to library databases online and UnCover fax request service for articles. PC computer software available on request from book distributor. All students given computer accounts on university network. It is recommended that students equip themselves with PC, modems, and appropriate communications software.

Students are required to log on to computer for e-mail interaction, and, in the "Virtual Classroom," students are required to log on weekly; student-to-student interaction is part of typical course management.

Moderator of online discussions relate subject matter to a student's job. Many projects can be designed to involve student's employment interests or community resources.

Program effectiveness is determined through retention reports, surveys of withdrawn students, and postcourse surveys to access student satisfaction and instructor performance.

Thomas Edison State College

101 W. State Street
Trenton, NJ 08608
Phone: 609-292-9992
Fax: 609-984-8447
E-mail: imartini@call.tesc.edu

Degrees Offered

Associate in Arts; Associate of Science in Management; Associate in Science in Applied Science and Technology; Bachelor of Arts; Bachelor of Science in Business Administration; Bachelor of Science in Technology; Bachelor of Science Human Services; Bachelor of Science in Nursing; Master of Science in Management

Program Mission

To serve the educational needs of adults. As part of the New Jersey State College system, Thomas Edison is structured to provide alternative delivery options including guided independent study, online courses, contract learning, portfolio assessment, testing, and transfer credit as vehicles for degree completion.

Accreditation

Middle States Association of Colleges and Schools; National League of Nursing (for RN)

Admission Requirements

High school diploma/GED diploma; some programs require licensure

Credit Hour Requirements

60 semester hours for associate's degrees; 120 semester hours for bachelor's degrees

Minimum Campus Time

Master's program requires three short-term residency sessions

Tuition and Fees

In-state $51 per credit; out-of-state $76 per credit

Credit Awards for Examination

ACT-PEP: Regents College Examinations Program; CLEP general exams; CLEP subject exams; DANTES subject tests; College Board AP exams; Defense Language Institute proficiency tests; guided study examinations; TECEP examinations; contract online examinations

Credit Awards for Prior Learning

Transfer credits from accredited, degree-granting institution; ACE military recommendations; ACE/PONSI recommendations; portfolio type assessment; department/institutional exams

Description

Support services include student advisement center toll-free number; accessible Monday–Friday 12:00 pm–4:00 pm (for enrolled students). Saturday appointments available once per month 8:00 am–2:00 pm.

Distance education opportunities include DIAL (guided study courses); video-supported, contract online courses; and Internet access to the college's Web page and CALL Network system.

Students use local resources. Students may access computers on loan through the college. Academic advisors/faculty mentors are available to assist students.

Interaction between faculty and students include faculty participation in pregraduation conferences, evaluating submissions for portfolio credit, and mentoring students courses.

The graduate program was designed to allow for interaction between students as they participate throughout the curriculum. Students participate as a cohort and are able to contact one another through the college's CALL Network system. Limited residency requirement allows for personal interactions face-to-face with faculty and students.

Students are encouraged to apply work-related experiences to course work as appropriate. The Master of Science in Management program was designed specifically to encourage a partnership with the workplace.

Students may complete degree requirements through contracted learning, which has some degree of self-design to their structure. This is a limited option for students.

A credit-banking service is available.

Program effectiveness is determined through measures such as student evaluations, faculty evaluations, and intermittent surveys.

NEW YORK

New York Institute of Technology

Online Campus
Box 9029
Central Islip, NY 11722
Phone: 516-348-3059
Fax: 516-348-0299
E-mail: mlehmann@nyit.edu/olc

Degrees Offered

Bachelor of Professional Studies; Bachelor of Arts; Bachelor of Science in Interdisciplinary Studies; Bachelor of Science in Business (Management option); Bachelor of Behavioral Sciences in Psychology, Sociology, Criminal Justice, and Community Mental Health

Program Mission

To make college courses possible for students who choose not to attend a conventional campus.

Accreditation

Middle States Association of Colleges and Schools

Admission Requirements
High school degree or GED

Credit Hour Requirements
None

Minimum Campus Time
Bachelor of Behavioral Science 128 semester hours; all other degrees 120 semester hours

Tuition and Fees
$295 per credit

Credit Awards for Examinations
ACT-PEP: Regents College Examinations Program; CLEP general exams; CLEP subject exams; DANTES subject tests; College Board AP exams; Defense Language Institute proficiency tests; ACE-evaluated certification exams

Credit Awards for Prior Learning
Transfer credits from accredited, degree-granting institution; ACE military recommendations; ACE/PONSI recommendations; portfolio type assessment; department/institutional exams

Description
Students earn credits toward their degrees by instruction using computer conferencing. A personal computer and modem are used to log on to the host mainframe at New York Institute of Technology. Students interact both independently and in organized groups with instructors and classmates at times that are convenient to all. It is an asynchronous system with no residency requirement.

Support services include free tutoring, counseling, 24-hour technical support, and personal academic advisor.

All course work communication is by computer text-based asynchronous system.

Students may access library resources through the program Web site.

Interaction between faculty and students include telephone, computer, as well as the support of academic chair for troubleshooting and suggestions.

Interaction between students is available through a text-based system that provides an open forum for students.

Learning experiences may be designed to relate to the student's work or other life contexts.

Program effectiveness is determined through such measures as student and teacher evaluation. Evaluation by others of high academic standing with no vested interest is also used.

Rochester Institute of Technology

Distance Learning
Educational Technology Center
91 Lomb Memorial Drive
Rochester, NY 14623-5603
Phone: 716-475-5089
Fax: 716-475-5077
E-mail: ritdl@rit.edu; disted@rit.edu

Degrees Offered
Bachelor of Science in Applied Arts and Science with concentrations in Telecommunications, Applied Computing, Management, Health Systems Administration, Emergency Management, and Solid Waste Management Technology; Bachelor of Science in Electrical/Mechanical Technology; Master of Science in Health Systems Administration; Master of Science in Information Technology with concentrations in Telecommunications Technology, Telecommunications Management, Software Development and Management, Computer Integrated Manufacturing, Training and Human Performance, Interactive Multimedia Development, and Technology Man-

agement; Master of Science in Software Development with concentrations in Applied Computing and Communications, Telecommunications Network Management, Voice Communications, Data Communications, Health Systems Administration, Solid Waste Management, and Emergency Management

Program Mission
To offer interactive distance learning programs based on flexible and affordable technology.

Accreditation
Middle States Association of Colleges and Schools

Admission Requirements
Requirements vary by program and level (BS/MS). The admission procedures are the same for distance learning students and on-campus students.

Credit Hour Requirements
BS in Applied Arts and Science 180 quarter hours; BS in Electrical/Mechanical Technology 193 quarter hours; MS in Health Systems Administration 57 quarter hours; MS in Information Technology 48 quarter hours; MS in Software Development and Management 48 quarter hours; Professional Certificate Options: Applied Computing and Communications 24 quarter hours; Telecommunications Network Management 16 quarter hours; Voice Communications 12 quarter hours; Data Communications 12 quarter hours; Health Systems Administration 24 quarter hours; Emergency Management 24 quarter hours; and Solid Waste Management Technology 24 quarter hours

Minimum Campus Time
BS in Electrical/Mechanical Technology is site based. This program is currently limited to students located near a designated community college or corporate extension site. MS in Health Systems Administration

program requires three one-week on-campus sessions during the 21-month course of study.

Tuition and Fees
All graduate programs $458 per credit hour for 1–11 credit hours and $5437 per quarter for 12–18 credit hours; day programs $350 per credit hour for 1–11 credit hours and $4890 per quarter for 12–18 credit hours; evening and distance learning programs (100, 200, and 300 level) $211 per credit hour, (400, 500, and 600 level) $231 per credit hour

Credit Awards for Examinations
ACT-PEP: Regents College Examinations Program; CLEP general exams; CLEP subject exams; DANTES subject tests; College Board AP exams; Defense Language Institute proficiency tests; ACE-evaluated certification exams

Credit Awards for Prior Learning
Transfer credits from accredited, degree-granting institution; ACE military recommendations; ACE/PONSI recommendations; portfolio type assessment; department/institutional exams; educational experiences in noncollegiate organizations

Description
Over 3,000 students each year enroll in Rochester Institute of Technology (RIT) distance learning programs throughout New York, the United States, and overseas.

Courses range from flexible formats to site-based options. Distance learning courses offered in the flexible format are regular RIT courses designed to be taken without coming to campus. Convenience for the student is a main objective.

The BS in Electrical/Mechanical Technology is currently limited to students located near a designated community college or cooperate site. Other RIT distance learning programs can be offered or designed to meet the needs of industry/corporate clients as necessary.

Advising is available to students via toll-free 800 number 8:30 am–8:00 pm. Advisors are also available via e-mail or the RIT online services option. All other service departments (bursar, bookstore, registrar, etc.) are available during regular business hours (8:30 am–4:30 pm with some variations) and online 24 hours a day.

Every RIT distance learning course is created by a professional development team that works with faculty to plan, design, produce, and deliver each course. The team includes specialists in the television production, software development, information science, student services, and educational technology areas of campus. The team works with the RIT college offering the course and departments such as the library, academic computing, and the bookstore, to provide the required support services. Other on-campus units also provide a network of convenient services for distance learning students.

Course materials are delivered using a combination of three primary technologies: videotapes take the place of classroom lectures; scheduled telephone conferences support classroom interaction; and computer communication via e-mail and FirstClass conferencing allows class interaction and access to course information. Courses also use the audiotapes, fax, electronic blackboards, cable, satellite, compressed video, and the Internet for delivery of course materials and information.

Videotape and/or audiotape is used to present lectures and other instructional presentations. Mail order is used for textbooks, videotapes, course materials, modems, and software (students provide their own computers). Tests are taken online, faxed, or mailed. Long-distance students arrange for an approved proctor for their exams. Homework is sent online (via computer), mailed, or faxed. Professors on campus can be reached through electronic mail and toll-free numbers. Class discussions are held using telephone and computer conferences. Library catalogs at RIT and around the world are available online. For long-distance students, materials from RIT and other schools are delivered through interlibrary loan. Online services include campuswide information, campus discussion groups, and 24-hour messaging to departments such as the distance learning office, the bursar, the registrar, and part-time enrollment services. Print materials are distributed to students in course packets with pertinent course information, textbooks, lecture notes, and special reading materials. Internet is used for delivery of some course materials and access to resources.

Course design and content fall under the responsibility of the faculty member and offering department. Level of interaction is determined by the subject mater and the need for high or low levels of interactivity between the faculty member and class members.

Primary means of interaction by students is via e-mail and Lotus Notes conferencing. Level of interaction is determined by the subject matter and the need for high or low levels of interactivity between the faculty member and class members.

Most graduate students must prepare a final project or report, which is often related to the student's work—especially in the areas of software development and health systems administration. This type of academic/work relationship is encouraged.

It is possible to satisfy any degree requirements through new self-designed courses, but provisions for this must be made with the approval of the department and the program chair.

Other than the number of registrations and students enrolled, Distance Learning conducts several surveys and evaluations during each academic quarter. A midquarter evaluation is sent to each student containing questions about their course, course materials, professor, distance learning services, and student demographics. A drop-withdrawal survey is sent to students who have dropped or withdrawn from a distance learning course during a given quarter to determine the reason for their drop/withdrawal. Final course evaluations are administered by the institute with questions about the course, distance learning services and technology, and course faculty.

SUNY–Empire State College
Center for Distance Learning

2 Union Avenue
Saratoga Springs, NY 12866
Phone: 518-587-2100
Fax: 518-587-5404
E-mail: mcraft@sescva.esc.edu

Degrees Offered

Associate in Arts and Bachelor of Arts in Community and Human Services, and in Interdisciplinary Studies; Associate in Science in Business, Management, Economics, Community and Human Services; Bachelor of Science in Business, Management, Economics, Community and Human Services, and Interdisciplinary Studies; Bachelor of Professional Studies in Business, Management, Economics, and Community and Human Services. A concentration in Fire Service Administration is available at either the associate or bachelor's level. The college is in the process of expanding telecommunications options for associate's and bachelor's degrees in the following areas: the Arts, Cultural Studies,

Educational Studies, Historical Studies, Human Development, Labor Studies, Science, Mathematics and Technology, Social Theory, Social Structure and Change.

Program Mission

To offer courses and programs leading to associate's and bachelor's degrees, requiring no on-site classes or travel.

Accreditation

Middle States Association of Colleges and Schools

Admission Requirements

High school or GED diploma, interview, and entrance essay

Credit Hour Requirements

Associate's degree, 64 semester hours; bachelor's degree, 128 semester hours

Minimum Campus Time

None

Tuition and Fees

Matriculated students, $113 per credit; nonmatriculated students, $137 per credit

Credit Awards for Examinations

ACT-PEP: Regents College Examinations Program; CLEP general exams; CLEP subject exams; DANTES subject tests; College Board AP exams; Defense Language Institute proficiency tests; ACE-evaluated certification exams

Credit Awards for Prior Learning

Transfer credits from accredited, degree-granting institution; ACE military recommendations; portfolio type assessment; and New York State Education PONSI

Description

Each student is expected to engage in the educational planning process, through which each student, under the guidance of an academic advisor, examines his or her own background, prior learning, strengths, goals, and needs in order to design the most effective degree program possible.

Each student is assigned a faculty mentor, with whom he or she undertakes a credit-bearing educational planning activity. This activity identifies a student's prior learning (formal and informal) as well as learning skills, goals, and interests. Each student develops a degree program responsive to the identified goals and learning needs. The mentor provides ongoing guidance and support through to graduation. Mentors and students establish appropriate communication times and channels.

Distance learning opportunities include faculty-guided independent study courses via text, videotape, telephone, mail, e-mail, asynchronous computer conferencing, and FirstClass. The term structure permits online peer learning and simulations.

The center's computer menu provides a full range of access to public and private library and database resources, including full-text article retrieval services, supported by institutional funds.

Courses are offered over 15-week terms, with course tutors assigned to sections of no more than 25 students. Course tutors are oriented to be proactive with students, maintaining contact and setting expectations throughout the course term. (The center holds required tutor development workshops each term to improve the quality of the faculty-student interaction.)

The center's online courses (currently 20%–25% of courses offered each term) utilize asynchronous computer conferencing, which permits working adult students with busy schedules to interact with their classmates on their own time schedules. As more students get online, the center plans to increase its online course offerings.

Center courses are designed to encourage students to incorporate elements of their own experience and prior knowledge into the fabric of the course. The center uses problem-centered learning, drawing on students' own experiences as a common pedagogical strategy.

Degree programs are individually designed to meet the needs and goals of each student. When appropriate, students and faculty may design up to 16 credits of a program as unique independent study.

Program effectiveness is assured through each student's active involvement in the academic design of his or her program. Students work directly with both a program advisor or mentor, as well as with the individual faculty tutors for each course of study. An advisor coordinator and a tutor coordinator provide ongoing training and support to these faculty. Students are surveyed throughout their programs on the effectiveness of various components of their education (administration, course design, course tutoring, and academic advising). The center actively encourages students, both formally and informally, to contact center representatives in the event of any concerns.

SUNY–Empire State College
FORUM

28 Union Avenue
Saratoga Springs, NY 12866
Phone: 518-587-2100
Fax: 518-587-4382

Degrees Offered
Associate's degrees and bachelor's degrees in management

Program Mission
To make higher education accessible to nontraditional students not served by traditional institutions. FORUM is specifically

designed for first-level and middle managers.

Accreditation
Middle States Association of Colleges and Schools

Admission Requirements
Written statement and recommendation of employer; high school diploma (most students also have previous college experience). Prior learning: school, in life, and on the job. Participants must have management experience and be sponsored by a corporation.

Credit Hour Requirements
128 semester hours at least 32 "in program" for BS/BA degree; 64 semester hours at 24 "in program" for a AA/AS degree

Minimum Campus Time
One-day orientation and six weekend residencies per year

Tuition and Fees
$3500 comprehensive fee per 24-week term (average of 12 course credits plus 10 prior learning credits per term)

Credit Awards for Examinations
ACT-PEP: Regents College Examinations Program; CLEP general exams; CLEP subject exams; DANTES subject tests; College Board AP exams; Defense Language Institute proficiency tests; ACE-evaluated certification exams

Credit Awards for Prior Learning
Transfer credits from accredited, degree-granting institution; ACE military recommendations; ACE/PONSI recommendations; portfolio type assessment

Description
Educational planning with assigned mentor by appointment; degree program and assessment consultations 8:30 am–4:30 pm Monday–Friday; credit by evaluation services by appointment; assessment, development, application of managerial competence by appointment; regularly scheduled writing clinics, workshops, consultations.

Distance education opportunities include such nonresidency-based activities as credit-bearing seminars, workshops, individualized tutorials, internships, and directed projects.

Students learning at a distance access academic resources through phone, mail, and e-mail contact with faculty and staff, and at writing clinics; e-mail access to Writer's Complex—a hypertext writing support environment; Internet access to libraries and other information sources around the world; and use of all State University of New York libraries.

Students access to faculty via frequently scheduled and unscheduled phone consultations. Faculty are evaluated on student perception of accessibility and quality of service.

Students interact with each other in subject and interest matter caucuses, e-mail connections between individuals and in groups, and conference calls.

Work-related projects supervised by faculty are encouraged, particularly application of managerial competencies in support of, or as the core of, the student's educational plan.

All students are eligible for self-designed courses or projects. Recent examples include: trade and investment assessment of Baltic economics; uses of information technology in the human resource function; and financial communications.

All program elements are ultimately learner-centered. Students develop individualized degree plans (under faculty guidance) according to college curricular guidelines.

Program effectiveness is determined through such measures as intensive, regular feedback from students and alumni; cross-sectional and longitudinal surveys; and discussions with corporate sponsors.

SUNY–Empire State College
Master of Arts

28 Union Avenue
Saratoga Springs, NY 12866
Phone: 518-587-2100
Fax: 518-587-4382
E-mail: gradprog@sescva.esc.edu

Degrees Offered
Master of Arts in Business and Policy Studies; Master of Arts in Labor and Policy Studies; Master of Arts in Social Policy; Master of Arts in Liberal Studies

Program Mission
To serve adult students who seek a challenging, accessible graduate education. The programs offer several alternative ways to earn a degree. They are arranged so that most of the student's studying can be done outside of a classroom setting, as an independent learner.

Accreditation
Middle States Association of Colleges and Schools

Admission Requirements
Official transcript showing an undergraduate degree from an accredited university or college; standard biographical information; record of previous employment and/or education; personal essay describing academic and professional goals; an analytical essay; three letters of reference from appropriately qualified persons who can attest to the applicant's ability to pursue graduate study.

Credit Hour Requirements
36 credits

Minimum Campus Time
Three- or four-day residencies, held three times per year, during completion of required courses

Tuition and Fees
$213 per credit for NY residents, $351 for out-of-state residents, $50 per term telecommunications fee, $.85 per credit college fee, $2.50 per credit ($10 maximum) student activity fee, and $60 residency fee (per residency attended)

Credit Awards for Examinations
ACT-PEP: Regents College Examinations Program; DANTES subject tests

Credit Awards for Prior Learning
Transfer credits from accredited, degree-granting institution; ACE military recommendations; ACE/PONSI recommendations; New York PONSI

Description
Each student is assigned a faculty advisor on admission who is usually available by telephone four days per week. The faculty chairs of each program are available by telephone to talk with students in the program during the normal workday. The assistant director is available for general discussion of educational goals and to answer questions. All faculty and professionals are available via electronic mail. A writing assistance option is available via electronic mail; a writing assistance option is available via computer 24 hours a day for those people who have VAX computer accounts (available to all students); a writing tutor is accessible 10 hours per week via telephone. Staff registration and records assistance is available from 8:30 am–5:00 pm Monday–Friday via telephone; all support staff are on e-mail.

Distance education opportunities include electronic mail, Internet access, computer conferencing, and independent study.

Students with a computer and modem have access to the computer network of ESC (the software is provided by the college). At each residency, workshops are held to assist students in understanding the range of computer services available and a handbook is sent with each disk. Via this VAX account, students can access libraries, the Internet, electronic mail to faculty and other students, computer conferencing courses, and the Writer's Complex, among other resources. Modem banks throughout the state offer local calls to nearly all students. Access using an 800 number is available to others. Over 90% of faculty use electronic mail.

Students and faculty are expected to connect via telephone or e-mail at least four times per term. In computer conferencing courses, faculty and students are expected to interact several times per week. Students mail, fax, or e-mail assignments to faculty. Telephone numbers, e-mail addresses, and mailing addresses are provided in each registration booklet.

All students with e-mail accounts can look up the e-mail names of another student on the computer. With permission, students are listed in a telephone book mailed to all students each term. For some courses, group projects are required. Some of this interaction occurs online; interaction also occurs during the residencies or via telephone conference calls.

Learning experiences may be designed to relate to the contexts of the student's life. For example, Organizational Behavior students are asked to analyze their work setting or volunteer organization. In the Economic and Financial Analysis course, students are asked to select an industry for a microeconomic analysis; many choose the industry in which they work. For their final project, students frequently select topics that are a part of their work life, or they find an internship that relates to their work or volunteer interests.

Students are encouraged to design electives that are not already offered and that will provide them with additional knowledge specific to their needs. Many do so. All final projects are the design of the student, who must provide a proposal for approval before starting.

Where appropriate to their program, students are encouraged to design contracts that build on their work experience and in which it is possible to provide recognition of prior learning. Students are also encouraged to establish bulletin boards or discussion groups online that provide opportunities for interaction on a personal level.

Program effectiveness is assessed via continual feedback from the students and reviews by panels of faculty teaching in the graduate programs. In the policy programs, all master's exams are read by at least two program faculty; in the liberal studies program, a faculty review committee approves each individually designed program and rationale essay, which is the program exam. Each final project must have a second reader and an oral defense, which provides integrating, evaluative comments. Extensive pre-enrollment, self-assessment data are collected and used to inform program design. Several years ago, a study chronicled graduation rates and other statistical outcomes. The college plans a follow-up study.

SUNY–Empire State College/ SUNY–New Paltz

SUNY Learning Network: Mid-Hudson Region
State University Plaza

Albany, NY 12246
Phone: 518-443-5331
Fax: 518-443-5167
E-mail: sdumas@sln.esc.edu

Degrees Offered
Bachelor of Arts in Liberal Studies from SUNY-New Paltz; Bachelor of Arts in Business Management and Economics (concentration: Business Administration) from SUNY-Empire State College

Program Mission
The SUNY Learning Network is an association of eight colleges in the mid-Hudson region (New Paltz, Empire State, Ulster, Rockland, Orange, Sullivan, and Columbia-Green Community College) who have joined together to offer online college courses leading to two bachelor's degrees.

Accreditation
Middle States Association of Colleges and Schools

Admission Requirements
SUNY-New Paltz: minimum of 60 credits and meet SUNY-New Paltz general education requirements or hold an Associate of Arts or Associate of Science from a SUNY or CUNY Community College

Credit Hour Requirements
SUNY-New Paltz, 120 credits; Empire State College, 128 credits

Minimum Campus Time
None

Tuition and Fees
NY residents $1700 full-time per semester and $137 part-time per credit; nonresidents $4150 full-time per semester and $346 part-time per credit

Credit Awards for Examinations
CLEP subject exams and College Board AP exams

Credit Awards for Prior Learning
Transfer credits from accredited, degree-granting institution; portfolio type assessment; department/institutional exams

Description
All courses are conducted via computer and each course uses Lotus Notes software. This software creates an electronic forum where students have access to libraries at participating campuses and to fully equipped computer learning centers on each campus (hours vary from campus to campus).

Students need a home computer, access to a computer at work, or access to a computer at a SUNY Learning Network Campus. An office or home computer must have a modem (9600 baud or higher) and meet certain minimum requirements. IBM compatible: 4 megabytes of RAM, 20 megabytes of free hard disk space, 80386 (or higher) processor, Windows 3.1 or higher. Macintosh: 5 megabytes of RAM, 20 megabytes of free hard disk space, running system 6.04 (or higher) or system 7 (or higher).

Except for books and library resources, academic resources are available online. Some courses offer at least one face-to-face meeting between faculty and student, otherwise the interaction is online.

Regents College
The University of the State of New York

7 Columbia Circle
Albany, NY 12203-5159
Phone: 518-464-8500
Fax: 518-464-8777
Internet: http://www.regents.edu

Degrees Offered
Associate of Applied Science in Nursing; Associate of Science in Nursing, Business,

Liberal Studies, Computer Software, Electronic Technology, Nuclear Technology, and Technology; Bachelor of Science in Nursing, General Business, Accounting, Accounting CPA, Finance, International Business, Management, Human Resources, Management Information Systems, Marketing, Operations Management, Liberal Studies, Computer Information Systems, Computer Technology, Electronic Technology, Nuclear Technology, and Technology; and Bachelor of Arts in Liberal Studies

Program Mission
Regents College is founded on the premise that what a person knows is more important than how or where that knowledge was acquired. The college believes that college-level learning that has been acquired in a variety of settings can be documented objectively and comprehensively through transcripts, written or performance examinations, and other academically sound assessment procedures. It also believes that adults' needs for further learning can be met in a variety of ways, both traditional and nontraditional, from taking college courses to independent study followed by proficiency examinations. The final responsibility for that learning lies with the student rather than with the faculty or the institution.

Accreditation
Middle States Association of Colleges and Schools; National League for Nursing

Admission Requirements
Open admission, with no high school or GED requirements. In nursing, students must document acceptable clinical experience and background.

Credit Hour Requirements
Associate degree, 60 semester hours; baccalaureate degree, 120 semester hours; Nuclear Technology degree, 124 semester hours

Minimum Campus Time
None

Tuition and Fees
Enrollment/initial evaluation fee $565. For other fees, contact the college.

Credit Awards for Examinations
ACT-PEP: Regents College Examinations Program; CLEP general exams; CLEP subject exams; DANTES subject tests; College Board AP exams; Defense Language Institute proficiency tests; ACE-evaluated certification exams; GRE

Credit Awards for Prior Learning
Transfer credits from accredited, degree-granting institution; ACE military recommendations; ACE/PONSI recommendations; portfolio type assessment; department/institutional exams; Federal Aviation Administration certificates; and teaching a course at a regionally accredited college

Description
Student support services are available Monday and Wednesday 8:30 am–8:00 pm, Thursday and Friday 8:30 am–5:00 pm. Advising services include: program planning, course selection, and course approval; learning style analysis; career guidance; decision making; stress reduction; affirmation and encouragement; self-assessment; learning resource identification; and referrals to other agencies.

Print-based learning packages are provided to students who are preparing for Regents College examinations; these learning packages include audio- and videotapes, software, CD-ROMs, and other appropriate materials, depending upon the examination. Also offered are optional online study groups led by faculty to support students preparing for examinations. Students are referred to distance learning courses that utilize all forms of print-based and electronic delivery systems.

Students access academic resources via phone, mail, fax, and e-mail, and have access to a variety of learning resources via the Regents College electronic bulletin board. Students are referred to library resources in their own communities. Faculty prepare reading anthologies for hard-to-find primary resources and students purchase these and other learning resources through the college mail-order bookstore. Students may purchase computer equipment and software through the college.

Students participating in some guided learning experiences access faculty via electronic conferencing, telephone, and regular mail. Audio teleconferences are provided as a component to some guided learning experiences. Students interact directly with faculty. Students are provided with e-mail addresses for staff and faculty and advisors as appropriate. As an assessment institution, students are provided with materials that they use to prepare independently.

Students are able to join the Regents College learning network, which provides them with a directory of student names, addresses, phone numbers, and other information that they can use to contact fellow students. Students are able to enroll in guided learning experiences that have electronic discussion groups as a component. Students participate face-to-face in a variety of workshops delivered in several regions throughout the country. These workshops are designed to assist students in preparing for examinations and sharpening their study skills.

Program effectiveness is determined through such measures as graduate follow-up studies and regular program evaluation. Program effectiveness is also assessed through self-reported graduate follow-up studies and through follow-up studies with students' employers and graduate school advisors. There is also direct assessment of student performance in critical thinking and synthetic and analytic skills.

NORTH CAROLINA

North Carolina State University College of Textiles

Textile Off-Campus Televised Education (TOTE)
Box 8301
Raleigh, NC 27695
Phone: 919-515-1532
Fax: 919-515-8578
E-mail: teresa_langley@ncsu.edu

Degrees Offered
Master of Science in Textiles

Program Mission
To provide continuing, high-quality educational opportunities to textiles employees who reside in areas where no textile education is available. The student is able to take specialized classes pertaining to his or her area of employment, such as textile chemistry, textile management, among others.

Accreditation
Southern Association of Colleges and Schools

Admission Requirements
Bachelor of Science

Credit Hour Requirements
33 credit hours

Minimum Campus Time
None

Tuition and Fees
Undergraduate: in-state $400 per credit hour, out-of-state $500 per credit hour; graduate: in-state $500 per credit hour,

out-of-state $600 per credit hour. Out-of-state students pay mailing costs to return videos and homework, etc.

Credit Awards for Examinations
None

Credit Awards for Prior Learning
None

Description
The graduate student, after being accepted into the Master of Textiles program, is in contact with the graduate administrator and the student is assigned an advisor (committee chair) who they are in touch with by phone and fax. Faculty normally give their office hours and phone numbers during taping of the first lecture. Students are free to call the professor with questions or problems and will receive help.

Videotaped lectures are prepared for both undergraduate and graduate classes. A small number of independent study courses are available to graduate students in the Master of Textiles degree program.

Students living within a reasonable driving distance are able to access the College of Textiles at any time. They also can obtain a NCSU all-campus card for use at the NCSU D.H. Hill Library, with proper identification. Students living at a great distance are encouraged to use the resources available in their local city libraries and university or college libraries.

Communication between the instructor and the student is explained clearly in student guidelines mailed to each student at the start of the semester. Students are strongly encouraged to communicate with their professors by phone, fax, or by regular mail. Faculty often address the distance learners through comments as the class is being videotaped.

There are no processes designed to provide for interaction between students. The only exception would occur when two or more students are enrolled in the same class and are employed by the same company. Since TOTE is entirely a textiles program, the students enrolled are employed in textiles or textile-related companies and positions.

Program effectiveness is determined through such measures as follow-up student satisfaction surveys, as well as statistical course enrollment studies.

NORTH DAKOTA

University of North Dakota
Corporate Engineering
Degree Program

P.O. Box 9021
University of North Dakota
Grand Forks, ND 58202-9021
Phone: 800-342-8230
Fax: 701-777-4282
E-mail:
    lynette_krenelka@mail.und.nodak.edu

Degrees Offered
Bachelor of Science in Mechanical Engineering, Electrical Engineering, and Chemical Engineering

Program Mission
To offer Bachelor of Science degrees in mechanical, electrical, and chemical engineering through videotape combined with on-campus labs.

Accreditation
North Central Association of Colleges and Schools; Accreditation Board for Engineering and Technology

Admission Requirements
There are two types of admission: admission to the University of North Dakota (UND) and admission to a School of Engineering and Mines (SEM) degree program.

Admission to UND must occur first. It allows students to take CEDP courses. Admission to a SEM degree program occurs after appropriate requirements are met, which is normally the completion of most lower division courses. Specific admission requirements can be obtained from UND through the Division of Continuing Education. Currently, the program is offered to employees of companies who have joined the Corporate Engineering Degree Program consortium as voting or nonvoting members. This policy may change in the future (open enrollment may be possible).

Credit Hour Requirements
Mechanical Engineering, 139 credits; Electrical Engineering, 136 credits; and Chemical Engineering, 136 credits

Minimum Campus Time
Students are required to attend on-campus summer labs for those classes that have lab requirements (approximately one week per credit hour is a guideline)

Tuition and Fees
There are two different tuition costs, depending on the company consortium membership, (1) nonvoting and (2) voting. Nonvoting membership, $375 per credit hour fall/spring courses and $500 per credit hour summer laboratory; voting membership, $225 per credit hour fall/spring courses and $500 per credit hour summer laboratory.

Credit Awards for Examinations
ACT-PEP: Regents College Examinations Program; CLEP subject exams; DANTES subject tests; College Board AP exams; Defense Language Institute proficiency tests; SAT and TOEFL

Credit Awards for Prior Learning
Transfer credits from accredited, degree-granting institution; ACE military recommendations; portfolio type assessment; department/institutional exams

Description
Once a student is admitted into UND, an academic advisor from the School of Engineering and Mines is assigned. The student works with the assigned advisor to develop a program of study. Students not yet admitted to UND who need academic advisement first contact the CEDP Coordinator through the Division of Continuing Education.

Engineering distance education courses are videotaped on campus and distributed to students via their company or sent to the student's home. Students are required to attend summer labs on the University of North Dakota campus as part of the engineering distance education degree. Students may also enroll in correspondence study courses through the University of North Dakota's Division of Continuing Education (without being admitted to UND). Many students interested in the engineering degrees offered through CEDP begin taking some of the lower-level courses through correspondence study.

All services provided to on-campus students are available to distance learners in the CEDP. The services include full library services (including interlibrary loan).

Engineering distance education students have access to faculty through telephone, e-mail, and fax. Interaction is encouraged.

With students' permission, their e-mail address, phone number, and address are provided to other students in their class.

UND faculty are currently working with CEDP students to develop a capstone design course (two semesters in length) that will actually be completed at the student's workplace. Students will work with a company representative in establishing an engineering design team to complete the capstone with the student taking the lead.

School of Engineering and Mines faculty are in the process of piloting the development of student portfolios to assess experiential learning. Many of the CEDP students have been working in industry for a number of years and may have an opportunity to develop a student portfolio to receive credit for work experience or show that the learning outcomes have been met in specific courses.

In order to measure program effectiveness, students participate in focus groups during the summer while attending summer labs. CEDP faculty and staff meet with the students to identify program areas that are successful and those areas that require improvement. In addition, students complete written evaluations on each course for which they have enrolled.

University of North Dakota
Space Studies

P.O. Box 9008
Grand Forks, ND 58202-9008
Phone: 701-777-3164
Fax: 701-777-3711
E-mail: borysewi@aero.und.nodak.edu

Degrees Offered
Master of Science in Space Studies

Program Mission
To offer in-depth study of the implications of humankind's entry into space: the scientific, technical, political, medical, and legal impacts, on national and international levels, that are associated with the exploration and development of space. The goal is to integrate traditional space-related disciplines. While specialized technical training will remain essential, the all-encompassing nature of space development also requires people who possess a broader background that links policy, business, law, science,

and technology. This perspective makes the Department of Space Studies unique in the United States.

Accreditation
North Central Association of Colleges and Schools

Admission Requirements
Must have a baccalaureate degree with a major in one of the following fields: engineering, science, business, social science, or communication and information systems; or have four years of postbaccalaureate work experience in space-related activities. In addition, applicants must have one course in statistics, calculus, or a programming language at the college level; one course in sociology, psychology, or political science; and one course in a science. Those who do not meet these requirements may be admitted on a qualified basis until the deficiencies are completed.

Credit Hour Requirements
32 credits and a comprehensive exam are required for graduation

Minimum Campus Time
Each distance student will attend a short (approximately two weeks) summer session at the UND campus in Grand Forks, as a capstone to their distance learning experience. The summer session will allow students to meet their professors and fellow students face-to-face, possibly for the first time. The goal of the capstone course is to integrate, extend, apply, and test knowledge learned in earlier Space Studies courses and readings.

Tuition and Fees
$260 per credit including cost of videotape lectures and shipping in the United States

Credit Awards for Examinations
None

Credit Awards for Prior Learning
None

Description
Distance students have the same level of opportunities for discussion and advisement as on-campus students. Faculty is available by telephone during normal business hours and by e-mail at any time.

Lecture videotapes offer a great deal of flexibility to the distant student, allowing the individual to tailor instruction time to fit his or her schedule. Each student receives a complete set of lecture tapes and lecture study guide at the start of each term. Students can assimilate the information at their own pace, as long as they keep up with the material covered in the scheduled interactive sessions.

A student's regular interaction with faculty and other students clarifies understanding and provides opportunities for the presentation and discussion of new ideas. To this end, regularly scheduled group discussion periods are conducted via the Internet. Class assignments and testing are conducted over the Internet to the fullest extent possible.

With their faculty advisor's permission, students can take up to eight credits of independent study.

Students access academic resources via SPACE.EDU, the virtual campus on the World Wide Web. SPACE.EDU has links to the UND library where students can search the online card catalog and download full-text documents or use interlibrary loan to check out books. SPACE.EDU also has links to other online resources, such as NASA Web pages and Internet-related software.

A student's regular interaction with faculty and other students clarifies understanding and provides opportunities for the presentation and discussion of new ideas. To this end, regularly scheduled group discussion periods are conducted via chat sessions on the Internet. Students "go to class" once a week for an online discussion with their instructor and fellow classmates. Instructors and fellow students are also easily reached by e-mail or phone.

Many distant students work in the aerospace industry. They seek to integrate their independent study with their work needs and experiences.

OHIO

Case Western Reserve

Weatherhead School of Management
George S. Dively Center
11240 Bell Flower Road
Cleveland, OH 44106-7166
Phone: 216-368-2042
Fax: 216-368-4793
E-mail: edm@pyrite.cwru.edu

Degrees Offered
Executive Doctorate in Management (EDM)

Program Mission
To integrate concept and practice within the context of today's emerging and pressing global issues.

Accreditation
North Central Association of Colleges and Schools

Admission Requirements
Master's degree, 15 years work experience, and letter of recommendation. Description of time availability and intensity of learning objectives are also required.

Credit Hour Requirements
54 semester hours

Minimum Campus Time
14 days per semester

Tuition and Fees
$21,000 per year

Credit Awards for Examinations
None

Credit Awards for Prior Learning
None

Description
The EDM is available to a small, select group of experienced executives who possess an MBA or the equivalent and are committed to pursuing formal, rigorous study as practitioner-scholars. It is designed to address practicing executives' specialized needs for advanced knowledge and skills, and to explore new horizons of executive leadership within their organizations and beyond.

Student support services available through small program class size; advising/support by director and program faculty.

Distance education opportunities available are e-mail and independent study for limited purposes.

Access to the university's library is by modem dial-in to university network.

Interaction between students is facilitated by program purchase of five hours per month of connect time through commercial Internet service for all students and faculty.

Learning may be related to the contexts of a student's life. For example, a vice president of a Cleveland Growth Association focuses program project requirements on regional human resource planning, which is his organizational responsibility.

Program effectiveness will be determined in terms of long-run intellectual and policy influence of graduates.

Cleveland Institute of Electronics

1776 E. 17th Street
Cleveland, OH 44114
Phone: 800-243-6446
Fax: 216-781-0331

Degrees Offered
Associate of Applied Science (AAS) in Electronics Engineering Technology

Program Mission
To educate individuals in technical skills through home study methods.

Accreditation
Distance Education and Training Council

Admission Requirements
A high school diploma or GED is required for admission to the associate degree program.

Credit Hour Requirements
106 quarter credit hours

Minimum Campus Time
None

Tuition and Fees
AAS program costs $1200 per six-month term. Students pay only for those terms they use, as they may study as quickly as they wish. Most students complete in an average of five terms. Students are allowed eight terms to complete program.

Credit Awards for Examinations
None

Credit Awards for Prior Learning
Transfer credits from accredited, degree-granting institution and transfer credits from military training

Description
General student services (i.e., billing, shipments, etc.) are available to students Monday–Friday 8:30 am–5:00 pm. Instructional

services are available to students (via telephone) Monday–Thursday 8:30 am–9:00 pm, Friday 8:30 am–7:00 pm, and Saturday 8:30 am–5:00 pm. Students may fax exams or other paperwork 24 hours a day. All exams, faxed or mailed, are returned within 48 hours of receipt by the school.

All courses are offered via independent study. All lesson books, textbooks, and study guides are included, as is all lab equipment and computer disks, if used.

Students are given all materials they need for usual study. Certain programs require a student to own a computer or to have access to one on a regular basis. The school will pay for a library membership of the student's choice, if requested. Students also have access to additional reading materials, computer software, and laboratory equipment through the bookstore.

Students who are falling behind in studies are contacted by the faculty. Faculty are accessible by telephone for over 12 hours most days.

Many students are currently employed in the field of electronics and bring to their studies knowledge of the topic as learned in their jobs.

Graduates are surveyed to learn if their studies have resulted in any job advancements, pay increases, or placement in the field of electronics (if not employed in the field at the time of enrollment). They are also surveyed so that the school may learn if the student's individual learning objectives were met and their assessment of the learning materials, instructors, and student services.

Defiance College

Design for Leadership
701 N. Clinton Street

Defiance, OH 43512
Phone: 419-783-2465
Fax: 419-784-0426
E-mail: dhoward@tdc.edu

Degrees Offered
Associate of Arts in Religious Education; Bachelor of Science in Religious Education; Bachelor of Arts in Religious Education

Program Mission
To offer a program for mature nontraditional students seeking a career in religious education.

Accreditation
North Central Association of Colleges and Schools

Admission Requirements
High school or GED diploma; evidence student can do college-level work (transcript from other colleges/universities); three letters of recommendation; an autobiographical sketch; an ability to work well with people; ability to work independently, to be self-starters; ability to manage time well; and commitment to the field of religious education

Credit Hour Requirements
120 semester hours for BS/BA; 61 semester hours for AA

Minimum Campus Time
None

Tuition and Fees
Guided independent studies fee $96 per semester; supervisor/service fee per semester $370; extended service fee $125; application fee $25

Credit Awards for Examinations
CLEP general exams; CLEP subject exams; DANTES subject tests; College Board AP exams

Credit Awards for Prior Learning

Transfer credits from accredited, degree-granting institution; ACE military recommendations; ACE/PONSI recommendations; portfolio type assessment; department/institutional exams

Description

The major includes a series of guided independent studies (Foundations of Religious Education, Old and New Testament, Theology, Curriculum, Leadership and Group Work Theory, Age Level Studies [children, adolescents, adults], Administration and Planning, World Religions, Church History, and Special Topics). The major also includes supervised field experiences (three semesters for AA and four for BA/BS students). General education and elective courses to complete the 120 semester hours (61 for AA) may be taken at accredited colleges/universities in the student's geographic area. Faculty endeavor to blend theory and practice. Students are prepared to serve as directors/coordinators of religious education in churches or (if BA/BS graduates) enroll in graduate education.

In areas where there is more than one student, the group gathers for area seminars four times a semester (spring/fall). Questions are received by the coordinator and staff and are managed via letter, fax, or telephone. Summer Learning Center provides opportunities for support.

Supervised field experience includes conference, observations, and (where there are two or more students in a geographic area) area seminars. Adjunct instructors provide these services. Guided independent studies are conducted by mentors who are usually the writers. Comments on learning activities flow back and forth over the months each is in process.

To access secondary academic resource services students simply write the coordinator and order. Only return postage or UPS costs required. Secondary resources include books, audiotapes, and videotapes. Primary resources are purchased by students locally or from the Defiance College bookstore. Each guided independent study is composed of a series of learning activities that the student completes. These are sent to the coordinator and on to the mentor who reviews and comments, evaluates and returns them. In addition to written comments, telephone communications are initiated by either the student or mentor from time to time. In supervised field experience, there is direct person-to-person conversations plus telephone calls, plus interaction with 5- to 7- person advising groups from the field experience setting.

Each summer the Summer Learning Center, an optional week-long experience, is held on campus and students come, meet each other, form professional relationships, and often keep in contact with each other, share resources, ideas, concerns, etc. These relationships sometimes continue well after graduation.

This experience includes a series of introductory workshops on the guided independent studies. In addition, nationally known educators present in one-day workshops that focus on elements of field experience or research issues in the field of religious education. Guided independent studies and supervised field experience are completed in the student's community. Supervised field experience in religious education yields a total of 12 semester hours and may be the student's current employment in a church or service agency. On some occasions portions of the guided independent studies may involve life experiences. One element of the guided independent study group is called Special Topics. A student may design a study (in turn approved by faculty) for which 1–3 semester hours of credit may be awarded.

In addition to the 12 semester hours (four semesters usually) of supervised field experience and the guided independent studies (13–15), students complete their general education and elective courses at colleges and universities in their geographical areas and transfer credit to Defiance College.

The McGregor School of Antioch University

800 Wivermore Street
Yellow Springs, OH 45387
Phone: 937-767-6325
Fax: 937-767-6461
E-mail: admiss@unibase.antioch.edu

Degrees Offered
Individualized Master of Arts in Intercultural Relations

Program Mission
This program offers adult students from all over the world the opportunity to earn a master's degree without relocating from their home community.

Accreditation
North Central Association of Colleges and Schools

Admission Requirements
Bachelor of arts, bachelor of science, or commensurate experience

Credit Hour Requirements
60 quarter hours

Minimum Campus Time
Two one-week seminars and two two-week seminars

Tuition and Fees
$1800 per quarter; $75 seminar fee; $100 enrollment fee; and room and board during residency (variable)

Credit Awards for Examinations
ACT-PEP; Regents College Examinations Program; CLEP subject exams; College Board AP exams; CLEP general exams; and DANTES subject tests

Credit Awards for Prior Learning
Transfer credits from accredited, degree-granting institution; credit-by-exam; ACE/PONSI recommendations; ACE military recommendations; and portfolio type assessment

Description
Advising may take place via fax or telephone and is usually done 9:00 am–5:00 pm Monday–Friday. Advising through e-mail may take place at other times.

The faculty advisor guides the students to degree/learning components completion. Advisor-student interaction is integral to learning success. This interaction is increased through frequent review of the learning components that make up the student's program.

Limited residency programs with opportunities to study independently, via e-mail, videotape, or through local university study, depending on student's design.

Students may enroll 4 times per year: October, January, April, and July.

Distance learning opportunities include e-mail, videotapes, and self-directed learning.

Students provide support for each other through e-mail interaction, further strengthening the learning community.

Relating learning experiences to a student's employment through program practicums, learning components, and thesis development are all areas in which a student can tie work to theory.

A student may earn 128 quarter credits through individually designed learning components.

Program effectiveness is determined by student feedback.

Ohio University

External Student Program
301 Tupper Hall
Athens, OH 45701-2150
Phone: 800-444-2420
Fax: 614-593-0452
E-mail: extdegprog@ohiou.edu

Degrees Offered

Associate in Arts; Associate in Science; Associate in Individualized Studies; Associate in Applied Business in Business Management Technology

Program Mission

To allow students to complete course work—without coming to campus—by using services offered through the Office of Lifelong Learning.

Accreditation

North Central Association of Colleges and Schools

Admission Requirements

High School diploma or GED certificate. If previous college credit has been earned, student must have a 2.0 GPA on a 4.0 scale for admission.

Credit Hour Requirements

192 quarter hours for the Bachelor of Specialized Studies; 103-105 quarter hours for the Associate in Applied Business in Business Management Technology; 96 quarter hours for the Associate in Arts, Associate in Science, and Associate in Individualized Studies degrees

Minimum Campus Time

Student attend campus for one to three weeks to earn college credit, meet other people in the program, and meet and learn from Ohio University faculty. This program is currently offered three times a year: summer, winter, and spring.

Tuition and Fees

$58 per quarter hour for independent study courses by correspondence plus a $10 enrollment fee per course; $31 per quarter hour for course credit by examination; $67 per quarter hour for independent study projects; and $35 per quarter hour for special course credit by examination

Credit Awards for Examinations

CLEP subject exams

Credit Awards for Prior Learning

Portfolio type assessment

Description

The staff of the External Student program will assist the student to determine a course of action for accomplishing his or her degree goals and then guide the student through a degree program. A staff member also serves as a link between the student, faculty, and other university personnel.

Support services include the assignment of an advisor. The advisor can be reached via phone, on a toll-free number, Monday–Friday 8:00 am–5:00 pm. Students may also contact their advisors by fax or regular mail.

Students complete all Ohio University course work through correspondence via independent study or course credit by examination. Faculty contact is routed through the independent study office, which serves as a liaison for faculty-student communication. Students may contact their advisors by e-mail.

Students enrolled in courses by correspondence have all their lessons graded by the faculty member teaching the course; they receive written comments and feedback regarding their work. Students are also provided with an optional opportunity to come to campus three times a year for special "Institutes for Adult Learners."

Active students in the program were surveyed last year as a measure to determine program effectiveness.

The Union Institute Center for Distance Learning

440 E. McMillan Street
Cincinnati, OH 45206-1947
Phone: 513-861-6400
Fax: 513-861-0779
Internet: http://www.tui.edu

Degrees Offered
Bachelor of Arts and Bachelor of Science in Liberal Arts and Science-based curriculum

Program Mission
To focus on learners as individuals, recognizing and respecting their career orientation and their personal and academic potential. As a university, The Union Institute provides alternative programs in higher education for independent, self-motivated, adult learners who are unable or do not desire to meet the time and place requirements of traditional universities. The Union Institute's mission is to provide educational opportunities and service of exemplary quality to traditionally underserved adult populations, to develop nontraditional yet rigorous strategies for the support of learning and the delivery of instruction, and to foster change in higher education. The principal purpose and tasks of the Center for Distance Learning, as part of the College of Undergraduate Studies, are to offer individualized baccalaureate studies in the arts and sciences, culminating in the award of the bachelor of arts (BA) or bachelor of science (BS) degree; to offer opportunities

for highly motivated adults to complete their degrees in carefully supervised, individually designed degree programs, each of which includes a general education requirement; to continue the search for more effective and productive systems of adult education; and to encourage and support practitioner research in the area of adult learning.

Accreditation
North Central Association of Colleges and Schools

Admission Requirements
Structured essay, three letters of recommendation, interview, high school diploma and official transcripts, and application form and fee ($50 nonrefundable). Evidence of the ability to do college-level work as demonstrated by transcripted course work and experience; high motivation to complete the degree; capacity for self-directed learning; a basic level of computer literacy.

Credit Hour Requirements
A minimum of 128 semester hours is required for the degree

Minimum Campus Time
Five-day entry colloquium (at which the final admission decision will be made)

Tuition and Fees
$242 per semester credit hour

Credit Awards for Examination
ACT-PEP: Regents College Examinations Program; CLEP general exams; CLEP subject exams; College Board AP exams; ACE-evaluated certification exams

Credit Awards for Prior Learning
Transfer credits from accredited, degree-granting institution; ACE military recommendations; portfolio type assessment; department/institutional exams

Description

Learners have access by telephone (9:00 am–5:00 pm) to the staff of the Center for Distance Learning; they may also communicate via the university's electronic bulletin board system or Internet e-mail. Learners are in regular contact with their faculty advisor, who serves as advisor, mentor, colleague, and evaluator; as well as with the two adjunct faculty/instructors for each course. The scope and time(s) of contact are determined by agreement between the learner and the individual faculty member, since the center's faculty are somewhat of a dispersed community (i.e., located throughout the United States, not limited to the university's headquarters in Cincinnati, Ohio).

Since all Center for Distance Learning programs are individually designed, the scope and types of distance education opportunities are determined by the individual learner, working in conjunction with her/his faculty advisor. All programs involve some degree of independent study at their core. The university provides: electronic bulletin board (via toll-free number), e-mail (via Internet) available at very low cost, and toll-free telephone communication with the Cincinnati, Ohio offices.

Center faculty assist and advise learners in identifying and locating the academic resources best suited for their programs, as well as helping them learn how to conduct library research. The university covers the cost of a valid library card at a university library in the area in which the learner lives. Learners access online bibliographic databases (e.g., ERIC and Ohio Net) via the university's electronic bulletin board system. They access the libraries of the world via the Internet's World Wide Web. They access public, university, medical, and specialized library collections as needed. The university provides the appropriate letters of recommendation to facilitate such access. Research assistance is provided by The Union Institute's information specialist.

Learners' first contact with faculty is during the application process, when they schedule an in-person or telephone interview. Faculty frequently provide assistance in the application process. At the entry colloquium, newly matriculated learners meet with the faculty conveners and guests. At seminars, learners meet with faculty conveners. The level of interaction between a learner and faculty will vary, defined by the individually designed courses and the level of faculty assistance that the learner desires and needs.

Learners are encouraged, beginning with the entry colloquium, to establish a peer support network. Learners meet with their peers through their participation in group learning agreements, and at seminars. Learners interact regularly on the university-supported electronic bulletin board.

Learners may, and often do, design programs that build upon their current professional or community involvement. Many learners seek degrees in academic areas directly related to their current employment or their community involvement.

Learners, with the advice and assistance of their faculty advisor, develop a Learning Agreement for each course: one that is specifically tailored to individual learning goals. The majority of courses taken by learners are one-on-one tutorials. The center requires a minimum of 64 semester credits in the four dimensions of learning (language/communications, social sciences, humanities/arts, and science/mathematics), but there are no required courses in these areas or in the learner's chosen area of concentration.

Learners provide written evaluations of each course taken toward the degree. They also evaluate the program as a whole prior to graduation. These mechanisms, along with faculty evaluations, and the tiered survey program ensure an ongoing evaluation of the effectiveness of the center's program.

The average age of center learners is 38; the program's design stems from recognition of the maturity of the learner population. The use of the term "learner" rather than student is an important distinction, recognizing the responsibility and ability to participate actively in the design and execution of the program, learning outcomes, and experiences.

The Union Institute Graduate School

440 E. McMillan Street
Cincinnati, OH 45206-1947
Phone: 513-861-6400
Fax: 513-861-0779
Internet: http://www.tui.edu

Degrees Offered
Doctor of Philosophy in Interdisciplinary Studies in the Arts and Sciences and Interdisciplinary Studies in Professional Psychology

Program Mission
To focus on learners as individuals, recognizing and respecting their career orientation and their personal and academic potential. As a university, The Union Institute provides alternative programs in higher education for independent, self-motivated, adult learners who are unable or do not desire to meet the time and place requirements of traditional universities. The Union Institute's mission is to provide educational opportunities and service of exemplary quality to traditionally underserved adult populations, to develop nontraditional yet rigorous strategies for the support of learning

and the delivery of instruction, and to foster change in higher education. The principal purposes and tasks of the graduate school are to provide high quality, interdisciplinary doctoral studies culminating in the doctor of philosophy (PhD) degree in the arts and sciences; to respond to the educational needs of mature, self-motivated adults by providing individually designed graduate programs; to continually refine and improve through self-evaluation; to promote the intellectual and professional development of its faculty; and to promote national networks of individuals, groups, and organizations that share a common educational mission.

Accreditation
North Central Association of Colleges and Schools

Admissions Requirements
Three letters of recommendation; three detailed, narrative essays; official transcripts; and application form and fee ($50, nonrefundable); clear evidence of applicant's motivation and ability to undertake a self-directed program of independent, doctoral-level study

Credit Hour Requirements
Program is not based on credit hours

Minimum Campus Time
25 days, consisting of one 10-day entry colloquium and three five-day seminars. Colloquia and seminars are scheduled throughout the year and are held at various locations in the United States, including The Union Institute's headquarters in Cincinnati.

Tuition and Fees
$3660 per semester

Credit Awards for Examination
None

Credit Awards for Prior Learning
None

Description
Learners have access by telephone (9:00 am–5:00 pm) to the Dean and Assistant Dean of the Graduate School; they may also communicate via the university's electronic bulletin board system or Internet e-mail. Learners are in regular contact with their faculty advisor, who serves as advisor, mentor, colleague, and evaluator, as well as with the two adjunct faculty serving on the learner's doctoral committee. The scope and time(s) of contact are determined by agreement between the learner and the individual faculty member, since the center's faculty are somewhat of a dispersed community (i.e., located throughout the United States, not limited to the university's headquarters in Cincinnati, Ohio).

All graduate school programs are individually designed, so the scope and types of distance education opportunities are determined by the individual learner, working in conjunction with her/his faculty advisor. All programs involve independent study at their core. The university provides: electronic bulletin board (via toll-free number), e-mail (via the Internet) available at very low cost, and toll-free telephone communication with the Cincinnati, Ohio offices.

Faculty members on the doctoral committee assist and advise learners in identifying and locating the academic resources best suited for the individual's program. Learners access online bibliographic databases (e.g., ERIC and Ohio Net) via the university's electronic bulletin board system. They access the libraries of the world via the Internet's World Wide Web. They access public, university, medical, and specialized library collections as needed. The university provides the appropriate letters of recommendation to facilitate such access. Research assistance is provided by The Union Institute's information specialist.

Learners' first contact with faculty is during the application process, when they may be referred to a faculty member for assistance. At the entry colloquium, newly matriculated learners meet with the faculty conveners and a number of faculty guests. At seminars, learners meet with faculty conveners. The degree of interaction between the learner and the faculty members on the doctoral committee varies by the nature of the individually designed program and the different roles played by each committee member. Minimally, the entire doctoral committee meets, face-to-face, at three points during the program. Learners interview and nominate their doctoral committee members, subject to review and approval by the Dean of the Graduate School. This ensures the best possible interaction between the learner and her/his faculty advisor(s).

Learners are encouraged, beginning with the entry colloquium, to establish a peer support network. Learners are required to meet with their peers at least 16 times during the program through their participation in 10 peer days (learner-designed mini-seminars), the entry colloquium, and the required five seminars. Learner Council, an elected group, provides additional support and networking opportunities. Each doctoral committee has two peer members, nominated by the learner. Learners interact regularly on the university-supported electronic bulletin board.

Although the doctoral research cannot be "business as usual," learners may, and often do, design programs that expand upon their current professional or community involvement.

All graduate school programs are individually designed (no established curricula or course catalog). Learners work with their doctoral committee to identify the various ways in which they will acquire the knowledge needed to attain the PhD degree. This can be done through any number of ways, including self-designed courses.

Throughout the course of the program, learners provide written evaluations of their various learning experiences (colloquium, seminars, peer days, internship); they also evaluate the program as a whole in their program summary prior to graduation. These mechanisms, along with annual faculty evaluations and the tiered survey program, ensure an ongoing evaluation of the effectiveness of the graduate school program.

It is important to note that, in addition to being responsible for identifying and nominating all members of the doctoral committee, the learner also serves as chair of that committee. The average age of graduate school learners is 46; the program's design stems from recognition of the maturity of the learner population. The use of the term "learner" rather than student is an important distinction, recognizing the responsibility and ability to participate actively in the design and execution of the program, learning outcomes, and experiences.

OKLAHOMA

Oklahoma State University

University Extension
470 Student Union
Stillwater, OK 74075
Phone: 405-744-6606
Fax: 405-744-7923
E-mail: nivens@okway.okstate.edu

Degrees Offered
Master of Science in Computer Science, Business Administration, Telecommunications Management, Chemical Engineering, Electrical Engineering, Mechanical Engineering, Natural and Applied Sciences, and Health Care Administration

Program Mission
To facilitate the dissemination of the teaching, research, and professional expertise of the university faculty and staff to people who would otherwise be unable to continue their education and to promote economic development in the state by providing a highly educated workforce.

Accreditation
North Central Association of Colleges and Schools; Accreditation Board for Engineering and Technology

Admission Requirements
MS in Computer Science: to qualify for admission to the MS Program, an applicant must poses a BS degree in computer science or equivalent from a recognized college or university and have a "B" average in undergraduate work. Students who have a continually increasing grade point average will be considered for admission under academic probation. International students must also have a TOEFL score of at least 550.

The following materials must be submitted before an application will be considered for admission: completed OSU Graduate College application form, two official copies of transcripts from all institutions previously attended, and three letters of recommendation. Applicants with degrees in closely related fields are also accepted, but remedial undergraduate course work may be required.

Successful completion of an eight-hour calculus sequence is required.

Credit Hour Requirements
MS in Chemical Engineering, 30 hours; MS in Mechanical Engineering and Health

Care Administration, 33 hours; MS in Computer Science, 24 hours; MS in Business Administration, 48 hours; and MS in Telecommunication Management and Electrical Engineering, 36 hours

Minimum Campus Time
MS in Business Administration, six Saturday sessions done within first two years; MS in Telecommunication Management, four days

Tuition and Fees
$175 per credit hour (10 or more students combined total at all sites) and $195 per credit hour (less than 10 students combined total at all sites)

Credit Awards for Examinations
ACT-PEP: Regents College Examinations Program; CLEP subject exams; DANTES subject tests; College Board AP exams; ACE-evaluated certification exams

Credit Awards for Prior Learning
Transfer credits from accredited, degree-granting institution; ACE/PONSI recommendations; department/institutional exams

Description
The focus of most programs is in Oklahoma. Some delivery modes (such as compressed video) must be used at specifically equipped company/community sites in the state.

Student support services are available 8:00 am–5:00 pm Monday–Friday, 8:00 am–8:00 pm Wednesday. Students can contact the university extension staff by phone, fax, or e-mail and will be put in contact with all the resources that are available or be referred to the appropriate authority.

Distance education opportunities include satellite video courses, videotaped courses, compressed video courses, broadcast television–assisted courses, e-mail–assisted courses, independent study courses, correspondence study courses, and audio-assisted courses.

In accessing academic resources at a distance, students contact the staff at university extension program units who will direct them to the specific services needed.

Faculty have regular office hours and may be reached electronically by telephone, fax, and e-mail.

Many courses have regular electronic class meetings for live student interaction, plus e-mail discussion options. Most degree programs have professional project options that encourage applications to an individual's job and/or community. Many of these projects allow self-designed undertakings.

In determining program effectiveness, both faculty/staff observations and course evaluations from students are monitored for formative and summative judgment about revising or replacing courses.

Oral Roberts University

School of Lifelong Education
7777 S. Lewis Avenue
Tulsa, OK 74171
Phone: 918-495-6238
Fax: 918-495-6033
E-mail: slle@oru.edu

Degrees Offered
Bachelor of Science in Business Administration, Christian Care and Counseling, Church Ministries, Elementary Christian School Education, and Liberal Studies

Program Mission
To enable mature adults to obtain a bachelor of science degree through an accredited nonresident program. Recognizing that learning is an ongoing, lifelong process, the School of Lifelong Education is designed for adult learners who seek to better equip themselves educationally, but find it im-

possible to leave homes, jobs, and ministries to attend Oral Roberts University in Tulsa, Oklahoma.

Accreditation
North Central Association of Colleges and Schools

Admission Requirements
High school diploma or GED certificate, must be 22 years of age or older

Credit Hour Requirements
129 semester hours

Minimum Campus Time
12 hours

Tuition and Fees
$105 per credit hour

Credit Awards for Examinations
CLEP general exams; CLEP subject exams

Credit Awards for Prior Learning
Transfer credits from accredited, degree-granting institution; portfolio type assessment; department/institutional exams

Description
Toll-free line provided to students to facilitate faculty contact, enrollment in classes, advisement, etc.

Distance education opportunities utilize correspondence study, and online Internet services are being developed.

Faculty provide written feedback on course work and can be reached by telephone to discuss problems and needs.

The various degree programs are developed in such a way so as to promote practical "life experience" learning opportunities, in counseling, education, ministry, and the business community.

Every student, upon completion, is given an opportunity to provide feedback through an exit interview.

University of Oklahoma College of Liberal Studies

Bachelor of Liberal Studies/Master of Liberal Studies
1700 Asp Avenue, Suite 226
Norman, OK 73072-6400
Phone: 405-325-1061
Fax: 405-325-7698

Degrees Offered
Bachelor of Liberal Studies; Master of Liberal Studies; Master of Liberal Studies, Museum Emphasis

Program Mission
To provide coherent, interdisciplinary, liberal arts programs of high quality through innovative formats that serve the needs of nontraditional students. Academic degrees and other programs of the college share the common goal of focusing on the study of issues and the examination of ideas from multiple, interrelated perspectives.

Accreditation
North Central Association of Colleges and Schools

Admission Requirements
GED or high school diploma and application essays in both programs. Student's probability for success based on life accomplishments and other identified criteria.

Credit Hour Requirements
Bachelor of Liberal Studies (BLS), 126 credit hours; Master of Liberal Studies (MLS), 32 credit hours; and Master of Liberal Studies/Museum Emphasis, 32 credit hours

Minimum Campus Time
BLS, 3 seminars = 25 days; and MLS, 3 seminars = 30 days

Tuition and Fees
BLS lower division, resident $54.50, nonresident $170; BLS upper division, resi-

dent $58, nonresident $188.50; MLS, resident $75, nonresident $235

Credit Awards for Examinations

ACT-PEP: Regents College Examinations Program; CLEP subject exams; DANTES subject tests; ACE-evaluated certification exams

Credit Awards for Prior Learning

Transfer credits from accredited, degree-granting institution; ACE military recommendations; ACE/PONSI recommendations

Description

Faculty usually available Monday–Friday 8:00 am–5:00 pm. Students are allowed to arrange advising times on an individual basis with faculty advisors.

Distance education opportunities include e-mail, independent study courses, and college listserv.

Library holdings are available online for literature searches. Students are encouraged to use local libraries and interlibrary loans when appropriate.

The college is developing technology to provide for discussions (via the Internet) for students. Students are encouraged to maintain contact with faculty advisors via phone, e-mail, and regular mail.

It is recommended at the introductory seminar that students form a study group in their area or at least interact with a "study buddy." The on-campus seminars provide student interaction, as well as advising workshops and annual receptions organized by the college. Students in the BLS program complete a study in-depth senior capstone project. They are allowed, within parameters, to design the project themselves. Many elect work-related topics. MLS students are allowed to design the entire program around their own goals or interests, within certain limits.

Program effectiveness is determined by formal assessment of in-depth studies (senior thesis) of graduating students by faculty assessment teams, formal questionnaires on effectiveness sent to alumni, exit interviews with graduating students, and unsolicited comments and reports of students and alumni.

OREGON

Chemeketa Community College

Chemeketa Online
4000 Lancaster Drive N.E.
Salem, OR 97305
Phone: 503-399-5191
Fax: 503-399-5214
E-mail: donnac@chemek.cc.or.us

Degrees Offered

Associate of Arts; Associate of General Studies; Associate of Applied Science in Fire Suppression

Program Mission

To provide students with alternative forms of delivery, such as CTV, modem-based classes, and other distance delivery options, as part of the overall mix of learning choices. These delivery methods are no longer peripheral or experimental, but are becoming an integral part of how we deliver education. Alternative delivery is an imperative, not an option, for the college's continued viability. We increase our flexibility in meeting learning needs because a "lifelong" approach to learning requires more flexible forms of delivery, and because learners want control over their learning environment.

Accreditation

Northwest Association of Schools and Colleges

Admission Requirements

Take college placement test (covers reading, writing, math, spelling, and study skills) or have test waived based on previous college course work

Credit Hour Requirements

93 credit hours for AA; 90 credit hours for AGS; 99 credit hours for AAS in Fire Suppression. Must complete at least 30 credit hours of Chemeketa courses to earn a degree.

Minimum Campus Time

None

Tuition and Fees

$33 per credit hour plus fees up to $47 per course

Credit Awards for Examinations

CLEP subject exams

Credit Awards for Prior Learning

Transfer credits from accredited, degree-granting institution; portfolio type assessment; department/institutional exams

Description

In-person service available on campus Monday and Tuesday 8:00 am–7:00 pm, Wednesday and Thursday 8:00 am–5:00 pm, and Friday 8:00 am–4:00 pm. In-person service one day each week at satellite campuses in Dallas, McMinnville, Santiam, and Woodburn. Counselor assigned to work with distance education students is available by phone, fax, and Internet e-mail. Services include career planning, career counseling, academic advising, and some personal counseling.

Distant education opportunities include computer online courses, videotaped telecourses, interactive TV, and correspondence courses.

Students access academic resources through the college library via mail and the Internet, and bookstore materials can be mail-ordered.

Faculty state how students can reach them in their syllabi: office hours, phone number, e-mail address.

Online and interactive TV classes include student interaction as an integral component of the course.

Geology classes have individualized site-based labs. Fire Suppression students use their own fire department work site as their lab.

Individualized study credits available in various disciplines.

Program effectiveness is determined through statistical information devised from student success information, student evaluation, and employer feedback.

PENNSYLVANIA

The American College

2705 Bryn Mawr Avenue
Bryn Mawr, PA 19010-2196
Phone: 610-526-1368
Fax: 610-526-1310
E-mail: gmcmilla66@aol.com

Degrees Offered

Master of Science in Financial Services and Management

Program Mission

To advance learning and professionalism in financial services.

Accreditation

Middle States Association of Colleges and Schools

Admission Requirements

Undergraduate degrees

Credit Hour Requirements
36 semester hours

Minimum Campus Time
Two one-week residencies

Tuition and Fees
$490 per distance course; $1300 tuition per residency; $700 room and board

Credit Awards for Examinations
None

Credit Awards for Prior Learning
Transfer credits from accredited, degree-granting institution

Description
Each student is assigned a faculty member to monitor their progress. Student counselors are available from 8:30 am–5:00 pm Monday–Friday.

Distant education is through independent study and case analysis.

Library is accessible through mail or e-mail.

Students must complete a research paper with a faculty advisor.

Local study groups may be arranged.

Program effectiveness is determined through student feedback and peer review.

Bucks County Community College

Distance Learning
Swame Road
Newtown, PA 18942
Phone: 215-968-8052
Fax: 215-968-8005
E-mail: bradleyj@bucks.edu

Degrees Offered
Associate in Liberal Arts and Business Administration

Program Mission
To enable capable, self-motivated adults to obtain postsecondary education outside the traditional classroom structure.

Accreditation
Middle States Association of Colleges and Schools

Admission Requirements
High school or GED diploma

Credit Hour Requirements
60 semester hours

Minimum Campus Time
The average on-campus time per courses: three-hour orientation, three-hour mid-term, and three-hour final examination. However, if travel to the campus is impossible, alternative arrangements are made in almost all courses.

Tuition and Fees
$66 in-county; $132 out-of-county; $198 out-of-state

Credit Awards for Examinations
CLEP general exams; CLEP subject exams; ACE-evaluated certification exams

Credit Awards for Prior Learning
Transfer credits from accredited, degree-granting institution; portfolio type assessment; department/institutional exams

Description
All students are assigned an advisor upon registration.

A full range of distance learning methods are used including the Internet, e-mail, voice mail, computer-assisted programs, video, and print.

Students have reciprocal borrowing privileges with 30 college libraries.

Faculty require early and constant interaction with students.

Interaction between students is through e-mail and voice mail accounts.

Program effectiveness is determined by teacher evaluations and student evaluations.

ICS Learning Systems

Center for Degree Studies
925 Oak Street
Scranton, PA 18515
Phone: 717-342-7701
Fax: 717-961-4038
E-mail: icsprof@aol.com

Degrees Offered
Associate in Specialized Business; Associate in Specialized Technology; programs are offered in Business Management, Accounting, Electronics Technology, Applied Computer Science, Finance, Marketing, Hospitality Management, and Mechanical, Civil, Electrical, and Industrial Engineering

Program Mission
To offer postsecondary career education in business and technology. Established to provide a learning system based on guided independent study, the center offers an opportunity to earn an ASB or AST degree for those unable or unwilling to pursue their educational goals through traditional means. The center aims to provide specialized education designed to fulfill practical needs—career, job advancement, self-improvement—without sacrificing the ultimate goals of education: personal growth and enrichment.

Accreditation
Distance Education and Training Council

Admission Requirements
High school diploma or GED

Credit Hour Requirements
Business Management, Finance, Marketing, Accounting and Hospitality Management, 60 credits; Applied Computer Science, 61 credits; Industrial Engineering, 64 credits; Electronics Tech and Mechanical Engineering, 67 credits; Electrical Engineering, 68 credits; and Civil Engineering, 69 credits

Minimum Campus Time
Two-week resident laboratory training session for technology programs only

Tuition and Fees
The total cost for all four semesters ranges from $2956 to $3566

Credit Awards for Examinations
CLEP subject exams; ACE-evaluated certification exams

Credit Awards for Prior Learning
Transfer credits from accredited, degree-granting institution; ACE military recommendations; ACE/PONSI recommendations; and portfolio type assessment

Description
Student can contact instructors Monday–Friday 8:00 am–9:00 pm. After hours student may leave a message for instructors and will be contacted the next business day. Customer service can be contacted Monday–Friday 8:00 am–9:00 pm and on Saturday from 9:00 am–3:00 pm. Examination grading via telephone is available Monday–Saturday 8:00 am–12:00 am. Automated services available 24 hours.

Distant education opportunities include independent study courses and e-mail.

Students are given a toll-free number to contact instructor via Dial-A-Question. Instruction services are available Monday–Friday 8:00 am–9:00 pm. Instruction answering service available other hours.

Students can also access libraries through the Internet and other online services.

Providing a toll-free assistance line and 24 hour services allows the student every opportunity for faculty interaction. The use of subjective exams in some courses requires instructor input and feedback.

Some writing assignments involve opportunity for individual student input. The resident lab experience in technical programs also provides "real-life" relational experiences. All study materials are designed to help students teach themselves. The instruction is built into the materials. This allows students to learn independently and at their own pace.

Surveys, exam completion reports, graduation reports, exam item analysis reports, and interaction on the phone with students are measures used to determine program effectiveness.

Luzerne County Community College

Tele College
1333 S. Prospect Street
Nanticoke, PA 18634
Phone: 717-740-0423
Fax: 717-735-6130

Degrees Offered
Associate of Arts in General Studies

Program Mission
To make college credit courses available to learners whose time constraints (and other factors) make it difficult for them to attend regularly scheduled courses in the classroom.

Accreditation
Middle States Association of Colleges and Schools

Admission Requirements
Open admission

Credit Hour Requirements
62 semester hours

Minimum Campus Time
Time required on campus may include orientation sessions, exams (midterm and final exams), or optional review sessions prior to midterm or final exams. Exams may also be sent to students to complete.

Tuition and Fees
In-state $144 per three credit course ($48 per credit), application fee $20, general services fee $15, telecourse production fee $10, video rental fee $20

Credit Awards for Examinations
CLEP subject exams; DANTES subject tests

Credit Awards for Prior Learning
Transfer credits from accredited, degree-granting institution; ACE military recommendations; portfolio type assessment

Description
Student services or counseling, telecollege personnel, and library services.

An interactive video classroom site is now in development.

Students are provided with information at the orientation; that is, services that are available and how to access them. They may use the college library or libraries located nearer to their homes.

Interaction between faculty and students begins initially with an orientation letter. Students and faculty are encouraged to contact each other as frequently as they desire or need to. Faculty have voice mail at the college and/or at home to receive messages from students and are encouraged to respond within a day or two at the most.

Mailings throughout the semester include a newsletter focusing on the program and information that would be of special interest to distance students.

Interaction between students is at the discretion of each telecourse facilitator. Students may be given the opportunity at the orientation session to exchange names and telephone numbers. Learning experiences may be related to various contexts of the student's life. Papers may be assigned, for example, to students enrolled in a telecourse, such as Principles of Management, which encourage students to think critically and to utilize research to discuss such topics as diversity in the workplace, ethics in the workplace, leadership, teamwork, and a host of other practical and relevant topics directly related to their experiences as an employee or community volunteer.

Attrition of students enrolled in telecourses was compared with that of the general population and found to be lower. Students have an opportunity, both written and orally, to provide feedback or recommendations. Suggestions for change are encouraged.

Marywood College

Off-Campus Degree Program
2300 Adams Avenue
Scranton, PA 18509
Phone: 717-348-6235
Fax: 717-961-4751
E-mail: pmunk@ac.marywood.edu

Degrees Offered
Bachelor of Science in Business Administration; Bachelor of Science in Accounting

Program Mission
To meet the special needs of adults through individual, guided study.

Accreditation
Middle States Association of Colleges and Schools

Admission Requirements
High school or GED diploma, reside 25 miles or more from Scranton, PA; personal/professional statement

Credit Hour Requirements
126 credits

Minimum Campus Time
Four weeks in residency in one- and/or two-week increments

Tuition and Fees
$237 per credit; $80 text/materials fee per course; $40–$75 registration fee dependent on number of registered courses

Credit Awards for Examinations
ACT-PEP: Regents College Examinations Program; CLEP general exams; CLEP subject exams; DANTES subject tests; College Board AP exams; ACE-evaluated certification exams

Credit Awards for Prior Learning
Transfer credits from accredited, degree-granting institution; ACE military recommendations; ACE/PONSI recommendations; portfolio type assessment; department/institutional exams

Description
Advising available via a toll-free number Monday–Friday 8:30 am–4:30 pm. Voice mail available at all other times.

All courses are independent study, with the exception of 12 credits in residency.

The library can be accessed through an Internet account.

Faculty feedback is included with each lesson examination (4–7 per course). Faculty are available via phone, fax, and/or e-mail.

Monthly bulletins and residency functions provide opportunities for interaction between students.

Learning experiences may be designed to relate to the contexts of the student's life. For example, a required marketing plan may be related to student's employment.

Program effectiveness is determined through such measures as student course evaluations, grade tracking, faculty course evaluations, and course revisions/upgrades.

Northampton Community College

College-at-Home Program (CAHP)
3835 Green Pond Road
Bethlehem, PA 18017
Phone: 610-861-5358
Fax: 610-861-5378
E-mail: sbj@pmail.nrhm.cc.pa.us

Degrees Offered
Associate in Business Administration

Program Mission
To allow students who cannot come to regularly scheduled on-campus courses a way to start or complete their educational program.

Accreditation
Middle States Association of Colleges and Schools

Admission Requirements
High school or GED diploma. Program is currently restricted to Pennsylvania and eastern New Jersey residents.

Credit Hour Requirements
60 semester credits

Minimum Campus Time
None

Tuition and Fees
$70 per credit, residents of sponsoring school districts; $146 per credit other PA school district; and $222 per credit for out-of-state students

Credit Awards for Examinations
ACT-PEP: Regents College Examinations Program; CLEP general exams; CLEP subject exams; DANTES subject tests; departmental challenge exams

Credit Awards for Prior Learning
None

Description
College-at-home students have access to all college services. Normal business hours are 9:00 am–7:00 pm Monday–Thursday, 9:00 am–5:00 pm Friday. Library is open Monday–Thursday 8:00 am–10:00 pm, Saturday 8:30 am–4:30 pm, and Sunday 1:00 pm–8:00 pm during academic year. Summer 8:00 am–10:00 pm Monday, Tuesday, and Thursday, and 8:00–6:00 pm Wednesday.

Distance education opportunities include printed materials, e-mail, videotaped lectures, independent study, video conferencing, and telecourses.

Library has computers and software and provides testing facilities.

Faculty receive name, address, and phone number of students. Students receive name, address, phone number, and e-mail address of faculty. Some instructors have required phone conferences, regular exchange of written materials. Students have at least three phone numbers to leave messages for faculty.

Program effectiveness is determined by evaluations by students who complete or withdraw from each course. CAHP is reviewed annually, and every five years there is an audit with outside evaluation.

The Pennsylvania State University

Department of Distance Education
211 Mitchell Building
University Park, PA 16802
Phone: 814-865-5403
Fax: 814-865-3290
E-mail: psude@cde.psu.edu

Degrees Offered
Associate of Arts in Letters, Arts, Science, and Sociology; Associate of Science in Dietetic Food Systems Management

Program Mission
To serve students in all parts of the world, increasing student flexibility regarding the time, place, and pace of study and creating a highly interactive, learner-centered environment that is marked by increased access to faculty expertise and increased access to information resources. Distance education is integral to the research and service elements of the university's mission; it helps the university reach out to a broader community and, at the same time, brings worldwide expertise to Penn State students. Distance education is not simply the addition of technology to instruction; instead, it uses technology where appropriate to make possible new approaches to the teaching/learning process.

Accreditation
Middle States Association of Colleges and Schools

Admission Requirements
High school or GED diploma

Credit Hour Requirements
Associate in Letters, Arts in Science, and Associate in Sociology requires 60 semester credits; Associate in Dietetic Food Systems Management requires 67 semester credits; and Associate in Business Administration requires 68 semester credits

Minimum Campus Time
None

Tuition and Fees
$98 per credit hour, $28 processing fee for cost of materials

Credit Awards for Examinations
None

Credit Awards for Prior Learning
Portfolio type assessment under review and department/institutional exams, College of Business

Description
The Department of Distance Education comprises a variety of delivery research and development units that support the mission.

Advisors are available 8:00 am–5:00 Monday–Friday via toll-free number

Distance education opportunities include e-mail lesson submissions for independent study courses, audio and video conferencing, and teleconferences.

The department plans to set up a system for students to have electronic access to university resources.

Interaction between faculty and students includes the use of e-mail, telephone, and correspondence.

For some courses, students may use job- or community-related experience as the basis for research papers.

Program effectiveness is determined through course and program evaluations as well as periodic interviews with clients and organizations.

RHODE ISLAND

Roger Williams University

Open Program
University College
Bristol, RI 02809
Phone: 401-254-3530
Fax: 401-254-3560
E-mail: jws@alpha.rwu.edu

Degrees Offered
Bachelor of Science in Administration of Justice, Business Management, Industrial Technology, and Public Administration

Program Mission
To offer courses and degree programs to students unable to be served by traditional education programs. It enables students to enroll not only in classroom courses but also in a variety of external courses and to receive credit for nontraditional learning experiences.

Accreditation
New England Association of Schools and Colleges

Admission Requirements
High school or GED diploma; interview. Students should enter with advanced standing based on credits already acquired from previous college attendance, military training; creditable employment /life experiences; CLEP and/or other exams. Students should have educational resources available to them in the event such resources need to be incorporated into their programs.

Credit Hour Requirements
BS degree programs require a minimum of 120 semester hours of credit; 30 hours academic enrollment requirement (hours that must be earned through enrollment at the institution exclusive of credit-by-exam, transfer credit, etc.)

Minimum Campus Time
No required residency. On-campus interview, advisement, and program assessment sessions, as needed.

Tuition and Fees
Depending on type of course selected, $185–$325 per credit; application fee $35; graduation fee $35

Credit Awards for Examinations
ACT-PEP: Regents College Examinations Program; CLEP general exams; CLEP subject exams; DANTES subject tests; College Board AP exams; Defense Language Institute proficiency tests; ACE-evaluated certification exams

Credit Awards for Prior Learning
Transfer credits from accredited, degree-granting institution; ACE military recommendations; ACE/PONSI recommendations; portfolio type assessment; department/institutional exams

Description
Support services include personal academic advisement (any time—in office or at home/in person, by telephone, fax, e-mail); career counseling/testing; financial aid; job placement; orientation; student services Monday–Friday 9:00 am–4:30 pm.

Distance education opportunities include audio/video cassettes and independent study courses; and external course program plans on offering selected courses through the Internet.

Students learning at a distance access academic resources by having library books sent to them; Interlibrary loan program; and direct line and modem contacts to institutional computer systems. The program plans to use Web sites on the Internet, with instructions to students about the availability of resources.

Students interact with faculty through periodic in-person meetings and/or by communications by telephone, e-mail, and fax; some faculty and advisors meet students at off-campus sites.

When requested, students enrolled in the same degree program or the same courses may be placed in contact with one another and may communicate by phone, mail, e-mail, fax, or in-person sessions.

Learning experiences may be related to various contexts of the students' life through selection of topics within courses, selection of topics for research papers and projects, case studies, internship and fieldwork assignments, and student selection of general electives and elective courses within an academic major or program.

The advisement process allows students to focus on their learning interests and objectives and incorporate these into their academic programs, to the fullest extent possible. The credit documentation process—the program's procedure for the granting of credit for life and work experience—requires students to focus on their prior learning experiences as well as on their current and future learning, education, personal, and career goals.

Program effectiveness is determined through such measures as student evaluations of all faculty and courses; student questionnaires regarding program, educational and instructional strengths and weaknesses; alumni achievement and evaluations of the success of their education; employer responses about program graduates; peer evaluations of faculty and courses; responses about results of employer and military-sponsored/initiated education and training programs; internship and co-op supervisor evaluations of student performance.

Salve Regina University

Graduate Extension Study
100 Ochre Point Avenue
Newport, RI 02840
Phone: 800-637-0002
Fax: 401-849-0702
E-mail: mistol@salve3.salve.edu;
   mistol@aol.com

Degrees Offered
Master of Arts in International Relations and Human Development; Master of Science in Management

Program Mission
To provide an alternative process to the traditional classroom approach to learning.

Accreditation
New England Association of Schools and Colleges

Admission Requirements
Student must possess an undergraduate degree from an accredited institution. Best scores of MAT, GRE, LSAT, or GMAT.

Credit Hour Requirements
36 semester hours/12 courses

Minimum Campus Time
Five-day institute, usually from Saturday to Wednesday in early June. Students may attend more than one institute if desired.

Tuition and Fees
$900 per course; graduation fee $150; application fee $25; commitment fee $100; transcript fee $3; and book fee $125 per course

Credit Awards for Examinations
ACE-evaluated certification exams and ACE-evaluated courses

Credit Awards for Prior Learning
Transfer credits from accredited, degree-granting institution; ACE military recommendations

Description

Detailed study guides, prepared by faculty members, provide a structured, step-by-step approach to learning while allowing students flexibility in time and place of study. The process involves a one-on-one relationship with instructors who guide the learning and monitor the student's progress through the courses via the exchange of written comments, telephone conversations, and electronic mail.

Administrative support available by toll-free number 24 hours a day. Office staff person available weekdays from 8:00 am–5:00 pm. Faculty available by phone and e-mail. Administration and faculty assistance is also available by e-mail.

Distance education is through independent study courses, e-mail, and computer bulletin board.

Students access the university library via the Internet.

Interaction with faculty is through matriculation interview via telephone, feedback on student papers, candidacy status via telephone, and exit review.

Students may incorporate outside learning experiences into research papers or projects.

Students receive a news bulletin twice a year that contains news and information about the university and its programs. Students also receive mailings from the university reminding them of deadlines, informing them of new courses, etc.

Students are encouraged to complete a course evaluation form when they have received a final grade. Students must submit an exit review detailing how the program has enabled them to attain their stated goals.

SOUTH CAROLINA

University of South Carolina

College of Library and Information Science
Davis College
Columbia, SC 29208
Phone: 803-777-3887
Fax: 803-777-0457
E-mail: gayle.douglas@sc.edu

Degrees Offered
Master of Library and Information Science

Program Mission
To provide and promote education and leadership in library and information science, services, and studies through the highest levels of teaching, research, and service. With the state of South Carolina as its primary focus, the college reaches out to the southeastern region and beyond with educational programs characterized by excellence and innovation.

Accreditation
Southern Association of Colleges and Schools; American Library Association

Admission Requirements
USC admissions application form and fee, CLIS supplemental application form, official transcripts, official score reports (GRE or MAT), letters of reference, and interview

Credit Hour Requirements
36 semester hours

Minimum Campus Time
Two Saturday classes per course per semester

Tuition and Fees
South Carolina residents, $160 per semester hour; Georgia, Maine, and West Virginia residents, $225 per semester hour

Credit Awards for Examinations
None

Credit Awards for Prior Learning
Transfer credits from accredited, degree-granting institution

Description
Enrollment is limited to residents of South Carolina and those in the following contract states: Georgia, Maine, and West Virginia. Distant learners in South Carolina are advised through the college's system of district advisement. Each faculty member travels twice a year to meet with students in his or her district. Advisement also may take place by telephone or through electronic mail. Students enrolling in the MLIS program through distance education have two separate avenues of student services support available to them, both of which are accessible through toll-free telephone numbers. Student services personnel in the USC Office of Distance Education provide assistance with registration, billing, and the provision of all textbooks and materials needed for each course. Videotapes of classes may be obtained through the Office of Distance Education in cases of technical difficulties, illness, or family emergency.

The majority of courses presented in the MLIS program via distance education consist of a combination of live interactive satellite transmission and on-site delivery. Some courses contain a videocassette component and others may be presented on-site in their entirety. Regardless of the delivery format, the instruction in each of the courses encompasses the same learning objectives as the classroom instruction of the same Columbia campus courses. Live instruction originating from studio classrooms at USC-Columbia is broadcast simultaneously to viewing sites in South Carolina and other contract states. Students at these sites watch television monitors and interact with the instructor and fellow students through a two-way audio "talkback" system. On-site class meetings are held on the Columbia campus for students in South Carolina and at centrally located sites in other contract states. For these required meetings, students travel to the designated site and meet with the instructor in person for an intensive, day-long series of activities such as examinations, group discussions, panel presentations, etc. On-site meetings are normally scheduled for two Saturdays during the semester.

South Carolina residents have access to the university system statewide (eight campuses). Out-of-state contracts include arrangements for use of necessary resources within those states.

Interaction between faculty and students include two-way audio talk-back system for class meetings, e-mail and class listserv, toll-free telephone line, and on-site visits.

Interaction between students is provided at approved viewing sites where groups of students participate as well as through group assignments, e-mail, class listserv, and on-site visits.

In partial fulfillment of class requirements, students may engage in various learning activities that are job-related. For example, students may write a job-related grant, design a job-related survey, prepare materials for a portfolio, participate in a storytelling festival, or attend a workshop.

Program effectiveness is determined through such measures as accreditation and placement of graduates.

TENNESSEE

American Academy of Nutrition

1200 Kenesaw
Knoxville, TN 37919-7736
Phone: 800-290-4226
Fax: 423-524-1692
E-mail: aantn@aol.com

Degrees Offered
Associate of Science in Applied Nutrition

Program Mission
To provide comprehensive independent study, while maintaining the highest academic standards.

Accreditation
Distance Education and Training Council

Admission Requirements
High school or GED diploma

Credit Hour Requirements
60 semester hours

Minimum Campus Time
None

Tuition and Fees
$290 per individual course; $1285 for one semester (five courses), including all books and videos

Credit Awards for Examinations
ACT-PEP: Regents College Examinations Program; CLEP general exams; CLEP subject exams; DANTES subject tests; College Board AP exams; ACE-evaluated certification exams

Credit Awards for Prior Learning
Transfer credits from accredited, degree-granting institution; ACE military recommendations; ACE/PONSI recommendations

Description
Student support services are available Monday–Friday, 10:00 am–6:00 pm.

All courses are through independent study. Many include videos.

Interaction between faculty and students occurs through regular faculty-student telephone conferences.

Seven courses allow credit for additional outside learning projects (four credits for each course rather than three).

Program effectiveness is determined by questionnaires to students, graduates, and telephone conferences.

All nutrition courses include case studies and assignments on comparing and analyzing alternative viewpoints.

Johnson Bible College

7900 Johnson Drive
Knoxville, TN 37998
Phone: 423-573-4517
Fax: 423-579-2337
E-mail: rbeam@jbc.edu

Degrees Offered
Master of Arts in New Testament Exercises and Preaching; Master of Arts in New Testament Exercises and Research; Master of Arts in New Testament Exercises and Contract

Program Mission
To encourage renewal in the church by increasing the depth and quality of New Testament study among those engaged in church leadership, with emphasis on the preaching ministry.

Accreditation
Southern Association of Colleges and Schools

Admission Requirements

Professing Christian with a serious purpose; 2.5 or better undergraduate GPA from an accredited college with a bible major; Accrediting Association of Bible Colleges bible test score; GRE score; three letters of reference; six hours of Greek or the equivalent.

Credit Hour Requirements

30 semester hours.

Minimum Campus Time

Two three-day on-campus experiences

Tuition and Fees

Application $15; orientation $125; tuition $125 per credit hour; graduation fee $50.

Credit Awards for Examinations

None

Credit Awards for Prior Learning

Transfer credits from accredited, degree-granting institution

Description

The program is limited to Christians engaged in church leadership.

Support services include toll-free telephone calls 9:00 am–5:00 pm five days a week and e-mail 24 hours a day.

Distance education opportunities include videotaped lectures primarily, e-mail interaction, and toll-free telephone interaction.

Interaction between faculty and students include toll-free telephone, e-mail, mail, and two on-campus experiences.

Interaction between students is provided through two on-campus experiences and the student directory, which includes addresses, phone numbers, and e-mail addresses.

It is assumed that students are serving in ministries and that work is directly related to their ministries.

Students complete the 21-hour core curriculum and may select nine hours from the college's curriculum or may transfer them from another institution. A project designed by the student integrates the core curriculum and the corollary studies.

Program effectiveness is determined through such measures as course grades, comprehensive exam, integrating project, and surveys of graduates.

University of Tennessee

Engineering Management
UT Space Institute
Tullahoma, TN 37388
Phone: 615-393-7529
Fax: 615-393-7201
E-mail: garriso@utsi.edu

Degrees Offered

Master of Science in Industrial Engineering (IE), with a concentration in Engineering Management

Program Mission

The Engineering Management Program is a concentration within the Department of Industrial Engineering at the University of Tennessee and leads to a master's degree in industrial engineering.

Accreditation

Southern Association of Colleges and Schools; Accreditation Board for Engineering and Technology (ABET)

Admission Requirements

Bachelor's degree in engineering or in a related scientific or technical field from ABET-accredited program; minimum GPA of 2.7; industrial experience is desired. Applicants with a 2.5 GPA or better may be admitted on a probationary status. Applicants with extended industrial experience where undergraduate degree is more than five years old may be given special consideration if they do not meet the above requirements. These are evaluated on a case-by-case basis.

Credit Hour Requirements
36 semester hours completed within a 6-year time frame. This includes 9 hours in core courses, 12 hours in management concentration courses, 6 hours of technical electives, 6 hours of management electives, and 3 hours for capstone project

Minimum Campus Time
On-campus defense of the capstone project before the faculty committee is required

Tuition and Fees
In-state $505 per three-hour course; out-of-state $996 per three-hour course

Credit Awards for Examinations
None

Credit Awards for Prior Learning
Transfer credits from accredited, degree-granting institution

Description
The 36-semester-hour course of study has been designed to integrate the knowledge, the quantitative and qualitative skills, and the attitudes needed by engineers and scientists who wish to succeed in management. The curriculum blends theory with practice, conceptual frameworks, and practical applications. Flexibility is built into the program. The course work can be scheduled to meet the student's needs, whether on campus, off campus, full time, or part time.

Staff and faculty can be reached by phone or fax 8:00 am–5:00 pm Monday–Friday. Classes are taught in the evening, so in some cases faculty may be available until 9:00 pm. E-mail can be used to access staff and faculty.

Access to academic resources can be obtained by phone, fax, or e-mail. Software may be transferred by Internet or by disk.

Phone, fax, and e-mail are used intensively for the videotaped classes to assure faculty and student interaction. Interactive classes (two-way audio/video) are available at selected sites.

Assignments are made that require the student to analyze or evaluate issues in their place of work. Most of the management courses have projects that require application of theory to real-world situations. Students are encouraged to work in teams on certain assigned projects.

Students evaluate course content and instructor effectiveness each semester and are asked to provide constructive criticism of the total program.

TEXAS

Dallas County Community College District

Distance Learning
LeCroy Center for Educational Telecommunications
9596 Walnut Street
Dallas, TX 75234
Phone: 214-669-6400
Fax: 214-669-6409
Internet: http://ollie.dcccd.edu

Degrees Offered
Associate in Arts and Science in General Studies

Program Mission
To provide greater access to learning by serving the educational and instructional needs of students in Dallas County and worldwide through the delivery of quality distance learning opportunities.

Accreditation
Southern Association of Colleges and Schools

Admission Requirements
Application, high school and college transcripts

Credit Hour Requirements
61 semester hours

Minimum Campus Time
None

Tuition and Fees
$75–250 per semester hour, varies with residency; materials/resources vary with course; some courses have special fees

Credit Awards for Examinations
CLEP subject exams; College Board AP exams

Credit Awards for Prior Learning
Transfer credits from accredited, degree-granting institution; ACE/PONSI recommendations; portfolio type assessment; department/institutional exams

Description
Student support services available by telephone: 8:00 am–5:30 pm Monday–Friday. Voice mail and online information 24 hours. Admissions counseling, registration, and course planning are provided. An online learning skills laboratory also is available to students.

Distance education opportunities include telecourse, online courses, and one-way video, two-way audio.

Students access bibliographic information from multiple libraries online.

Interaction between faculty and students occurs through audiobridge conferencing, telephone, voice mail, and e-mail.

Program effectiveness is determined through mid- and end-of-semester evaluation by students; in-house research on test banks and tests used; and comparative studies with on-campus courses.

ICI University

University Degree Program
6300 N. Belt Line Road
Irving, TX 75063
Phone: 214-751-1111
Fax: 214-714-8185
E-mail: info@ici.edu

Degrees Offered
Bachelor of Arts in Bible/Theology and Religious Education; Associate of Arts in Religious Studies; Bachelor of Arts honors program in Bible/Theology

Program Mission
To offer programs for ministers, ministerial students, and lay people who are serious in their desire for a biblical education. The purpose of ICI academic programs is to train leaders for the various ministries of the church. Such leaders become pastors, evangelists, educators, missionaries, or fulfill other ministries to which God has called them. A strong spiritual commitment is encouraged throughout these programs.

Accreditation
Distance Education and Training Council

Admission Requirements
GED diploma, high school diploma. Provisional admission in certain circumstances to non-high school graduates. When studying outside the United States, a national ICI director coordinates the application, unless the applicant is enrolling via Internet.

Credit Hour Requirements
BA, 128 credits; AA, 64 credits

Minimum Campus Time
None

Tuition and Fees
$69 per credit hour plus books

Credit Awards for Examinations
ICI exam

Credit Awards for Prior Learning
Transfer credits from accredited, degree-granting institution; ACE /PONSI recommendations; portfolio type assessment

Description
Student services support office is open from 8:00 am–4:30 pm Monday–Friday. Students can also seek student support using fax and e-mail (24 hours a day). Included in this support is program evaluations, review, and recommendations.

Distance education opportunities include independent study courses, e-mail, and asynchronous classes.

In most cases, students study in a learning center context where they have access to library materials and course work support and counseling.

Interaction between faculty and students is provided through regular mail and by e-mail. Also, telephone access is possible (toll-call).

Interaction between students occur in courses offered using e-mail interaction with a listserv feature.

Each course requires a project, most of which are to be conducted in reference to the student's environment and cultural context.

Program effectiveness is determined through such measures as graduate follow-up surveys (it has been determined that over 80% of graduates are engaged half time or more in ministry positions), and focus groups of local and national leadership to verify program relevance and determine areas for improvement.

Midwestern State University

Radiologic Sciences
3410 Taft Boulevard
Wichita Falls, TX 76308
Phone: 817-689-4337
Fax: 817-689-4513
E-mail: radiology@nexus.mwsu.edu

Degrees Offered
Bachelor of Science in Radiological Science; Master of Science with majors in Radiologic Education or Radiologic Administration

Program Mission
To prepare registered radiologic technologists for management and teaching positions. Through a holistic approach to the major areas of study, the program provides a transition for the working technologist into higher levels of technology and supervision.

Accreditation
Southern Association of Colleges and Schools

Admission Requirements
Bachelor of Science, American Registered Radiologic Technician (ARRT) credentials; Master of Science, ARRT credentials and bachelor of science degree, one year professional experience, admission index of 1400 (200 x GPA of last 60 hours plus verbal and quantitative GRE scores). Completion of general academic courses, university and program applications, and letters of recommendation.

Credit Hour Requirements
BS, 130 semester hours; MS, 36 semester hours

Minimum Campus Time
BS: two-day orientation, one-day seminar, and one-day per course each semester; MS: two days twice each semester for six semester hours

Tuition and Fees
BS: three credit hours TX resident $300, three credit hours nonresident $920; MS: three credit hours TX resident $325, three credit hours nonresident $875

Credit Awards for Examinations
CLEP subject exams; DANTES subject tests; College Board AP exams

Credit Awards for Prior Learning
Transfer credits from accredited, degree-granting institution; department/institutional exams

Description
Registrar's office, business office, financial aid office, and veteran's affairs office available Monday–Friday 9:00 am–5:00 pm.

Distant education opportunities include independent study modules, videotaped lectures, e-mail, Internet access, and phone conferences.

Students learning at a distance access academic resources through Texshare services within Texas university libraries; Internet access, mail, and interlibrary loans.

A toll-free number is available for students to call faculty, and faculty routinely correspond or call students.

Interaction between students is provided through assignments that require students to share information with their classmates.

In most of the radiologic sciences courses, students will be able to use or apply course content at their place of employment.

Program effectiveness is determined through such measures as student/graduate feedback, employer feedback, and graduate job progression.

Texas Wesleyan University

Master of Education via Distance Learning
1201 Wesleyan Street
Fort Worth, TX 76105-1536
Phone: 800-336-4954
Fax: 800-604-6088
E-mail: joyedwards@aol.com

Degrees Offered
Master of Education Degree in General Education

Program Mission
To offer a master of education degree through multilearning modalities.

Accreditation
Southern Association of Colleges and Schools

Admission Requirements
Undergraduate degree from an accredited institution; GPA of 3.0 (overall or last 60 hours), full-time teaching status, and at least one year teaching experience.

This MEd Program via distance learning is for classroom teachers only. To qualify for the program, full-time teacher status in Texas must be verified.

Currently, participants must live within the state of Texas.

Credit Hour Requirements
Six semester hours continuous enrollment and 36 hours total program for degree.

Minimum Campus Time
None

Tuition and Fees
$239 per semester hour, $65 materials fee per semester, and $55 general fee per semester.

Credit Awards for Examinations
None

Credit Awards for Prior Learning

Transfer credits from accredited, degree-granting institution

Description

Each course includes videotaped presentations that feature nationally recognized specialists in education, as well as written texts and materials. Faculty mentors are available via toll-free numbers and e-mail. Registration is completed by phone. Students work in study teams of two to five to watch the video programs and complete assignments.

Students can call the library; however, because of recent changes in copyright laws, copy materials are not sent to students.

Students are required to contact their faculty mentor and have a conference call between mentor and study team three times during each semester.

Students can enroll only after they have a study team to work with. No one is allowed to progress through the program alone.

Students are required to relate course material to their actual classroom teaching. Assignments have been designed to create this kind of practical application.

Graduate surveys are sent yearly, and there are course evaluations in each course.

Trinity University

Executive Master's Program in Health
  Care Administration
HCAD #58
715 Stadium Drive
San Antonio, TX 78212-7200
Phone: 210-736-8107
Fax: 210-736-8108
E-mail: shubenak@trinity.edu

Degrees Offered

Master of Science in Health Care Administration

Program Mission

To offer a three-year executive master's program designed for students who already have a responsible position in a healthcare organization, but who want to enhance their career opportunities by obtaining a master's degree in healthcare administration.

Accreditation

Southern Association of Colleges and Schools; Accrediting Commission on Education for Health Services Administration

Admission Requirements

A bachelor's degree from an accredited college or university; be currently employed in a healthcare setting; complete, prior to entrance, a three-hour undergraduate course in each of the following areas: accounting, economics, and statistics. Students must complete the three-hour undergraduate level courses with a grade of A or B. (C grades will be evaluated on an individual basis.) Individuals who petition to the Admissions Committee for any exceptions will be considered on an individual basis; submit aptitude test scores from either the GRE or the GMAT.

Applicants must also complete the Executive Program Admission Form and submit $25 nonrefundable application fee. Official transcripts, not more than one year old, from all colleges and universities previously attended, résumé or autobiographical sketch detailing educational background and employment experience are required. A brief statement of purpose indicating specific reasons for seeking further education in health care administration and two letters of recommendation from individuals who are familiar with the applicant's academic and/or employment performance must be submitted. Access to an IBM-compatible computer is necessary.

Credit Hour Requirements
42 semester hours

Minimum Campus Time
Six days in calendar year—three days at the beginning of each fall and spring semester

Tuition and Fees
Application fee $25; tuition for all graduate students enrolling for 1–11 semester hours in the 96-97 academic year $562.50 per semester hour; advance deposit (which is applied toward tuition) $200

Credit Awards for Examinations
Evaluated on individual basis

Credit Awards for Prior Learning
Transfer credits from accredited, degree-granting institution and evaluated on individual basis

Description
This is a long-distance learning experience: students come to the Trinity campus at the beginning of each fall and spring semester for three days of intensive course work, with the remainder of the course requirements being accomplished via written assignments, use of e-mail, and class telephone conference calls. Because students are working in healthcare organizations, course assignments often focus on the application of conceptual knowledge to a particular real-world situation. In addition, a series of seminars over the final year and a half of the program allows students to develop projects that will meet their own educational needs.

Health Care Administration Department faculty members are available for consultation during office hours, Monday–Friday 8:00 am–5:00 pm and by appointment.

Interaction between faculty and students occurs through on-campus sessions, comments on written assignments, individual phone calls, group conference calls, and e-mail.

Several courses require job-oriented projects.

Program effectiveness is determined through such measures as course evaluations, accreditation reports, placement and advancement of graduates, and a continuing stream of qualified students.

VERMONT

Burlington College

Independent Degree Program
95 N. Avenue
Burlington, VT 05401
Phone: 800-862-9616
Fax: 802-658-0071

Degrees Offered
Bachelor of Arts in Psychology, Transpersonal Psychology, Human Services, Humanities, Writing and Literature, or individualized major

Program Mission
To provide a degree program designed for adults who cannot or do not wish to attend weekly classes, but are interested in a program that treats them as independent adults with support from faculty in areas that are of interest to them.

Accreditation
New England Association of Schools and Colleges

Admission Requirements
45 previously completed college credits of C or better, phone interview, three references, and writing sample

Credit Hour Requirements

45 in general education, 36 in upper-level major, 15 in upper-level outside of major, and 24 electives

Minimum Campus Time

Four-day residency

Tuition and Fees

Full-time $3,400 per semester; part-time $2,000 per semester; weekend residency $85 per semester; admission fee $50; and graduation fee (optional) $75

Credit Awards for Examinations

CLEP general exams; CLEP subject exams; DANTES subject tests; and ACE-evaluated certification exams

Credit Awards for Prior Learning

Transfer credits from accredited, degree-granting institution; ACE military recommendations; ACE/PONSI recommendations; portfolio type assessment

Description

This is a low-residency, frequent-contact, independent BA degree program for upper-level students. Burlington College believes that learning is a dynamic process of sharing information, experience, and knowledge.

The college's Educational Resources Center (ERC) has tutoring assistance available, arranged per student's convenience, generally during regular college hours 9:00 am–5:00 pm Monday–Friday, but can be arranged during evening hours. Career and graduate school counselor available two days weekly. Students arrange meetings with mentors per individual schedules.

Learning is structured in self-designed modules under the direction of faculty. Each student has an individually assigned mentor who will guide him or her through the program and help design a degree plan.

Students communicate at regular predetermined intervals with their mentors and faculty by telephone, mail, fax, and/or modem.

Students access through academic resources and services available in their respective geographical areas.

IDP has two semesters per year, each beginning with a four-day residency in Burlington, Vermont. The residency is held at a retreat center where students share rooms. The residency is paced with activities for students to interact with other students undertaking similar learning activities as well as with mentors, faculty, the IDP director, and other people from the college. By the time students leave, degree plans are revised, next semester's learning modules written and approved, schedules for faculty and mentor contacts in place, and students are ready to begin their work with a network of support people, including other students.

In the development of their learning modules, students have the opportunity to incorporate various kinds of learning activities that may include job- or community-related experiences.

Each learning module is self-designed and specifies learning goals, how they will be completed, and how the student and their instructor will evaluate their progress.

Program effectiveness is evaluated on an ongoing basis among mentors and the IDP director, based on individual student's participation, progress, and satisfaction. Exit interviews with the director of admissions, which address the effectiveness of the program, are also conducted with each graduating IDP student.

Goddard College

Campus BA and Low-Residency BA,
  MA, and MFA Programs
Plainfield, VT 05667
Phone: 802-454-8311
Fax: 802-454-8017
E-mail: peterb@earth.goddard.edu

Degrees Offered
Bachelor of Arts; Master of Arts in Liberal
Arts Studies; Master of Arts in Education
and Teaching; Master of Arts in Social
Ecology; Master of Arts in Psychology and
Counseling; Master of Fine Arts in Writing
and Literature

Program Mission
To advance the theory and practice of learning by undertaking carefully planned ex-
periments based on the ideals of democ-
racy and on the principles of progressive
education, developed by John Dewey and
those who worked with him. Goddard is a
small college in rural Vermont dedicated to
hard thinking and plain living. Founded in
1938, as successor to Goddard Seminary, a
prominent New England academy dating
back to 1863, Goddard is recognized for
innovation in education. At Goddard, students are regarded as unique individuals
who will take charge of their own learning
and collaborate with other students, staff,
and faculty to build a strong community.
Goddard encourages students to become
creative, critical, passionate, lifelong learners, working and living with an earnest
concern for others and the welfare of the
earth.

Accreditation
New England Association of Schools and
Colleges

Admission Requirements
Undergraduate: application plus fee, transcripts for high school or GED and any
colleges attended, three letters of recommendation, personal statement, and personal interview. Graduate: completed application and fee, college transcripts, three
letters of recommendation, personal statement, study plan, and bibliography.

Credit Hour Requirements
BA, 120 semester hours; MA in Liberal
Arts Studies, 36 semester hours; MA in
Education and teaching, 36 semester hours;
MA in Social Ecology, 36 semester hours;
MA in Psychology, 36 semester hours; MA
in Counseling, 48 semester hours; MFA in
Writing and Literature, 48 semester hours

Minimum Campus Time
A week-long residency is required at the
beginning of each semester

Tuition and Fees
BA off-campus student, $3948; BA study
leave, $210; MA $4504; MFA $4585; MA
in social ecology semester 1, $5304; MA in
social ecology semester 2, $5004; MA/In-
stitute for teaching summer 2, $2210; MA
off-campus education summer 1, $3035;
MA off-campus social ecology summer 1,
$2700; MA off-campus social ecology sum-
mer 2, $2806

Credit Awards for Examinations
CLEP general exams; CLEP subject exams;
College Board AP exams

Credit Awards for Prior Learning
Transfer credits from accredited, degree-
granting institution; ACE military recommendations; ACE/PONSI recommendations; portfolio type assessment

Description
Most students access Goddard's resources
during their residency, then use resources
in their home location upon their return. If
they are within driving distance of the college, they are able to use library facilities
throughout the semester.

Faculty contact is built into the design of the programs and the advisor/advisee relationship is key to the program's success. Students are assigned a personal educational advisor each semester. During their residency they meet with their advisor several times to develop and refine their study plans, then correspond through the mail (by letter or tape) every three weeks throughout the semester. Individual advisors set individual boundaries for contact beyond this, but many make themselves available by phone or e-mail or, when geography permits, by appointment. They are encouraged to contact them during usual working hours, 8:00 am–4:30 pm in most cases. Students in their final semester also have contact with a faculty who serves as second reader for their senior study or final product.

Different programs approach this in different ways, but networking is a spontaneous outcome of the intensity and intimacy of the residency periods. Many students meet for support groups, writing groups, etc. Correspondence by phone, mail, e-mail, and even visits also occurs frequently. In the psychology and counseling program, more and more use of e-mail is encouraged both for one-on-one discussions and chat groups.

Employment and involvement cannot supplant the learning, but they are important supplements in that they both provide opportunities for testing theory in practice. Student teaching, volunteering in literacy or after-school programs, or leading workshops are examples of ways students have tested their learning about education. Internships and practicums are also essential parts of the psychology and counseling programs, the school guidance program, and the MFA in writing program. At the undergraduate level, students can incorporate active learning projects in their study plans to test the ideas they learn in different study areas in practical situations. Ex-

amples include testing water quality locally, volunteering at a battered women's shelter, and working with a local herbalist. Students self-design their entire programs in consultation with faculty advisors.

At the undergraduate level, the attainment of the Goddard Bachelor of Arts degree signifies that its holder has wide knowledge, has demonstrated thoughtful action and positive self-development. Students must have completed 120 semester hours and their Senior Study, a major independent learning project. They must also complete and submit all necessary student-prepared records, and the final criteria is payment of any amounts due the college. On nomination of the student's advisor and second reader, the faculty of the off-campus program recommends the student to the president of the college for a degree.

Vermont College of Norwich University

Adult Degree Program
Montpelier, VT 05602
Phone: 800-336-6794
Fax: 802-828-8508
E-mail: vcadmis@norwich.edu

Degrees Offered
Bachelor of Arts in Liberal Studies (areas of faculty expertise are Writing, Literature, Social Sciences, History, Art, Holistic Studies, and Teacher Education)

Program Mission
To offer the bachelor of arts degree in liberal studies in a brief-residency format featuring student-designed, mentor-guided study projects.

Accreditation
New England Association of Schools and Colleges

Admission Requirements
High school diploma and sound writing skills, motivation, and ability to do independent study

Credit Hour Requirements
120 semester credits

Minimum Campus Time
Two weeks a year

Tuition and Fees
$3625 for 15 credits

Credit Awards for Examinations
ACT-PEP: Regents College Examinations Program; CLEP general exams; CLEP subject exams; DANTES subject tests; College Board AP exams; Defense Language Institute proficiency tests; ACE-evaluated certification exams

Credit Awards for Prior Learning
Transfer credits from accredited, degree-granting institution; ACE military recommendations; ACE/PONSI recommendations; portfolio type assessment

Description
Student support services are available 8:00 am–4:30 pm Monday–Friday and at any time via e-mail.

Distance education is through mentor-guided study conducted via written exchanges by mail and e-mail.

Academic resources may be accessed through Norwich University mainframe and e-mail.

There is high interaction between a student and faculty mentors.

Learning may be related to the contexts of a student's life. For example, a social worker can study sociology/psychology with focus on relevant job topics. All learning is self-designed.

Program effectiveness is determined through student evaluations, evaluation of faculty work, and periodic program evaluation by an outside team.

VIRGINIA

American Military University

9104-P Manassas Drive
Manassas Park, VA 22111
Phone: 703-330-5398
Fax: 703-330-5109
E-mail: amugen@amunet.edu

Degrees Offered
Master of Arts in Military Studies; Bachelor of Arts in Military History, Military Management, and Intelligence Studies

Program Mission
To provide distance education in military studies.

Accreditation
Distance Education and Training Council

Admission Requirements
MA Program: BA/BS degree and three letters of recommendation. BA program: 60 semester hours of college, meeting criteria of Virginia Transfer Module, satisfactory GPA. AMU has "whole person" philosophy for admissions. Personal/professional achievement is considered along with academic record.

Credit Hour Requirements
MA degree 36 semester hours; BA degree 120 semester hours (60 semester hours for admission)

Minimum Campus Time
None

Tuition and Fees
MA program tuition $425 per three semester hour credits and books; BA program

tuition $375 per three semester hour credits and books

Credit Awards for Examinations
CLEP general exams; CLEP subject exams; DANTES subject tests; Defense Language Institute proficiency tests; ACE-evaluated certification exams

Credit Awards for Prior Learning
Transfer credits from accredited, degree-granting institution; ACE military recommendations; ACE/PONSI recommendations; and portfolio type assessment

Description
Administrative help and general academic guidance: AMU offices 8:30 am–5:00 pm Monday–Friday. Specific course advice/counseling: each professor has telephone office hours to allow one-on-one access for all of his or her students. Days and times depend on individual faculty member's location and other factors.

Distance education opportunities include independent study, telephone contact with faculty, e-mail and Internet contact with faculty. Detailed guidance for directed study and research.

Research/supplemental reading materials are provided for all courses (sent to student). Students use local library resources for additional study and research. Major Military Studies resource centers are accessible through the Internet and through interlibrary loans.

Every course requires the student to have a minimum of four lengthy telephonic conferences with the professor. Purpose of these is to provide personal interface, guidance, mentoring, as well as instruction and assessment of student's mastering of the material/course content.

Student bulletin boards and chat groups on the Internet are planned. Student directory is published and faculty can provide class members with information to contact others in the same course.

Over 250 courses in military studies are offered. Students have the ability to structure the academic content of their individual program to meet their own individual needs.

Mary Baldwin College

Adult Degree Program
ADP House
Staunton, VA 24401
Phone: 540-887-7003
Fax: 540-887-7265
E-mail: adp@cit.mbc.edu

Degrees Offered
Bachelor of Arts in Art-Communications, Arts Management, Asian Studies, Business Administration, Business Administration/Economics, Computer Science/Business Administration, Economics, English, Health Care Administration, History, International Relations, Marketing Communications, Philosophy, Political Science, Philosophy/Religion, Political Science, Psychology, Sociology, Sociology/Social Work, Theatre

Program Mission
To provide adult learners an opportunity to pursue a rigorous liberal arts undergraduate education in ways that recognize their maturity, experience, life circumstances, motivation, and capacity for independent scholarship.

Accreditation
Southern Association of Colleges and Schools

Admission Requirements
21 years of age or older; high school diploma or GED; at least a 2.0 GPA in any

recent college course work; the ability to read discerningly and to write clearly; the ability to work independently. Some college experience strongly recommended. Applicants must reside in the Commonwealth of Virginia or bordering locations.

Credit Hour Requirements
132 semester hours

Minimum Campus Time
One-day orientation on campus, and must be able to get to regional center to meet with advisor in person twice a year

Tuition and Fees
$266 per semester hour, $25 application fee, $25 orientation fee, and $35 graduation fee

Credit Awards for Examinations
CLEP general exams; CLEP subject exams; DANTES subject tests; ACE-evaluated certification exams

Credit Awards for Prior Learning
Transfer credits from accredited, degree-granting institution; ACE military recommendations; ACE/PONSI recommendations; portfolio type assessment

Description
Each ADP regional center (Weyers Cave, Richmond, Roanoke, and Charlottesville, Virginia) is staffed by full-time faculty advisors, available by phone, fax, e-mail, or in person during regular working hours, and available evenings and weekends by appointment.

Distance education opportunities include independent tutorial courses, where students work one-on-one with faculty either in person or at a distance (via telephone and e-mail). With these courses, students can choose where and when to study. Some courses available via videotape, and putting courses online is underway. E-mail communication with faculty and advisors is available.

Each regional site has a computer lab. Writing Center and Learning Skills Center services are available by phone, or walk-in at the main campus. Library services are available by phone to the main campus, and computer access is in progress. There are also local library cooperative arrangements at each regional location.

A minimum of three extended interactions (faculty-student) are required for independent tutorials. Group tutorials require face-to-face class sessions held at regional sites.

Group tutorials distribute class lists to encourage interaction. Students may also contact other students on the program's networking service called "the Web." Each regional center also hosts get-acquainted events for students. Online connections are pending completion.

Senior projects can be designed to relate to the students' job as can prior learning portfolios, class projects, or papers. A student may work with an approved faculty member to design learning contract on a course topic of their choosing. Mary Baldwin College also carries the option of students designing their own major.

Each student is assigned a faculty advisor who specializes in advising adult students. The program is 20 years old (founded in 1977) and the staff and faculty are very experienced in working with adult students. Academic vigor and personal attention given to each student is emphasized.

Program effectiveness is determined through such measures as student performance on nationally normed exams, student GPA, alumni surveys, feedback from employers, and accreditation.

Old Dominion University

TELETECHNET and Graduate Engineering State Network
217 Administration Building
Norfolk, VA 23529
Phone: 804-683-5314
Fax: 804-683-3004
E-mail: RRR100U@Jefferson.na.odu.edu

Degrees Offered
Bachelor of Science in Business Administration, Criminal Justice, Professional Communication, Human Services Counseling, Interdisciplinary Studies, Middle School Education (Math and/or Science), Engineering Technology (Civil, Computer, Electrical, and Mechanical), Nursing, and Health Services Administration; Master of Science in Nursing (Family Nurse Practice), Education (Special Education), and Engineering Management

Program Mission
To offer 10 baccalaureate degree completion programs to place-bound adults. The program is a partnership with the Virginia Community College System (VCCS) with the VCCS providing the first two years on-site and the second two years by information technology from Old Dominion University.

Accreditation
Southern Association of Colleges and Schools; Accreditation Board for Engineering and Technology; National Council for Accreditation of Teacher Education

Admission Requirements
First two years college completed or health science certificate (e.g., RN, Dental Hygiene) or BS for MS degree

Credit Hour Requirements
Bachelor's, 120-124 depending on major; master's, 36 credits

Minimum Campus Time
None, unless engineering labs are required. These are offered in condensed summer sessions.

Tuition and Fees
$119 per credit hour

Credit Awards for Examinations
CLEP general exams; CLEP subject exams; DANTES subject tests; College Board AP exams; and Defense Language Institute proficiency tests

Credit Awards for Prior Learning
Transfer credits from accredited, degree-granting institution; ACE military recommendations; ACE/PONSI recommendations; department/institutional exams

Description
Student support services are available by e-mail with advisor and with site director where available; scheduled television sessions; staff available 8:00 am–6:00 pm Monday–Friday.

Distance education opportunities are provided by e-mail and videotaped lectures.

All distant sites are connected to the university mainframe. Using a computer, students access the Virginia Library Information Network and search databases online. If copies or books are needed, students may request them to be sent to the distant site and pay for copies by credit card. Each site serviced by a director can also access student records. Bimonthly workshops are held on television. Topics range from writing skills, internships, and curricula to assessment issues.

Interaction between faculty and students is through voice mail and the Internet. All students have e-mail and interact with each other on newsgroups.

All undergraduate students may participate in an internship if they choose. ODU awards credit for an internship experience and sets up that experience.

Program effectiveness is measured through the assessment process.

Presbyterian School of Christian Education

Extended Campus Program
1205 Palmyra Avenue
Richmond, VA 23227
Phone: 804-359-5031
Fax: 804-254-8060
E-mail: psce_con_ed@ecunet.org

Degrees Offered
Master of Arts in Christian Education; Doctor of Education

Program Mission
To prepare students for the challenges of educational leadership in the church and related professions.

Accreditation
Southern Association of Colleges and Schools; The Association of Theological Schools in the United States and Canada

Admission Requirements
Graduation from accredited college or university or equivalent preparation. If no degree, enrollee may take up to three courses as a limited enrollment student. Students must apply to the program after completion of three courses.

Credit Hour Requirements
90 quarter hours

Minimum Campus Time
Two weeks of on-campus classes; three hours per class per day during the last two weeks in June

Tuition and Fees
$132.50 per credit hour

Credit Awards for Examinations
None

Credit Awards for Prior Learning
Transfer credits from accredited, degree-granting institution

Description
The extended campus program is designed for working adults with limited time to spend in a classroom. This program combines directed study at home with two weeks of classes on campus. Courses in Bible, theology and ethics, and education and ministry constitute the curriculum.

Program coordinator serves as advisor and provides assistance to students enrolled in the program. Students who have been accepted into degree program are assigned a faculty advisor. Services are available during office hours, 9:00 am–4:30 pm Monday–Friday.

The extended campus courses use a variety of distance learning methods including written materials, audio- and videotapes, and telephone conferences. Computer courses will be added in 1998.

Students use libraries in their communities, if needed.

Written assignments are returned with instructor comments. Individual and conference telephone calls are often included during the directed study segment. Some students and instructors interact via e-mail.

For students already working in churches, activities such as designing curriculum for church school, teaching a class, planning a youth program or Wednesday night fellowship may be used as class projects.

Program effectiveness is determined by student evaluations of courses and different aspects of the program. Also, the faculty and program coordinator evaluate several aspects of the program.

Regent University

Center for Leadership Studies
1000 Regent University Drive
Virginia Beach, VA 23464
Phone: 757-579-4122
Fax: 757-579-4042
E-mail: clsphd@regent.edu

Degrees Offered
Doctor of Philosophy in Organizational Leadership

Program Mission
To provide a terminal research degree that synthesizes knowledge from diverse fields into a focused yet flexible plan of study that is useful to leaders in all forms of global organizations. The program is multidisciplinary in scope and through the Internet.

Accreditation
Southern Association of Colleges and Schools

Admission Requirements
A master's degree from an accredited institution; GRE, GMAT, or MAT scores from tests taken within the previous five years; applicants whose primary language is not English are required to take the Test of English as a Foreign Language (TOEFL); at least three years of relevant professional experience; evidence of reasonable potential to successfully complete the doctoral program, including the requisite electronic communication skills.

Credit Hour Requirements
60 semester hours

Minimum Campus Time
One week at the start of the program, and one two-week residency for each of the next two years

Tuition and Fees
Each two-course (six hours) trimester is $2200. One week on-campus residency is $400.

Credit Awards for Examinations
None

Credit Awards for Prior Learning
Transfer credits up to 15 hours from accredited, degree-granting institutions

Description
The center's learners are midcareer professionals who are not able to leave their current employment or geographical area to pursue such a degree. The goal of the program is to prepare its learners to assume key leadership positions in their organizations or government service. It is hoped that graduates of the program will model the principles of truth, justice, and love as described in Scripture, and follow them in an exemplary way in their leadership call. The doctoral program in Organizational Leadership integrates knowledge and research from business, divinity, and education, as well as allied disciplines.

Learners begin the program in cohorts of approximately 30 learners who are mentored by full-time staff and faculty advisors. Each learner has access to support services 24 hours per day via Internet connection and World Wide Web sites, as well as traditional methods.

The program is delivered primarily via computer mediated learning, including e-mail, course-specific World Wide Web sites, and Internet search engines. Faculty and staff assist the learners throughout the process.

Each learner completes a research facilities access survey during their initial one-week residency and receives specific training in necessary electronic research and Internet communication skills. Thereafter, full-time library staff are available to respond to inquiries via e-mail, fax, or telephone.

Each learner, as a component of each course, must respond to specific faculty inquiries and discussion. Additionally, faculty advisors and program staff are available for noncourse assistance to learners.

The entire concept of computer-mediated learning and this program are built on the foundation of learner interaction. The process is monitored to assure that no learner is "out of contact" with the program.

The program is designed for midcareer professionals who are encouraged to develop as scholars building upon the experiences and background each brings to the program.

Ongoing evaluation by the Office of Institutional Effectiveness as well as five-learners assessment team designated for each cohort specifically tasked to evaluate and recommend improvement in all aspects of the program are measures used to determine program effectiveness.

Virginia Commonwealth University

Medical College of Virginia
P.O. Box 980203
Richmond, VA 23298-0203
Phone: 804-828-0719
Fax: 804-828-1894

Degrees Offered
Master of Science in Health Administration

Program Mission
To provide graduate education in management for self-motivated, mature, and experienced professionals who are seeking continued career advancement. The Executive Program is an innovative, two-year course of study leading to a master of science health administration (MSHA). It can be completed in two years by individuals working full time, residing anywhere in the United States.

Accreditation
Southern Association of Colleges and Schools; Accrediting Commission for Education in Health Services Administration

Admission Requirements
Baccalaureate degree; GRE or GMAT exam; three letters of reference; résumé and statement of why the choice to enter health administration. Must have five years of progressively responsible administrative, supervisory, or clinical experience.

Credit Hour Requirements
44 semester hours

Minimum Campus Time
Five on-campus sessions

Tuition and Fees
The program consists of four six-month semesters. For Virginia residents, the cost of each semester is $3567; for out-of-state students, the cost is $7187 per semester.

Credit Awards for Examinations
CLEP general exams; CLEP subject exams; and College Board AP exams

Credit Awards for Prior Learning
Transfer credits from accredited, degree-granting institution; department/institutional exams

Description
The executive program is 24 months long. Students enroll in four six-month semesters of course work. Each semester is composed of both on- and off-campus sessions. During the off-campus session of each semester, students continue studies at their home/work site, using a carefully planned array of innovative learning technologies.

The mix of on-campus and off-campus study is designed to minimize time away from employment and home as well as travel expenses. During the five on-campus sessions (ranging from six to 14 days each), students attend executive program classes on the Medical College of Virginia Campus in Richmond. There is much collegiality that is engendered through on-campus sessions and group assignments online.

Career counseling and job placement services are provided when requested. In addition, all university support services are available to students when taking on-campus courses. Copies of articles can be provided by the university library at cost. Interlibrary book loans may also be requested through local institutions.

Distance education is provided by computer conferencing via the World Wide Web, which includes e-mail, audio conferences, and videotaped lectures.

Computer conferencing is set up for faculty-student interaction and is monitored by program directors and system personnel who notify directors of nonparticipation by either faculty or students.

The program is designed for health practitioners and many assignments, cases, etc. are based on their experiences.

Elective courses can be self-designed.

Students assess every course as well as do an overall program assessment at the time of completion/graduation. Referrals from alumni is another measure of program effectiveness.

Virginia Polytechnic Institute and State University
Commonwealth Graduate Engineering Program

College of Engineering
Blacksburg, VA 24061
Phone: 540-231-9762
Fax: 540-231-7248
E-mail: bsblanch@vtvm1.cc.vt.edu

Degrees Offered
Master of Science in Engineering, Electrical Engineering, and Systems Engineering; Master of Engineering Administration (all master's programs have "non-thesis" option)

Program Mission
To provide and deliver graduate engineering programs to qualified individuals throughout the state of Virginia, and beyond as necessary, to complete student program requirements. This capability is being offered through a cooperative statewide program, working with six other state institutions (University of Virginia, Virginia Commonwealth University, Old Dominion University, George Mason University, Mary Washington College, and Shenandoah University). Courses are offered "live" from the campus and extended via satellite (one-way video) with two-way audio utilizing a telephone bridging network.

Accreditation
Southern Association of Colleges and Schools

Admission Requirements
Bachelor of Science degree in appropriate field of engineering, or equivalent; GRE scores; undergraduate GPA; letters of reference; experience résumé (as applicable)

Credit Hour Requirements
30 hours for each program

Minimum Campus Time
None

Tuition and Fees
$771 per three-hour course (in-state) and $1147 per three-hour course (out-of-state)

Credit Awards for Examinations
None

Credit Awards for Prior Learning
Transfer credits from accredited, degree-granting institution

Description
Student support services include on-campus advising of off-campus students with program director (as required); individual course advising with faculty teaching a specific course (varies); off-campus advising through Northern Virginia Graduate Center (9:00 am–6:00 pm Monday–Friday).

Distance education opportunities include e-mail, videotaped lectures, telephone, fax, and regular mail (UPS and FedEx).

Student access academic resources through libraries, computer, World Wide Web, and course notes/textbooks.

Interaction between faculty and students, and between students, is provided through a two-way audio utilizing a telephone bridging network. Some courses are offered via two-way compressed video (VTEL).

In the systems engineering program, there is a final three-hour project and report requirement, resulting in a bound thesis-like format (but applications-oriented) that must be defended in front of a committee of three. Additionally, there are applications-oriented projects in many of the specific courses being offered.

In completing course requirements for degree, independent study (up to six semester hours) is available if approved.

The College of Engineering has offered 221 graduate courses through the "Commonwealth Graduate Engineering Program," involving 108 faculty and over 10,000 enrollees, from 1983 (when the program commenced) through the spring semester 1996. Additionally, several courses have been offered via VTEL. This is part of a larger off-campus graduate engineering program activity involving 800 to 900 part-time students located throughout the state of Virginia.

An annual program evaluation is submitted to the Virginia Council for Higher Education. Other measures used to determine program effectiveness are enrollments, number of program graduates, program/course evaluations, general feedback from students and organizations that are providing student support, and word of mouth.

Virginia Polytechnic Institute and State University
Pamplin MBA Program

1044 Pamplin
Blacksburg, VA 24061-0209
Phone: 540-231-6152
Fax: 540-231-4487
E-mail: rdjmba@vtvm1.cc.vt.edu

Degrees Offered
Master of Business Administration

Program Mission
To provide high-quality graduate business education to working professionals using live instruction and interactive audio capabilities. The focus of the program is to provide strong education in the basic business functions and to enhance that education with a broad set of additional courses.

Accreditation
Southern Association of Colleges and Schools

Admission Requirements
Undergraduate degree, official transcripts, letters of reference, résumé, official GMAT scores are all a part of the application process

Credit Hour Requirements
48 semester hours (16 courses)

Minimum Campus Time
The complete graduate degree program may be completed at official sites; not requiring any campus time.

Students currently may take classes at specific sites. All current active sites are within the state of Virginia.

Tuition and Fees
Current cost is approximately $775 per three-credit course. Tuition and fee rates are set each spring by the university's board of visitors.

Credit Awards for Examinations
None

Credit Awards for Prior Learning
Transfer credits from accredited, degree-granting institution

Description
Central office program staff are available from 8:00 am–5:00 pm daily. Advising staff also visit sites periodically. Advising staff may also be contacted by e-mail.

For this satellite MBA program, all instruction is broadcast live. Classes are taped at the sites for viewing by students who missed class due to work. Up to six credits of independent study can be included.

Library services are available via the Internet.

Faculty hold regular phone office hours, are available via e-mail, and occasionally stay on the audiobridge at the conclusion of the regular evening class.

All classes are interactive. In addition, at each site, team projects are typically used.

Independent study projects, designed with the consultation and approval of a faculty member, can be included in a student's program of study.

This program is included as part of the normal outcomes assessment done for all academic programs at the university.

World College

Bachelor of Electronics Engineering
   Technology
5193 Shore Drive, Suite 113
Virginia Beach, VA 23455
Phone: 800-696-7532
Fax: 804-464-3687

Degrees Offered
Bachelor of Electronic Engineering Technology

Program Mission
To offer a bachelor's degree in electronics engineering technology, via independent study, that allows students to learn at a rate, time, and place suited to their individual needs.

Accreditation
Distance Education and Training Council

Admission Requirements
High school diploma or GED diploma

Credit Hour Requirements
139 semester hours

Minimum Campus Time
None

Tuition and Fees

Students pay $2400 per 12-month term. Students may complete as many courses in the program as they can within each 12-month period. In other words, students pay only for the time used to complete the program. (Students may take a maximum of eight terms to complete the program.)

Credit Awards for Examinations

None

Credit Awards for Prior Learning

Transfer credits from accredited, degree-granting institution and transfer credits from military training

Description

General student services (i.e., billing, shipments, etc.) are available to students Monday–Friday 8:30 am–5:00 pm. Instructional services are available to students (via telephone) Monday–Thursday 8:30 am–9:00 pm, Friday 8:30 am–7:00 pm, and Saturday 8:30 am–5:00 pm. Students may fax exams or other paperwork 24 hours a day. All exams, faxed or mailed, are returned within 48 hours of receipt by the school.

All courses are offered via independent study. All lesson books, textbooks, and study guides are included, as is all lab equipment and computer disks, if used.

Students are given all materials they need for usual study. Certain programs require a student to own a computer or to have access to one on a regular basis. The school will pay for a library membership of the student's choice if requested. Students also have access to additional reading materials, computer software, and laboratory equipment through the bookstore.

Students who are falling behind in studies are contacted by the faculty. Faculty are accessible by telephone for over 12 hours most days.

Many students are currently employed in the field of electronics and bring to their studies knowledge of the topic as learned in their jobs.

One course in the program, the senior design project, requires the student to design an electronic device of his or her choice. The student must follow all stages of project design, from submitting a proposal to submitting written status reports on the project through its final completion.

Graduates are surveyed to learn if their studies have resulted in any job advancements, pay increases, or placement in the field of electronics (if not employed in the field at the time of enrollment). They are also surveyed so that the school may learn if the student's individual learning objectives were met and the student's assessment of the learning materials, instructors, and student services.

WASHINGTON

Washington State University

Extended Degree Program
202 Van Doren Hall
Pullman, WA 99164
Phone: 509-335-3557
Fax: 509-335-0945
E-mail: eap@wsu.edu

Degrees Offered

Bachelor of Arts in Social Sciences, emphasizes an interdisciplinary approach with possible major and/or minor course concentrations in Criminal Justice, Sociology, Psychology, Anthropology, History, Political Science, Business Administration, or Women's Studies

Program Mission
To offer a degree for students who have completed the equivalent of the first two years of college.

Accreditation
Northwest Association of Schools and Colleges

Admission Requirements
27 semester hours, 2.0 cumulative GPA

Credit Hour Requirements
120 semester credits

Minimum Campus Time
None

Tuition and Fees
Video courses $165 per credit out-of-state, $151 per credit in-state; correspondence courses $90 per credit

Credit Awards for Examinations
CLEP general exams; CLEP subject exams; DANTES subject tests; College Board AP exams

Credit Awards for Prior Learning
Transfer credits from accredited, degree-granting institution; ACE military recommendations

Description
Two academic advisors are available Monday–Friday 8:00 am–5:00 pm, via toll-free telephone or via e-mail. A student is assigned a specific advisor who assists throughout the program. A student services coordinator is also available Monday–Friday 8:00 am–5:00 pm via toll-free telephone or e-mail to resolve any support issue.

Distance education opportunities include videotaped lectures, e-mail, voice mail, correspondence/independent study courses, and audiotapes.

A librarian is available Monday–Friday 8:00 am–noon via toll-free telephone or e-mail for research assistance and borrowing materials.

Interaction with faculty is through a voice mail system that is available via a toll-free number for questions and discussion. A majority of the faculty is also available through e-mail.

Interaction between students is by a voice mail system, e-mail, and "circles of learning" in some courses.

Learning experiences may be related to the contexts of a student's life. For example, in English 402, Technical and Professional Writing, students write materials related to their jobs or personal or professional activities. This is also true for Sociology 301, Rural Sociology. There are also special topics courses developed between faculty and students. Internships are available in some disciplines.

Program effectiveness is determined through a comprehensive assessment following areas outlined by the Washington State Higher Education Coordinating Board.

WISCONSIN

University of Wisconsin–Madison

College of Engineering
432 N. Lake Street
Madison, WI 53706
Phone: 608-262-0133; 608-265-2083
Fax: 608-263-3160
E-mail: karena@epd.engr.wisc.edu
Internet: http://epdwww.engr.wisc.edu

Degrees Offered
Professional Development (PD) in Engineering

Program Mission

To offer the professional development degree for the practicing engineer, intended as an alternative to the traditional master of science degree. It is a postbaccalaureate degree that allows candidates to pursue courses specific to professional goals identified by each candidate.

Accreditation

North Central Association of Colleges and Schools

Admission Requirements

Applicants must have a BS in engineering from an Accredited Board of Engineering Technology program (or the equivalent) and four years of professional experience in engineering.

Credit Hour Requirements

120 continuing education units (CEU) earned in a five-year period after acceptance

Minimum Campus Time

None

Tuition and Fees

Cost of entire program ranges from $2500 to $5000

Credit Awards for Examinations

None

Credit Awards for Prior Learning

Transfer credits from accredited, degree-granting institution. All credit is converted to CEUs. A maximum of 60 CEUs may be transferred.

Description

Candidates utilize a variety of distance education media and may also choose face-to-face course work, if available.

Director and advisors are available by phone or fax or for on-campus visits. Voice mail and e-mail options available seven days per week, 24 hours per day.

University of Wisconsin-Madison offers a variety of courses via audiographics, Educational Television Network, seminars, videotape, correspondence, traditional classroom, and video teleconferencing.

Advisor regularly contacts active candidates. A newsletter is also used to notify students of program information.

A requirement of the PD degree is a 200-hour (minimum) independent study project based on projects related to the candidate's employment.

Each candidate is contacted at six-month intervals to determine rate of progress toward the goal of program completion in five years.

University of Wisconsin–River Falls

Extended Degree Program in Agriculture
410 S. Third Street
River Falls, WI 54022
Phone: 715-425-3239
Fax: 715-425-3785
E-mail: katrina.larsen@uwrf.edu

Degrees Offered

Bachelor of Science in Agriculture, with majors in Agricultural Business or in Broad Area Agriculture

Program Mission

To offer a program for the busy adult who wants to complete a degree but cannot attend regularly scheduled classes on campus due to work obligations, family responsibilities, geographical location, or all of these.

Accreditation

North Central Association of Colleges and Schools

Admission Requirements

High school graduation in the top 70% of their high school graduating class or GED. A transfer student must have at least a 2.0 GPA on a 4.0 scale and be able to return to the previous school attended (no scholastic or behavior reasons preventing reacceptance).

Credit Hour Requirements

120 semester credits

Minimum Campus Time

Most courses do not require any on-campus time. Some courses require a one-day visit.

Tuition and Fees

WI residents $85 per credit; MN residents with reciprocity $98 per credit. In addition to the tuition, there is an annual $50 contract fee and the charge for course materials, which varies by course.

Credit Awards for Examinations

CLEP general exams

Credit Awards for Prior Learning

Transfer credits from accredited, degree-granting institution; ACE military recommendations; portfolio type assessment; department/institutional exams

Description

Extended degree course work can be completed primarily at home using self-paced courses. Only occasional campus visits are required. The content of the courses and the faculty are the same as the traditional degree programs. The degree requirements are identical. The difference is the method by which learning takes place. Students can complete the degree by taking extended degree courses, by transferring courses taken at other accredited colleges and universities, departmental or CLEP exams, and credit for experiential learning in agriculture through the submission of a portfolio documenting their learning experiences.

Student support services, including advising, counseling, career services, library, and learning skills, are available from 8:00 am–4:30 pm Monday–Friday. Students can call a toll-free number, and they will be transferred to the appropriate department.

Distance education opportunities include independent study courses, videotaped lectures, and interactive television using fiber optic networks in Wisconsin.

Students may interact with faculty by calling the toll-free telephone number and be transferred to the appropriate department. They can also access the departments by e-mail.

Students may meet some degree requirements through self-designed courses or projects. Examples include one student who designed a computer program that dealt with estate planning and changes in Wisconsin marital property legislation. Another student designed a sanitation program for her food company and submitted it for credit in an introductory food science course.

Self-designed independent study courses numbered 490 are offered. Students can receive up to six credits of 490 courses.

Program effectiveness is determined through such measures as every course having a study guide that includes evaluation forms for the course itself and the Extended Degree Program staff.

University of Wisconsin–Superior

Extended Degree Program
1800 Grand Avenue
Superior, WI 54880
Phone: 715-394-8487
Fax: 715-394-8139
E-mail: extdegree@staff.uwsuper.edu

Degrees Offered

Individualized major—an interdisciplinary major planned by the student to meet educational goals

Program Mission

The University of Wisconsin–Superior Extended Degree Program serves degree-seeking students of Wisconsin and who have career commitments and/or family responsibilities or who live a distance from campus.

Accreditation

North Central Association of Colleges and Schools

Admission Requirements

High school or GED diploma minimum, most transfer credits from other universities/colleges

Credit Hour Requirements

128 semester credits; 54 credits in the major

Minimum Campus Time

None

Tuition and Fees

$85 per semester credit for Wisconsin residents and $98 semester credit for Minnesota residents.

Credit Awards for Examination

ACT-PEP: Regents College Examinations Program; CLEP general exams; CLEP subject exams; DANTES subject tests; College Board AP exams; Defense Language Institute proficiency tests; ACE-evaluated certification exams

Credit Awards for Prior Learning

Transfer credits from accredited, degree-granting institution; ACE military recommendations; ACE/PONSI recommendations; portfolio type assessment; department/institutional exams

Description

Student support services include advising 7:45 pm–4:30 pm and until 7 pm on Tuesday in the office. Also, advisors travel to sites throughout northern Wisconsin on a routine basis. Proctoring—in office or at sites—is offered by faculty/staff in addition to approved proctors at other locations. Access to university resources via e-mail.

Distance education opportunities include use of various media as supplemental or as enhancements to print. Depending upon the resources of the student, course guides can be obtained in print, on disk, or over the Internet.

Students learning at a distance access academic resources through library staff who are available via phone or e-mail. Computer labs on campus are open, many University of Wisconsin system campuses allow use of computer laboratories to extended degree students. Resources are on loan from the Extended Degree Program for many courses. Future resources and course guides will be on Internet.

Students are in direct contact with faculty and advisors via campus visits, phone, computer, or mail. Individual faculty determine the extent to which contacts are required for each course.

All faculty are available via e-mail; phone numbers and addresses of faculty are provided.

Self-designed courses or projects can be included in the individualized-major plan.

Program effectiveness is determined through such measures as having graduates complete a learning environment survey. A student satisfaction index is administered every two years. Faculty surveys are administered periodically. Student progress is tracked, and reasons for "drop-outs" or "stop-outs" are documented. Student course completion rates are continuously tracked.

WYOMING

University of Wyoming

School of Extended Studies and Public Service
P.O. Box 3106
University Station
Laramie, WY 82071
Phone: 307-766-3152
Fax: 307-766-3445
E-mail: draggon@uwyo.edu

Degrees Offered
Bachelor of Arts in Administration of Justice; Bachelor of Science in Nursing; Bachelor of Science in Agricultural Business; Bachelor of Arts or Science in Psychology; Bachelor of Arts of Science in Social Sciences; Master of Arts in Education with a specialization in Adult Learning; Master of Business Administration; Master of Public Administration; and Master of Science in Speech Language Pathology

Program Mission
To enhance people's lives through the delivery of quality informational, cultural, and educational programming.

Accreditation
North Central Association of Colleges and Schools

Admission Requirements
An associate degree is required for any of the undergraduate degree programs and a bachelor's degree for any of the graduate degree programs.

Credit Hour Requirements
Social Science, 120 semester hours; Administration of Justice, 120 semester hours; Psychology, 120 semester hours; RN-BSN, 130 semester hours; MAE, bachelor's plus 30 semester hours; MBA, bachelor's plus 30 semester hours; MPA, Bachelor's plus 39 hours; and Master's Speech Language Pathology, Plan A bachelor's plus 45 semester hours, and Plan B bachelor plus 47 semester hours

Minimum Campus Time
MPA course requires some intensive weekends in various locations throughout the state, sometimes on campus. Psychology requires one laboratory course. Master's in Speech Language Pathology requires one summer session.

Tuition and Fees
Undergraduate: resident $76, nonresident $235.50; graduate, resident $117, nonresident $361

Credit Awards for Examinations
CLEP subject exams; College Board AP exams; department credit by examination

Credit Awards for Prior Learning
Transfer credits from accredited, degree-granting institution, portfolio type assessment, department/institutional exams

Description
Support services include an advisor for off-campus students in Administration of Justice, Psychology, and Social Science. On-campus advising for MBA and MPA. Student orientation and training sessions to facilitate learning at a distance are provided.

Distance education opportunities include audio teleconferencing, videotaped lectures, e-mail, and two-way video conferencing.

Students learning at a distance access academic resources through e-mail, fax, toll-free number, academic coordinator's offices, and the library's CARL online system.

Interactive audio teleconferencing, interactive compressed video, phone, fax, and e-mail, and face-to-face when the instructor teaches from a site where students are registered.

Interaction between students occurs during audio teleconferencing and compressed video classes. Students are free to exchange phone and/or e-mail information if they choose to.

Teachers who enroll in education classes design lesson plans and projects to use in their classrooms.

Program effectiveness is determined through such measures as instructor evaluations and student evaluations.

INDEXES

INDEX TO PART ONE

INDEX TO PART TWO

Fields of Study

Letters in parentheses specify the level of degree offered. (A) indicates an associate's degree, (B) indicates a bachelor's degree, (M) indicates a master's degree, and (D) indicates a doctorate.

INDEX TO PART TWO

Alphabetical List of Institutions